The Life and Times
of
Frank Thornton Birkinshaw

Also by Barbara Rudoe

MANY JOURNEYS
(Book One of the Trilogy)

The Life and Times of Frank Thornton Birkinshaw

Book Two

Barbara Rudoe

'I love you to the moon and back; to infinity and beyond'

Rudoe Press

Published in 2010 by Rudoe Press
62 Court House Road, London N12 7PJ

Printed and bound in Great Britain by
www.printondemand-worldwide.com

British Library Cataloguing in Publication Data. A catalogue record for this book is available from the British Library

ISBN 978-0-9564431-1-3

For
Jonathan and Naomi

My father Frank

Contents

ACKNOWLEDGEMENTS

I am particularly grateful to the Imperial War Museum, the RAF Museum at Hendon and the National Archives at Kew for their help in finding relevant documents, war records and diaries, and for patiently answering my interminable questions. Thank you to Churchill Archives Centre, Churchill College, Cambridge, and all the libraries, museums, schools and universities who provided me with information.

My many recently discovered second cousins have been magnificent in supplying documents, identifying photographs and passing on family stories, and I thank them for their input. Thanks also to my first cousin Anne Mathieson, who gave me access to her mother's documents and papers and for her enthusiasm at my project. I am also grateful to my writing tutor Sonia Ribeiro for her help.

My heartfelt thanks go to my half-sister Fay, who has very generously shared information about our father and suggested the title to this book, and also to my brother Alan for his unstinting help with editing and photographs and for his encouragement. And not least, very many thanks to my husband Nick for doing the design and artwork, and for being so long-suffering and supportive. I could not have done it without him.

List of Illustrations

Frontispiece – My father Frank

Preface

When, in 2006, I started writing about the life of my father Frank, I decided to ask my half-sister Fay what her thoughts were about my project. Fay had already written quite extensively about Frank in her autobiography *Auto da Fay*. She had also known him for much longer than I had (he died when I was three) as she was the daughter of his first wife and was fifteen years older than me. Fay's response was to say that Frank's story was one that should be told and she was happy for me to tell it, as she felt I would do it with honesty and integrity. That is exactly what I have endeavoured to do.

This book, which is the second in my trilogy, is also the second part of my mother's story. As in the first book, *Many Journeys*, where I have gone into the background of my mother's ancestors, I have also gone into some detail about Frank's forbears. Again, my husband Nick and I spent much time travelling round the country gathering information, meeting newly discovered cousins and examining records in order to fill in the story. We spent a wonderful holiday in Northumberland with my cousin Anne Mathieson, who was well informed about the Hendersons of my grandmother Isabel's family (Isabel's mother was a Henderson) who came from that part of the country, discovering where and how they had lived. Isabel's paternal Garbutt family, who lived in the Tyneside area, were mostly well-documented by my second cousin Geoffrey Allen who, like Anne, and before her, her mother Sheona, has long been one of the Garbutt family historians.

On the other hand my grandfather Herbert Birkinshaw's family, who came from Yorkshire, were not documented by the family at all. I discovered from searching the records in the National Archives and finding one of my father's first cousins, that Herbert had nine siblings, who between them produced twenty offspring, all of whom my father would have known. Of my consequent fifteen second cousins I have managed to find and meet five, one of whom lives in Canada. I discovered seven others who had already died, and there was another one I have not been able to trace; there were two more who are still living, but I have not met them. Some of the Birkinshaw families were still living in Yorkshire in the 1950s during the time we lived there, but we never met them, and my mother appeared unaware of their existence.

My mother once told me that the happiest years of her life were those she spent with my father. Sadly he died in October 1949 in New Zealand after they had been married only nine years. My mother rarely talked about Frank as we were growing up - there were no photos of him around the house, no memories as far as I was concerned - it was almost as though he had never existed. The reason for this, I believe, was that Mother was of the generation that did not talk about such things and she found the topic difficult to discuss with me. I always knew he had another family - I met my half-sisters occasionally, but Frank was rarely mentioned. When I was a child I would visit his mother, my grandmother Isabel; she sent me a ten shilling note every birthday and Christmas. I also knew his two sisters and brother and their families.

When I was about thirteen, and living in Scotland, I came across a box of black and white negatives in a cupboard which turned out to be photos of my brother and me taken when we were very young in New Zealand. With my mother's help I went through them, had some printed and put them in an album. I had a great expectation that the box might contain photos of Frank, and perhaps some of us all together as a family; unfortunately they had all been taken by my father, so he did not feature in them at all, and again my mother divulged very little information about him.

After my mother died in June 1977 I decided it was time to find out about my father and his antecedents and to try and discover something about his life. To this end I started to do some genealogical research, looking through public records, trying to establish some sort of a family tree - to find a background. I met other people researching their Birkinshaw families and was generally introduced to the world of genealogy. I also wrote to my father's sister, my Aunt Sheona, and his brother, my Uncle Bill, to ask them for information, and we started a correspondence. However, it was not until after an interval of many years, when my children had grown up and I took up my search again, this time with the help of the web, that a picture finally began to emerge.

Before I embarked on this research I had no idea my father was such an interesting man - extraordinary almost. It has been a voyage of discovery and I hope the reader will enjoy the journey as much as I have.

Chapter One

War

One of the enduring memories of the First World War was the iconic pointing finger of Lord Kitchener on his recruitment poster, on which were written the dramatic words: 'Your Country Needs You.' War was declared on 4 August 1914 and Kitchener, the newly-appointed Secretary of State for War, was asking for young men between the ages of nineteen and thirty-four to join up and fight. Within a month my father Frank, although only sixteen, had joined the throng and signed up.

Frank Thornton Birkinshaw was born on 16 June 1898 at No. 6 The Terrace, in the village of Ovingham on Tyne, near Newcastle, to Herbert Birkinshaw, commercial traveller, and Isabella Henderson Birkinshaw, formerly Garbutt. He was the eldest of four children.

Frank's favourite sister, Jane Thornton, sometimes known as Jennie, but always Sheona to us, was born in January 1901, also at Ovingham. His next sister, Mary, was born in May 1903, by which time the family had moved to Bradford. Bill, Herbert and Isabel's fourth child, was born in March 1905.

The family's next move was to the suburbs of Birmingham, and in September 1909, at the age of eleven, Frank went to King Edward V1 Aston School. The school archivist sent me his pupil record card which noted that the fees were one pound ten shillings per term. Herbert's occupation was denoted as 'agent' and his address as Gravelly Hill and later Erdington.

Herbert, according to family letters, was a bully, both to his children and his wife. In contrast, the family always remembered Isabel as long-suffering, sweet and gentle. All the childhood photographs of Frank showed him to be well-dressed and he always looked well cared for. What Herbert and the family showed to the outside world, however, was quite different from what went on behind closed doors.

The Terrace, Ovingham

Number 6 is the house between the two far chimneys

Frank and Isabel

Frank

Mary, Bill and Frank

Frank left school in December 1913 at the age of fifteen and a half, as his father either could not, or more likely would not, pay the fees. Herbert found Frank an apprenticeship at an engineering company, probably the Dunlop Rubber Company in Erdington where they were living at the time. Leaving school was precisely what Frank did not want to do; he was clever and he would much rather have finished his education. However, the experience probably stood him in good stead during his coming War years, and he remained in his job until signing up 'to fight for King and Country', at the tender age of sixteen and not even a quarter. Frank lied about his age as did many other boys, who, for whatever reason, were keen to go off 'on an adventure' and fight for their country. The recruiting sergeants, who were paid for every person they recruited, often turned a blind eye to the age of their recruits. Many people believed the war would be over by Christmas and the young men perhaps thought they should not miss out on the fun. The legal enlistment age in 1914 was nineteen for those being sent overseas to fight, but, nonetheless, Frank joined the 8th Battalion of the Royal Warwickshire Regiment[1] as a boy soldier, his destination - the Western Front.

Malcolm Brown in his book, *Tommy Goes to War*[2], described the terrible conditions the soldiers had to endure. In the preface to his book he asked the questions:

> What was it like to serve on the Western Front in the First World War? To cope with rats, lice and endless, cloying mud? To go 'over the top' into battle? To be wounded, or to witness the death of friends? And how in all this did the soldier keep his sanity – and his rich dry humour?

Tommy Goes to War answered many of these questions; some of the answers being in the form of letters from soldiers to their families back home. Included in the book is a letter from my father to his parents. Frank wrote several letters home during his time in the Warwicks and later with the Royal Flying Corps in Arabia. Isabel gave the surviving letters back to Frank after the War and I discovered them amongst my mother's papers after she died.[3] Frank also wrote occasionally to his sisters Sheona and Mary. Censors always checked letters sent from the war zone and Frank was not allowed to say exactly where he was in case the letters were intercepted by the enemy. Most of his letters were dated, and those letters prior to August 1915 said 'Somewhere in France' although it turned out that on several occasions he was actually in Belgium. The Brigade War Diaries and the official 8th Battalion Officers' Diaries[4] are in the National Archives at Kew and I was able to view them there. These gave the date, location, movement and other details of Frank's battalion so I was then able to match the dates and the locations of the troops mentioned in the diaries with the dates on Frank's letters, and so work out almost exactly where he had been and what he had been doing. In September 2001, nearly ninety years later, I visited the World War 1 battlefields in northern France and was able to find some of the actual places where my father had been. It was a very moving experience.

Another military historian, Peter Caddick-Adams, wrote a history, *By God They Can Fight*[5], of the 143rd Infantry Brigade, of which the 8th Royal Warwickshire Battalion was a part, in which he included extracts from some of my father's letters. The title referred to a comment by Brigadier-General C B Prowse who was killed on the first day of the Battle of the Somme. His full quote was: 'I did not think much of Territorials, but by God they can fight!'

Frank's first three letters to his parents, written soon after he joined up, were from Coggeshall in Essex where the battalion was in training, and 'where they spent the winter ready to defend London in case of invasion'; they were billeted in private houses.[6] These were possibly the first letters Frank had ever had to write home. The first one read:

> My dear Father,
>
> I got your letter tonight. I am still staying with Mrs Grey, where I have all my meals. She just gives us what the army provides with a spot of milk and occasionally pudding. She also makes beef steak puddings with her own suet.

I do not think there is any special way of getting a stripe; of course one can 'earhole' the officers etc.

It is purely luck if I get a pair of khaki trousers. Some get them and some don't. I see the papers every day. I have had no rifle practice yet, but am afraid that I shall not be much good. I shall try and be 'extra smart' for a week or so.

I don't think my vaccination has taken properly. I have got drenched with rain for two days running.

I do hope I get promoted.

From your son, Frank.

PS I got letters tonight from you, Mr Valentine, A. Jennie, A. Gus.[7]

The second letter was to his mother:

My dear Mother

I am writing this letter to tell you that we have been given (myself included) *a pair of boots*, two pairs of pants and a jersey.

On Wednesday night we had a night alarm. At half past eleven we were all safely asleep in bed when we were awakened by a terrible row of bugles and whistles. Everyone seemed to have gone mad. We got up, dressed, ran down to the company alarm post and were all at the battalion parade ground *twenty minutes* after the alarm had sounded. The parade ground was *two miles* away. We did not know whether it was a real alarm or only a test one, but it was only the latter. It was the War Office which started the alarm. Everyone in Coggeshall thought the Germans had come. There was a guard on the post office and all motor cars had to put out their lights. We were told to expect a real one the next day and we are told to always keep our kit bags packed in case we have to move off.

Today we were taken to the trenches and were told to go there and lie in them at the next alarm. Everyone was served out with 100 rounds of ball ammunition and those who have not pouches have to carry them in their *pockets*.[8] Today an aeroplane has been passing and re-passing us.

I have got a pair of boots like the ones I had before. The pants are quite nice ones, only far too big. I hope we go for shooting on Monday. The jam we have is labelled 'plum and apple' but runs like water and tastes like 'strawberry and turnip'. Kippers cost 3d per pair in Coggeshall. What do you think of the doubled income tax? Will it ruin Daddy?????

Next time you see Auntie Georgie[9] would you thank her for the mittens again and say that I would freeze to death if it were not for them. It snowed all yesterday and it was tremendously cold. It was ever so cold today. I could hardly move this morning when we were drilling.

From your loving son – Frank

The third letter from Coggeshall, again to his mother, was dated 18 October 1914:

My dear Mother

I am writing this letter in the family circle with the gramophone playing marches, hymns and comic songs. Today we have had only church parade, but tomorrow we start work in earnest; route marches, trench digging at night and outpost duty.

My arm is quite better so we will now have to get up at 5.30 and keep on until 9.0pm. After this I will not be able to write as much as I did before. I wrote the last part of this letter yesterday. Today we had bayonet drill before breakfast and rifle drill right up to dinner time. We start again at two o'clock this afternoon.

I just got your parcel when I came home this morning. Thank you for the socks and handkerchiefs. I hope you got the walnuts all right. I tried to get a battery for my nickel-plated flashlamp today but can not get one down here. Would you please get or order one from Halfords in Birmingham. Would you also send my button brush. I can't afford to buy things myself this week or I would do so, as I only got 4s. this week. I am having my shirts, towels and handkerchiefs etc. washed.

When you think of sending a parcel, never mind cakes, *send butter.........*

At night there is not a light on, that is why I want a flashlamp so badly. We have to go up about 200 yards of a 2ft wide footpath with a ditch at each side and there seems to be a likelihood of a sprained ankle. We see the searchlights going all the time.

Everyone here is afraid of zeppelins. Please don't forget the field glasses if I can have them.

Love from Frank.

The 8th Royal Warwickshire Battalion sailed from Southampton to Le Havre on 23 March 1915; Frank was still only sixteen. They had thirty officers and nine hundred and ninety-eight men, seventy-five horses, twenty-three vehicles, nine bicycles, and two Vickers machine guns. It was estimated that for every ten members of the 8th Battalion who left Southampton, only three could expect to return 'in good order'.[10]

From Le Havre they entrained via Abbeville to Cassel, which is eighteen miles south of Dunkirk. The train journey was in French cattle trucks with about forty men to a truck with straw on the floor and no room to move. From Cassel they marched, with heavy packs on their backs, to Hardifort where they arrived on 26 March. The next stop was Le Bunder and Caestre where Sir Horace Smith Dorrien, GOC of the Second Army, inspected the brigade as it marched past. They continued on to Bailleul (which was twelve miles from Cassel) and dug trenches at Neuve Eglise on the Bailleul/Armentières road.

On 1 April they marched seven miles to Armentières which was near the front line; it was nearly three hours of hard marching on a cobbled surface but the weather was fine and cold. A German airship dropped three bombs on the nearby town but luckily no damage was done. (See page 13 for map.)

Their next break from marching was after another three miles at Erquinghem, due west of Armentières. It was from here that Frank wrote to his mother on 3 April:

> My dear Mother
>
> I have just received your second letter this afternoon, but cannot understand why you have not received my letters. I have written three and one postcard since I came out here, but perhaps the censor has stopped them 'as containing information likely to be of value to the enemy'. [There is a decisive 'No' written in brackets by the censor!]
>
> I am so glad that Valentine has come out. I expect that he will follow us up and perhaps I shall see him as we are both in the same division.
>
> We have again moved and are now well within range of the enemy's guns which are casually shelling a village close by. The inhabitants treat it as a joke and during bombardments simply collect their valuables and have a picnic a few miles away. We are billeted up in a loft, the floor of which is only composed of branches covered with straw which is quite exciting, for occasionally a man will drop right through onto a horse box 15 feet below.
>
> We have unfortunately not been paid this week; so many of us are in the sad condition of not being able to buy milk for tea, etc. Auntie J wanted to know what I wanted. To start with I want a supply of Oxo cubes which prove immensely useful for flavouring pontoon, etc. To continue, I want the weekly edition of the *Mirror* or *Sketch* posted regularly; two or three khaki handkerchiefs and as much in the way of edible luxuries as you care to send out. The French chocolate is absolutely rotten and one is charged extortionate prices. The bread made by the country people is in most

cases made of rye. It is however quite acceptable, as compared with the army biscuits. I honestly believe that one of these would keep an average man alive for about 8 days in case of emergency. When I go on the march I start to eat one and have just about finished it when we reach our destination. (I hope the censor won't erase this).

So far the only work we have done is trench digging, but it is quite exciting at night to watch the flare lights and star shells. What with the rattle of the rifles one is reminded of November the Fifth on a large scale.

We will very probably go in the trenches tomorrow night. Things are pretty quiet where we are, and one could hardly imagine that war is on; everything is so peaceful a certain distance from the firing line. The weather is absolutely glorious just at present.

With love from your Son – Frank.

Peter Caddick-Adams described the soldiers' first taste of trench warfare, learning 'how to patrol No Man's Land, conduct wiring parties (to replace barbed wire entanglements damaged by shelling, or make new ones), set up listening posts close to the enemy trenches, hand over and relieve trenches'. All these things had to be done by night. They also learned how to build comfortable bomb-proof dug-outs and of course they had to be careful of snipers and the 'random shell, rifle and machine gun fire' which often swept no man's land.

When the men were not in the trenches they were billeted in cramped quarters in Bailleul which had been left in a very unsanitary state by the previous units; the war diary reported the HQ as being 'a very fine house at 28 Rue de Lille' in Bailleul. During the march to Bailleul sixteen men from the battalion 'fell out' presumably due to exhaustion from carrying their heavy loads. The diary stated succinctly: 'Enemy held at Armentières 9/10/11 April.' It was also interesting to note in the diary that earlier in the month the King had sent his best wishes to all the troops.

Frank wrote a letter[11] to his eleven-year old sister Mary on 11 April:

My dear Mary

I was so pleased to get your letter this afternoon. It arrived at the same time as a bottle of HMM tablets, about the fourth I have had since coming out here. However, they prove very useful for putting in tea instead of milk.

I happened to read the article in the *Morning Post* before receiving your letter, but it is certainly an excellent description. We get plenty of your local papers out here but magazines such as the *Royal* and *London* are very rare and I have not even seen *Punch* since leaving Coggeshall. In answer to your query I can assure you that I am interested in anything *except* war topics.

We are leaving here tomorrow, 'destination unknown' as usual, but of course if we did know I could not tell you so it does not make much difference.

There is absolutely nothing doing here and as far as quietness goes we might as well be in Coggeshall as here, except that all the streets are lit here whereas in Cogg no lights are allowed for fear of invasion. We get better aeroplane displays here than at the Tally Ho grounds and have seen some really fine exhibitions of banking and volplaning [gliding].

At the present moment the Colonel is inspecting our billet which I think I have described before. The only recommendation I can give it is that it is large and airy (distinctly so).

You might ask Dad not to send any more cakes from Barrows, but to send sardines in tomato sauce, Oxo and any other such condiments rather than cake which is always pretty stale, besides being easily procurable out here. S.G. would appreciate a small box (say 25) of cigars, but please don't mention my name in the transaction.

From your brother, Frank.

On 12 April they were on the march again to billets at Romarin. On 16 April the battalion took over the Steenbeck trenches from the 7th Royal Warwicks where there was firing and sniping all night. They were now near Ploegsteert Village, fondly known as 'Plug Street', which was south of Ypres in Belgium. The HQ was at La Plus Douve Farm, Petit Pont. The battalions rotated spending four days in the trenches followed by four days' training and resting. As Peter Caddick-Adams said, there would be little opportunity for sleep while they were on trench duty: 'The cold, wet, rats, lice or artillery duels prevented sleep by day, and the nights were full of frenzied activity as the patrols went out and came back.'

On 19 April they captured their first prisoner. He was from the 5th Bavarian Reserve Regiment and was picked up by some of the battalion out on listening patrol at 2am; unfortunately one of their number was killed doing so (as was another friend of Frank the following night) as Frank reported in his next letter home which was dated 25 April. Although headed 'Somewhere in France', it was actually written from Moat Farm in Belgium:

My dear Mother

I am writing this letter in bed, so I expect you will have a certain amount of trouble in reading it. We were out all last night, so after getting up for breakfast this morning we all got back again to 'kip'.

We 'came out' again for four days on Tuesday night and are billeted in a large moated farm about a mile and a half from the trenches. In the moat there are hundreds of gold fish, some quite big. We find it an interesting and instructive amusement in netting them.

You will be sorry to hear that Sandy Hutton, the Scotchman you met at Brownings was killed on Sunday while out on 'listening patrol'. Three of them went right up to the enemy's parapets when a flare light went up and he was shot.

I was so pleased to get your letter and *Punch* yesterday and expect I will get your parcel tomorrow. Yesterday I got a parcel of cigarettes from Auntie Madge.[12] I really don't know what to do with them as we get about 25 cigarettes given us each week and I am by no means a smoker. I smashed my watch glass a few days ago and have not up to now been able to get another.

From your loving Son – Frank.

PS In the next parcel could you send Cadbury's cocoa and milk in tins. The postage on the smallest parcel is 1s while a big one may come for slightly more if addressed c/o the GPO.

We found Sandy Hutton's grave at La Plus Douve Farm Cemetery in Belgium when we visited the area in 2001. It was a pretty place surrounded by fields and contained three hundred and forty-five graves of which nine were German[13].

On 28 April the battalion was in Jonesville. A and B Company went to Nieppe to have a bath and C Company, which was the one Frank was in, to Moat Farm. At the end of April the war diary reported six men had been killed and one had died of wounds; twenty men and one officer had been wounded and one man was missing.

They were back in the Douve or Steenbeck trenches on 3 May. Frank wrote to his mother again on 7 May:

My dear Mother

I was so pleased to get your letter yesterday morning. I hope you will not be anxious about not receiving a letter but we have just been in the trenches for four days and it generally takes another day before writing letters, so you must not expect letters too often. We are in a very quiet part of the line, so as long as one does not take needless risks, such as surveying the enemy's lines over the parapet, he is quite safe. We are again billeted in the large farm, having a rest, and have all the day to ourselves, only go out at nights trench digging.

I was so pleased to hear that the knife and fork is coming on. It has been rather rotten without them. We had a bath a week ago. We had to march ten miles there and back to have it, but it was worth it. The baths were once a brewery and we got in the large brewing tub full of hot water. We were given four minutes to bathe, and if we were not out by that time a hosepipe of cold water was turned on us. Most of us were very punctual in getting out. We had an entire new set of underclothing. The weather was absolutely beautiful, indeed it was so hot that we had a shirt sleeve parade, that is without our tunics, with equipment.

The last few days have been rather wet and miserable, but on the whole we have had nothing to grumble at. I have heard from Valentine, and we are only ten kms away from each other, but we cannot arrange a half-way meeting place because we are not allowed to mention names of places in letters, so we are in rather a predicament.

As there is absolutely nothing to say I will write again in a couple of days' time.

From your loving Son – Frank.

PS S.G. has not received the tobacco yet. I am getting anxious.

Peter Caddick-Adams remarked: 'Despite Birkinshaw's comments about the quietness of the line, harassing shell-fire and snipers consistently whittled down the fighting strength of the brigade.' During May eleven men were killed and twenty-eight were wounded from the 8th Battalion and there were almost thirty sick soldiers.

Malcolm Brown in *Tommy Goes to War* said: 'By the winter of 1914-15 a continuous line of trenches ran some four hundred and fifty miles across Europe from the Belgian coast to the frontier of Switzerland.' He went on:

'The trenches': there can be little doubt that this phrase was the most emotive to emerge from the vocabulary of the First World War. For the generation of 1914-18 – as indeed for every generation since – the words had and have a unique ring. To have been 'in the trenches' put a permanent mark on a man; he had been admitted to a special, private world, the reality of which, as many were aware at the time, could only be fully understood by those who had been part of it.

Another letter was duly sent on 11 May:

My dear Mother

I have only a quarter of an hour to write this letter as we have to go out on night work, so please excuse scrawl. I was so pleased to get your parcel, including knife, fork and spoon and have since received *Punch*. The sardines were very useful and I did so enjoy the honey. I also received a parcel from Aunt Gus. We are by no means overfed by the army so you may guess that parcels prove most acceptable.

I am enclosing this letter in one of the new envelopes that has come out, so must say nothing military.

I was very sorry to hear of Grannie's death. It came as a great surprise to me, but it is a great consolation to know that she died peacefully. She always used to say to me – 'Frank, never be a soldier! And after all, it was the best thing that she could say.' [14]

We are working pretty hard on our so-called rest so I have not much time for writing. The weather is still pretty hot and sultry and it is a pity that there is not a lake in the vicinity to bathe.

I shall write again tomorrow.

With love from your son – Frank.

On 24 May Frank wrote to his sister Sheona, addressing her as 'My dear Jennie':

I was so pleased to get your letter this morning. I unfortunately dropped it somewhere behind the trenches before reading it and spent about an hour and a half (at two o'clock in the morning) looking for it. When I did find it it took another half hour to read it through the mud.

We are relieved tonight and go back for four days' rest. I think it must be a little joke to call it rest, for we really do twice as much work as in the trenches. Every night during the 'rest' we man the reserve trenches until two o'clock in the morning. After that we lie in the woods until six o'clock. Then we march back and sleep, eat, have rifle inspections and wonder why we ever joined the army, until six o'clock at night, when the same thing happens again. In our spare time we go out and mend roads or pick up jam tins which other regiments have left behind. So far we have had an exceptionally fine four days in the trenches. The weather is beautiful and the Germans are really quite quiet, in fact, I suppose they are doing the same as us, basking in the sun.

Some of us are digging gardens at the back, most of us are boiling the inevitable can of tea on charcoal and wood fires. This life, combined with free firework displays at night would be absolutely grand were it not for the shells which keep buzzing over. Of course it is quite interesting watching our shells knocking the enemy trenches down, but it is quite a different matter when they start. They come over making a noise something between the howling of a baby and a pan of water upset on a fire and explode with a plop! Bang (most lucid) and then we run like rabbits for the dugouts and not much of us is seen or heard for a bit.

I got a letter from Thrale who wants some shrapnel. It is a funny thing, that although we get thousands of bullets over it is quite a novelty to find one lying about, but I suppose they lodge in the ground.[15]

With love from your brother – Frank

Many years later my Aunt Sheona told me how poignant she felt it was that her big brother should spend an hour and a half at two in the morning searching for a letter from a mere sister, she being only fourteen at the time.

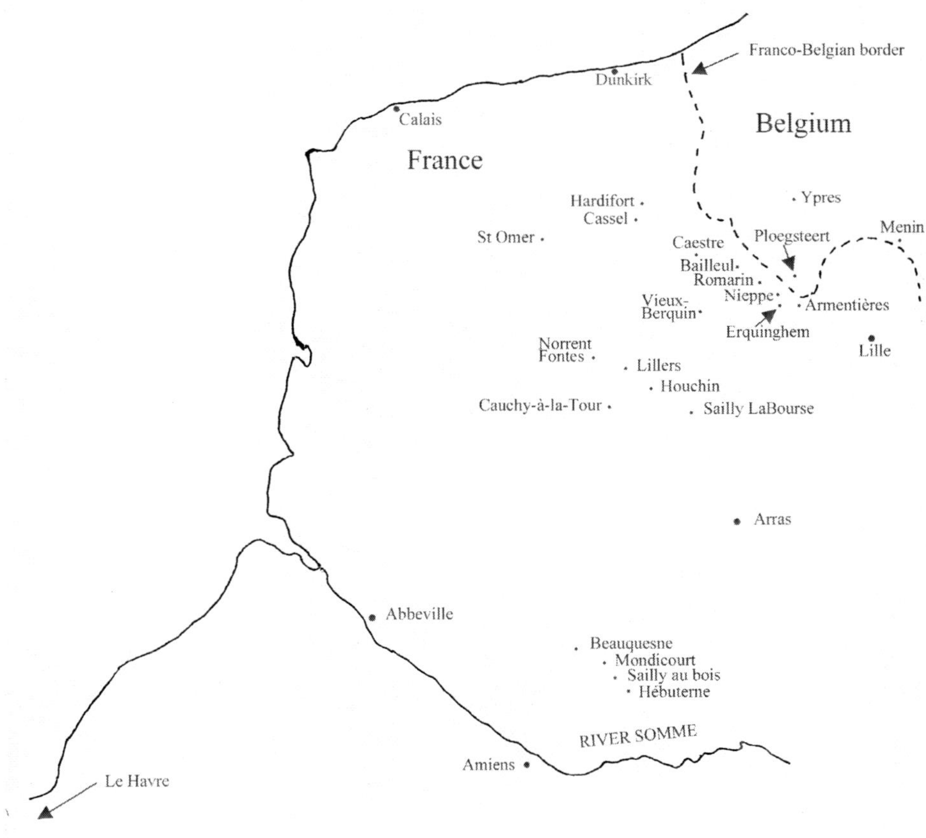

Map of France and Belgium showing some of the places where Frank was in 1915

On 25 May the Brigade War Diary revealed that some of the men were complaining of sore eyes; this was caused by the first use of poison gas on the Western Front by the Germans at Ypres. During the month of May nine men had been killed, two died of wounds and twenty-seven men and one officer were wounded.

Another private in Frank's battalion wrote that when drinking water was scarce they would 'dig a hole in the trench floor' to collect the water, then boil it and 'skim off the scum with an old envelope' in order to make tea. However, they soon gave up the practice when they noticed two wooden crosses not far away from their trench.[16]

The 8th Royal Warwicks stayed in the area of the Douve/Steenbeck trenches, Jonesville and Ploegsteert Wood through May and June. They were sent to have a bath at Pont Nieppe about once a month. Meantime they were in and out of the trenches. On 14 June they were inspected by Major-General Sir Robert Fanshawe, CB, DSO. Frank spent his seventeenth birthday in the reserve trenches in Ploegsteert Wood although it probably went by unnoticed. They were then on the move again and marched eight miles to Bailleul and on 26 June were inspected by General Pulteney. Another six miles took them to Vieux Berquin and another nineteen miles to Norrent Fontes where they arrived on 28 June at 4am. At 4pm that day they marched to Cauchy-à-la-Tour which was another ten miles.

On 1 July Sir Douglas Haig inspected the billets. An order of what discipline should be adhered to while marching was issued to the soldiers, including the instruction that 'no riding on wagons, nor equipment to be placed on them', is allowed, but 'singing and smoking are permitted for marching'. They had attack practice in Le Marquet woods.

There were no more letters from Frank until 10 July, but in the meantime Frank's father Herbert received one from a friend with whom they had lodged at Coggeshall, dated 4 July 1915:

> Dear Mr Birkinshaw
>
> Thought I would let you know that Mr Blyth is going on all right; he has not arrived home yet but expects to shortly, no doubt you found him a typical farmer. This war is no more or less than murder committed by those in authority the last seven years. They ought to be shot; it's their fair sentence, for sending the flower of the world to fight and nothing when they get there to fight with. It's double damnable. I have not the patience to read of our poor fellows facing death, against odds, not in men, but guns shells etc. etc. Talk about paying such scum £400 per annum. Oh my gracious, what for, Mr Birkinshaw. Is it not disgraceful?

Now about your dear boy. I only hope through God's grace he is all right. But a lot he was here with have gone home and some maimed, poor fellows, for life. Oh those lists every day.

We trust you are all quite well and bearing up with that spirit you showed here. Goodbye and hope good news in store for you all.

Yours sincerely – G Browning.

The 10 July letter from Frank was to his mother and described an inspection by the Secretary of State for War, Lord Kitchener, on the Lillers/ Choques Road on 8 July:

I was delighted to have your letter yesterday evening after expecting one for two or three days. Since I last wrote things are bucking up somewhat.

On Wednesday afternoon we went down the coal mine. It was really interesting; we went down in little coal buckets, three in each, and descended 600 feet. The buckets rolled and wobbled terribly and we were quite relieved when at last we reached the bottom where it was somewhat like a tube station with an electric motor for hauling the trucks along. We went about a mile along the galleries until we had to go on our hands and knees, and after picking some coal we came back and after about an hour we ascended to the surface, pretty black.

On Thursday we got up at three o'clock in the morning and marched about ten miles to form a guard of honour to Lord Kitchener and the Prince of Wales, who had come out to see the Warwicks (I don't think!). When we got back, after ten hours without anything to eat or drink, we were given our rations which consisted of one loaf of bread between a section [probably about eight men], six dates apiece and soap. It was really pitiful to watch the chaps endeavouring to spread the soap instead of butter.

Yesterday (Friday) we also got up at three o'clock and started out at five, returning at 3 o'clock in the afternoon. As one of our men said 'if this is our rest, God help us when we start work'.

The weather is really hot. I think that one of these days I will be found a drop of grease with my equipment lying by where I ought to be.

I am anxiously awaiting the socks as the only part left of mine is the tops. Also reinforcements in the way of shirts are urgently needed.

From your loving Son – Frank.
PS You would not like to see me starve (now would you?)

Frank's next letter dated 13 July was headed 'Somewhere' but the second page was missing:

> My dear Mother
>
> I told you in my last letter that we were most probably moving. Well last night we gathered together our belongings and putting them on our backs sallied forth into the unknown. We hadn't the slightest idea whither we were bound but made a pretty straight course towards the sound of the guns and flash of the flare lights and after marching for about six hours we at last turned off into a field, and after performing several intricate movements in the dark we were told to settle down for the night. It was quite a sight to see the field illuminated by the candles and small fires on which was boiling hot Oxo or tea and away on the horizon were the flashes of the guns. Occasionally the whole horizon would be lit up by multi-coloured lights.

They were now in Houchin and on 16 July there was a working party at La Bourse. On 17 July they returned to Cauchy-à-la-Tour and then to Lillers Station where they entrained for Mondicourt, and marched about seven miles to bivouac (sleeping in the open) at Beauquesne in Picardy on 20 July. Then another nine miles on to Courcelles to take over the trenches from the 93rd French Infantry Regiment where they were under enemy shelling. These trenches at Sailly au Bois, recently captured from the Germans, needed to be repaired as they were very wet and muddy because of the heavy rain.

By 7 August it was time again for their monthly bath. On 9 August thunderstorms flooded the trenches to two to three feet causing them to collapse. The war diary optimistically reported the trench situation 'well in hand' when inspected, and sure enough the next day the weather was fine and the trenches were drying out. The following day the 8th Warwicks killed and brought in a German soldier. On 15 August the battalion was relieved by the 8th Worcesters and they had another bath! Some of the men even helped the local farmers with the harvest.

Frank's next letter, dated 17 August, found him somewhat disgruntled:

> My dear Dad
>
> As we have just been issued with one of the famous green envelopes I am taking advantage of the privilege immediately.
>
> We have just come back from digging in the rain, so to start with I am not exactly in the best of humours. The parcel I had from Barkers was, I think, in most respects superior to those from Burrows. The cake was a revelation, but as I was at the time in mess with seven others it did not survive over a few minutes. Think of the

cake and then imagine eight hungry Warwicks living on an unvaried diet of bread and soap (more or less). Could you ask Mother if it is possible to send a *quantity* of home made greasy stodgy cake. It may sound a queer request but it would really prove very acceptable. You could ask Mrs Valentine for the recipe of her cake and then make it more or less greasy.

By the way Laurence is back in England. He is at the Earl of Derby's hospital in Warrington, the lucky beggar. In his letter he enthusiastically describes a golden-haired nurse and the people who come to visit him. He says that the cheering when the wounded soldiers passed through the town was worse than being shelled. He was originally booked to stay in France but there was one vacant berth on the hospital ship and of course he was picked. It is horrible without him; most of my pals are back at the base or in England.

Have just been informed that there is Bully-Beef for dinner tomorrow. Misery of Miseries!!!! etc. (language).

By the way would you see if it were possible for me to get a transfer now to the R.I.A. Royal Flying Corps or the A.S.C. or the R.G.A. or the Motor Transport. *This is important.* Please do your best.

From your loving son – Franky.

Frank was in the Hébuterne trenches on 24 August and he wrote to his father on the following day from the nearby ruined village of Sailly-au-Bois:

My dear Dad

I was delighted to have your letter this evening.

This afternoon we moved from the village mentioned in my letter of yesterday and are now in what was once a village just behind the trenches and at the beginning of our communication trenches. It is about the size of Coggeshall and about three months ago was in the possession of the Germans but when the French gunners started they did it very thoroughly. They absolutely smashed the place to bits. The church is scattered about in different parts of the village. Most of the houses are completely wiped out. Of some of them there remains but one wall. Opposite our billet the remains of a cottage consisting of a chimney and a bath, riddled with shrapnel and rifle bullets. In the road are great shell holes and loopholed barricades at frequent intervals. There is desolation everywhere and not an inhabitant in the village. The Germans are constantly shelling one part of the village but ours is practically untouched at present. Altogether it is quite a lively place. We were digging in front of the trenches last night until one o'clock in the morning. Tomorrow we move again, somewhere up the line, but I don't know where.

You ask if we saw the Lord Mayor? Unfortunately we were in the trenches at the time and as the communication trench was up to one's waist in water in most places he did not visit *us*. Besides he could not get up the narrow trench. However he inspected 'B' company (3 miles behind).

You say that Billy Laurence did not seem keen on soldiering. Be that as it may. He was one of the best NCOs in our company. He worked as hard as all the rest of them put together and one never heard him grousing. I can say no more than this.

You mention German helmets. The Germans don't wear helmets but little marine caps (very ugly). I once got a helmet only it hadn't a spike or badge so I threw it away.

From your loving Son – Franky.

PS Please don't imagine that I am fed up. I only desire a change for something more interesting or exciting.

In the autumn of 1915 Frank was evacuated from France to hospital in England suffering from rheumatic fever brought about from standing around in water in the trenches, sometimes waist-high as he had said in one of his letters. He had been in France about six months.

Part of a letter remained that he wrote to his mother from Ward Four of the Connaught Hospital, Aldershot:

I received your postcard with address this morning. I was moved to the main hospital on Saturday. Of course it is far better than the huts in every respect. The food is quite good, whereas down in the huts it was vile. The Doctor in this ward is the Harley Street man, Dr Abrams, the other Doctor is six feet two tall and has the French Legion of Honour. I have no idea when I am leaving here, but I am becoming more resigned now I am in the main hospital, though of course it is very tiresome having nothing to do for 15 hours every day. The nurses are awfully nice in here. One of them (the nicest) has the 'Royal Red Cross'. It was given her by the King at Buckingham Palace.

Frank must have recovered sufficiently to be back on duty by 6 December of that year as his next letter was written from Southminster where he was on guard duty:

My dear Mother

I was so pleased to have your letter on Saturday when on guard at Southminster. I don't know whether I told you that the rector has

> asked us up any time we feel so disposed. He is a very nice man and an enthusiastic bee keeper.
>
> I enclose four snapshots taken by my friend Brandrick. In most of the views you will find myself. I am easily identified – always smiling.
>
> My glove size is seven and a half and I take 'eight' boots. If you can't manage a large plum pudding, send a small one. If you remember, Auntie Jennie sent me one last Xmas. Please send me some Raphael Tucks Xmas cards in a box, they are so much nicer than the loose ones. A box costs about 1/- or 1/6. Please send the socks to P A Flowers, 10 Platoon, C. Coy and ask him to distribute them among Harvey, Boyd and Green and any others.
>
> From your loving son Frank.
> PS Don't forget pyjamas

His next letter, also from Southminster, was written on 4 January 1916, again to his mother:

> I thought that perhaps you might be pleased to hear we are moving to Newcastle on Friday night, arriving there some time on Saturday morning. The whole division is moving there so you may guess that things will be pretty busy. The advance party has already gone. As I thought it was probable that we might move this week I cycled over to Coggeshall on Sunday returning on Monday. I had quite a reception at the hands of the Coggeshall people, and am sure, had I wished, I could have got drunk at their expense. I stopped the night at Mr Browning's. Everybody, especially the children, looked aghast at seeing the once familiar Warwick Antelope and then came a chorus: 'Why, it's a Warwick, Jolly old Warwicks! Good old Warwicks!' And the shopkeepers said - 'We never had anyone like the Warwicks.'
>
> Mr and Mrs Jarvis, Mr Browning and family, the innkeeper and his wife at the Tilkey 'Lamb' all wish to be remembered to you and hope that 'you and Mr Birkinshaw' will again extend your patronage towards the town 'après la guerre'.

Despite all the hardships and dangers he encountered, Frank seemed quite pleased to go to war and, sadly, it also appeared his parents were happy for him to go, as they clearly did not try to stop him which they could easily have done, as he was well under age. Frank possibly felt his father at last respected him, and Herbert probably enjoyed the reflected glory of having a son fighting for King and country. It was somewhat reminiscent of the young Jack Kipling, only a little older than Frank, whose father Rudyard Kipling was desperate for his son to be seen to do his duty and secured him a commission in the Irish Guards. Jack too wrote letters home to his parents but tragically was killed on his first day of action at the Battle of Loos in September 1915, aged only eighteen.

Frank was indeed lucky to have got out of France before winter set in and before the massacre at the Battle of the Somme the following July, where the 8th Royal Warwicks suffered a fifty-five per cent casualty rate on the first day.

Frank, 1915

La Plus Douve Farm Cemetery, Belgium, where Sandy Hutton is buried. 2001

'Plug Street' wood, in Belgium, where Frank spent his 17th birthday
Photo taken in 2001

Frank's War Medals (front and back)

From left to right:

1914-15 Star Royal Warwickshire Regiment (Campaign Medal)

British War Medal; (Campaign Medal)

Victory Medal; (Campaign Medal)

Meritorious Service Medal; (RAF medal for meritorious service by ground crew)

Médaille d'honneur, RAF 1918; (awarded for service to the State of France)

Chapter Two

Arabia

Frank got his wish and left the Royal Warwicks and joined the Royal Flying Corps (RFC) on 23 February 1916 as an Air Mechanic, Second Class. He wrote to his mother from Larkhill Camp on Salisbury Plain in 'May or June 1916' where he probably spent his eighteenth birthday:

> Thanks so much for the letters and newspapers which I have received during the last week. I received *The Windsor* [a monthly magazine] this afternoon. We were taken out of isolation last week, only on Saturday we had another case in my hut so are now under special isolation for three weeks.
>
> I am feeling horribly fed up with everything and everyone in general. I can assure you that Salisbury Plain is infinitely worse than Essex. The only thing that we have to do is to clean up the hut, our only recreation is having a bath. Terrible isn't it?
>
> We are probably moving back to Farnborough in the near future. Thank goodness, then we will be only forty miles from London. We might possibly get leave in about a month's time as we will then have been three months in the RFC. I will be awfully glad when I get out of England for I feel anxious to 'do something' again and after all, England is horribly tame. I was inoculated last week and will probably be done again this week. My arm was pretty swollen.
>
> I will be *delighted* to receive cake or anything else *as soon as possible.*
>
> Your loving Son – Frank

Frank's war record, obtained from the National Archives, now described him as attached to a unit called 13 Depot with no more information to explain what sort of a unit it was or where it went. His letters were also sparse. However, he must have been sent back to France as he had a spell in a hospital in Boulogne with a knee problem. This was on 30 January 1917, following which he was transferred to hospital in Birmingham. There was a story my mother told me which was that Frank had been told on one occasion that he would have to have his leg amputated; this was possibly the time. He apparently asked the surgeon if he could have a say in the matter, and when told he could, refused the operation. He probably remembered the story about his namesake John Thornton[1] (Frank's middle name was Thornton) who lost his leg in the Peninsular War in 1813, and did not want to end up the same way. Frank was lucky and came through it and by April 1917 was ready to rejoin his squadron.

Frank in RFC uniform

Frank's next letter was written on 12 September 1917 from Italy; he was now nineteen:

> My dear Mother
>
> We are still waiting down here in this rest camp, eating, sleeping, and when it is impossible to avoid it, working. The weather is blazing hot and we spend most of the heat of the day on a rock with our feet dangling in the water. Every morning before breakfast we have a bathe and from four o'clock until seven in the afternoon we do the same. (Of course not all the time.) If it were not for the sea twenty-five yards from the tent I don't know what we should do, but as it is the camp is quite decent. We have had two impromptu concerts since we have been down here; the last being given by some men of a Welsh battalion who gave some ripping Welsh part songs. We couldn't understand the Welsh – it was absolutely worse

than Italian, but the singing was jolly fine. Until today we have been billeted in marquees, fifty in each, but today we shifted to tents, six in a tent, which is jolly comfortable.

I will have to stop now as it is getting dark and darkness only takes about ten minutes to fall down here and we are allowed no lights in the tents.

Your loving Son – Frank

In October 1917 Frank sent a postcard to his brother Bill from Taranto in Italy, saying that they were on the move again and that the family would probably not hear from him for a while. This time his destination was Arabia.

In September 1917 an RFC unit had been formed in Arabia, which was a detached flight known as 'X' Flight, under the auspices of No 14 Squadron, to fight alongside the Arabs. This was a Special Service Flight under the command of Lieutenant Colonel P C Joyce, Commander of the British section of the Arab Northern Army and Head of the Egypt Expeditionary Force, and was highly secret. Its aim was to give T E Lawrence and his Arab army the air support they needed. This was where Frank was sent and where he was to remain for the rest of the war.

I visited the RAF Museum at Hendon and found an article from *Cross & Cockade International*[2] about No 14 Squadron and 'C' Flight, from which 'X' Flight had emerged, although Frank was drafted in to it from another unit. 'C' Flight had been assembled at Suez in October 1916 and was known as the 'Arabian Detachment' of the Hejaz Expedition. The Hejaz was a Turkish Arab Province, the area running along the Red Sea in part of Saudi Arabia which included Mecca and Medina. Captain T E Lawrence (who was immortalised in the film *Lawrence of Arabia*) had asked for help to assist in the Arab revolt against the Turks in the Hejaz and 'C' Flight was made available to him. 'C' Flight had six aeroplanes which they referred to as 'machines', three Rolls Royce armoured cars, two Rolls Royce Tenders and at least three Crossley Tenders and Ford 'T' light cars; the latter Colonel Joyce described as 'galloping bedsteads'. The planes were shipped in crates in pieces and assembled at the base and their packing cases were used for hangers and workshops. Communication between planes and cars was by means of ground strips and smoke signals. In July 1917 Lawrence's forces had taken Aqaba and it was there that Frank went to join 'X' Flight a few months later.

On 8 November an entry in the war diary of 'X' Flight[3], announced that several NCOs and men had reported their arrival at Aqaba for duty. Amongst the thirty-five or so was 2/AM (Air Mechanic, Second Class) Birkinshaw FT. He was described as a driver mechanic.

One of the Commanders of 'X' Flight (from June 1918) was Captain V D Siddons who had been training for the Methodist ministry but became a pilot with the RFC and joined 'C' Flight (and later 'X' Flight) in the Hejaz. He was an occasional pilot for Lawrence and was awarded the DFC and the Order of Al Nahda (4th class) for 'his rendering glorious services and great tasks'. During the Second World War he became an army chaplain and was evacuated from Dunkirk; he eventually ended up in the Middle East and Egypt as a senior army chaplain.

The Reverend Siddons gave various lectures after the Second World War, one of which was on the subject of 'The Revolt in the Hejaz – 1916.' This I found amongst his papers in the Imperial War Museum.[4] Here he described the background to the Arab revolt. The Turks occupied the Hejaz, which was part of the Turkish Ottoman Empire, and the Arabs wanted rid of them. The narrow gauge Hejaz railway ran from Damascus to Medina and was built to carry pilgrims to Mecca, although the railway never quite extended that far. The Turks had garrisons at about twenty mile intervals to protect the railway line. Lawrence selected Feisal, son of Hussain, Sherif of Mecca, to help rally the Arabs. They captured Wedj and then moved towards Aqaba. On this expedition, with Lawrence and various Arab leaders, the railway line was cut and, as Siddons said, the 'telegraph wires broken by the simple means of cutting them and attaching the ends to several camels, the beasts then being driven until the weight of uprooted telegraph poles precluded any further movement'.

Captain Siddons, in his lecture, went on to talk about 'X' Flight. They had seven aeroplanes, one De Havilland DH2 and six Martinsydes (nicknamed Elephants as they were large and unwieldy), and three Crossley Light Tenders and trailers and two motor cycles and sidecars. He said that 'roads did not exist, the vehicles having to make their way as best they could, dodging the numerous sand dunes formed by the wind and scrub. The going was almost impossible in places and to surmount this difficulty ordinary wire mesh was pegged down, thus giving the car wheels some sort of grip.' The pilots were bombing Ma'an station and aerodrome and other stations along the railway line. Siddons described the 'extraordinary weather conditions' in the following terms: 'From November to March or April the clouds hang about on the mountains and make it impossible for aircraft to move freely', then after April 'the heat becomes so great after about 0900 hours, that aircraft cannot get off the ground with a good load on board'. He went on to talk about the difficulties which the motor vehicles had. The Crossley Light Tenders, which is what Frank would mostly have been driving, were found to be unsuitable for the area because large boulders made holes in the underside of the engines owing to the lowness of the sump, and the 'radiators were too small, causing repeated stops in order to fill up with water'. This was highly inconvenient as it meant extra water, which was scarce, had to be carried on long journeys and 'double driving wheels were found to be necessary in order to get a good grip of the extremely doubtful surfaces over which they had to pass'. These inhospitable surfaces included mud flats near Aqaba 'which in the rainy season are converted into veritable seas of mud, rendering them impassable for wheeled vehicles'. Siddons said that most of the transport was done by camels and donkeys. Camels could carry a 400lb load.

Crossley Tender somewhere in the desert (from Frank's collection of Arabian photographs)

On 17 December 1917 Frank wrote to his mother from Arabia:

> I am adding this letter to my last one as I kept it for several days waiting for a boat to come in, but one is due in tonight. We are of course quite excited when any boat is reported due in and we are now all expecting the Xmas mail. I received another letter from you three nights ago dated 12 November so evidently your letters are arriving here all right. I also got *Pearson's Magazine*[5] and was so pleased to get it because there is absolutely nothing to do in our hours of leisure except to argue and speculate as to the end of the war, that is when we have nothing to read. I am really afraid that I have, as usual, very little to say in this letter; you see we are so isolated here and apart from trivialities nothing ever happens; we haven't even had a pay day since we arrived in this place.
>
> Of course the inhabitants (if they could be called inhabitants) of this place (if it could be called a place) are very interesting. I am perfectly sure that they are the lost tribe of Israel, because the Israelites in their 40 years wandering toured this place I believe, pretty thoroughly. I am not very well up in Bible literature, but I bet that they were jolly glad when they got back to the Promised Land. The Arabs wander about two or three together, each with a camel, and usually a rifle and about two hundred rounds of ammunition, two revolvers, one walking stick, one nightdress and a complicated coloured duster round their heads, a skin of water and a bag of grub, and with these items apparently walk about in huge circles, returning to the same spot every five days or so. Occasionally, however, they all go mad, and a squadron of 100 or so of them come galloping down the hills on their camels, firing their rifles haphazardly in the air and waving banners or flags, and the 'resident' Arabs of the place turn out to greet them also firing rifles, and then everything is quiet for some time. Talk about Arabian nights!
>
> I told you I believe that I broke my 'Swan' pen. I am going to register it and send the two halves home fairly soon. I believe that the 'Swan' people will repair it for nothing but I do miss it fearfully. My watch stopped also but very few watches will go at all with such a tremendous amount of sand about, so I will send that home also as soon as possible.
>
> I must stop now as it is bedtime.
>
> Your loving Son – Frank.

The next letter to Frank's mother was undated but again from Arabia:

> I am afraid that I have been very backward just lately in my letters, but I will endeavour to make up for it from now onwards. The last five days I have been up at the advanced aerodrome, doing nothing except lying under my mosquito net and dividing my time between

swatting flies and wishing I were in the Arctic regions. Really it has been very hot just lately, even our drinking water is quite hot and I am sure that anyone who started an ice-cream industry would make his fortune.

I am enclosing several photos, all typical of the country, which were taken on one of my trips to the 'advanced drome'. The photo marked 'one' shows a train of camels going up through a pass in the mountain. The pass is the original road used by the pilgrims on their way to Mecca. The next photo shows one of the many dead camels which line the way. As a rule there are vultures round the dead bodies, but they did a bunk when I took the photo. No 3 shows the 3 cars stopping for lunch and the last is a photo of me speeding across the mud flats which I think I have told you about.

By the last mail I got the two books I asked for but no letter, neither did I get any letter by this mail, but we are now expecting another bout in a few days' time.

There has been quite a plague of Tarantula spiders about here lately. They are horrible big spiders about as large as a man's fist, and jaws that work sideways. I believe that they are poisonous.

I think that I had better stop now as we get up at four-thirty in the mornings nowadays and it is nearly half past nine – bedtime.

Your loving Son – Frank.

On 1 January 1918 Frank was promoted to Air Mechanic First Class. At one stage Frank asked his father to get him a machine gun manual as he was thinking of transferring to the machine gun section. On 3 March he wrote to his mother:

My dear Mother

I am sorry that I have not been able to write for nearly two weeks but the last ten days I have been up country. On my return I was jolly pleased to get two letters dated 13 October and 27 January, but as I didn't arrive at this place until November I suppose that you must have made a mistake and the date should read 13 January and not October. I was very much relieved to hear that you had at last got all my letters in a lump, you must have felt anxious not hearing for nine weeks, but I expect all my letters will arrive home more or less spasmodically. I believe that I have received most, if not all, of your letters, although they too arrive in inverted order.

If you received my last letter you will remember I told you that I was going on a little trip, partially by camel. I left the same day and had a ripping time. There was only myself and an officer, together with six or seven camel men, and as I had never ridden a camel before I had a most agonizing time the first two days. You see camels get up in three motions like a switchback and when they eventually get right up, one seems miles away from the ground. After the first day's ride I felt like a heap of cinders that has just been shaken through a sieve, but I soon got used to it and now I am quite an expert camel rider. We slept in all sorts of weird places, amongst them being a castle built by the Emperor Saladin, an old Turkish fort, a cave in the rocks, a ditch and a dry river bed, and we actually saw streams and green grass, both of course being absolutely foreign to the country around here. The last three or four days as we had run short of bread, but had plenty of flour, we lived on Arab bread, which is prepared as follows:

Ingredients: Flour, water, salt.
Directions: Get some flour, water and salt, and bang them about until you have a thick, sticky, dirty looking lump of dough, then flatten it out until it looks the shape of a …… [unfortunately there was a page missing, so we never get to know the full secret of Arab bread-making!]

Arabs making bread (from Frank's collection)

In fact this letter referred to a very interesting mission that Frank had just been on, led by one of the pilots, Lt. Makins, and which had been well documented in the war diary. It was not often that 'other ranks', the name given to those who were below commissioned officers, were mentioned by name, so to come across something with my father's name on it was particularly exciting. The date was 17 February 1918 and it was a report from 2/Lt. AD Makins on the search for a Turkish aeroplane which had been brought down by the Arabs east of Kalat Aneiza on the other side of the Hejaz railway line in enemy territory. The Arabs who shot down the plane had cut the wings off the machine so it could not fly, but now the British wanted to salvage the engine. The Turkish pilot had been captured and sent to a prison camp, and prior to the search for the plane Lt. Makins had been sent to find him. The Commanding Officer of 'X' Flight, Captain Furness-Williams, reported the situation in his weekly Summary of Operations:

> He [Makins] eventually found that the prisoner had been sent to Aqaba and traced him to the prisoners' camp. All his clothes had been taken away from him and he had been very badly treated. I obtained authority to get him away from the Turkish prisoners' camp and for the moment he is living with us before proceeding by ship to Egypt. I have interrogated him and information obtained is attached.

The pilot was nineteen years old and he was able to tell them how many planes the enemy had and where they were located and also how many guns and men they had.

Lt. Makins' report on the search for the aeroplane, addressed to the Officer Commanding 'X' Flight RFC, and later forwarded to Colonel Joyce[6] at Aqaba, was in the form of a diary:

Ismael Zaki, the Turkish pilot, third from left (from Frank's collection)

> Sir,
>
> Re above and in accordance with your orders I proceeded with 1/AM Birkinshaw FT by Crossley Tender on 17.2.18 to El Gueira [Guweira] where we spent the night.
>
> On 18.2.18, not being able to procure an interpreter, Major Maynard arranged for an officer and an Algerian of the French Army to proceed with us as interpreters. At 1100 I moved off from El Gueira with 13 camels and 11 all ranks and camped at the foot of the Nagb for the night.

Lt Makins went on to say that one camel man deserted during the night and the next day they proceeded to Mughaira where they camped. There he consulted with the Arab colonel in charge of the area about crossing the enemy line (denoted by the railway) and also getting a local interpreter, as his Algerian interpreter assumed all Arabs to be spies and even told them so, which made life very difficult. The Colonel lent them his Sergeant Major 'who speaks remarkably good English'. Makins added to the entry for that day – 'Raining all night.'

On 20 February the officer and the Algerian trooper returned to Guweira taking a report with them to say that Lt. Makins would be away for ten days. The party proceeded with eleven camels and ten 'all ranks' and arrived at Ain Basta at 1100 where they found 'a filled-in well, a spring and one brick house standing in a compound'. There was also plenty of water and about fifty cows 'grazing on excellent grass'. They camped in a big cave at El Arga one mile west of El Heisha. It rained all night. On 21 February they proceeded to a Bedouin encampment at Hassain El Dobie from where two Bedouins were detailed to help locate the downed enemy aeroplane as they knew where it was. Their journey continued through Nagel (Najl) three miles west of Shobak where the railway line runs from Aneiza to El Heisha.[7] Makins continued:

> We arrived at Shobak Castle and I reported to Sherif Abdul Main arranging with him to supply me with cavalry to take us across the line the following morning. Two Turkish prisoners were brought in and reported German cavalry patrolling the Ma'an and Jurf El Deruish Road and further that the Turkish officers along the line to a great extent had been returned to their regiments and German NCOs sent to replace them. Raining all night.

The entry for 22 February said that two camels had to be returned to Guweira as they were too sick to continue. One man went with them and he took a report from Makins to the Commanding Officer in Guweira. Lt. Makins proceeded with the three cavalry men who had been provided by the Sherif, his nine camels and nine 'other ranks', passing through a main camel road from Shobak on to the railway line which ran to Aneiza. They arrived at El Dosak where they had to remain for the rest of the day because of the rain and the 'general debility of men and camels'. The cavalrymen returned to Shobak

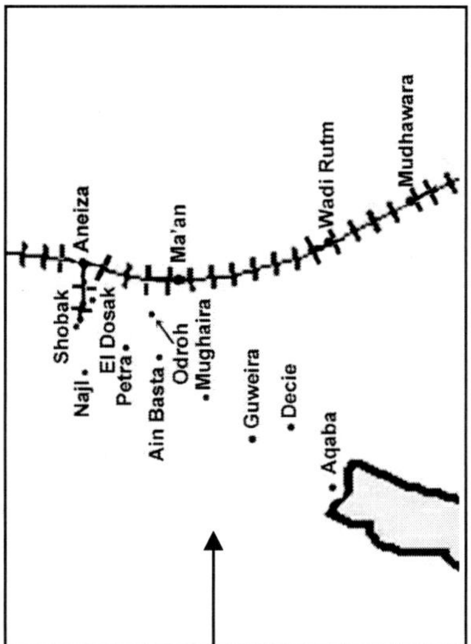

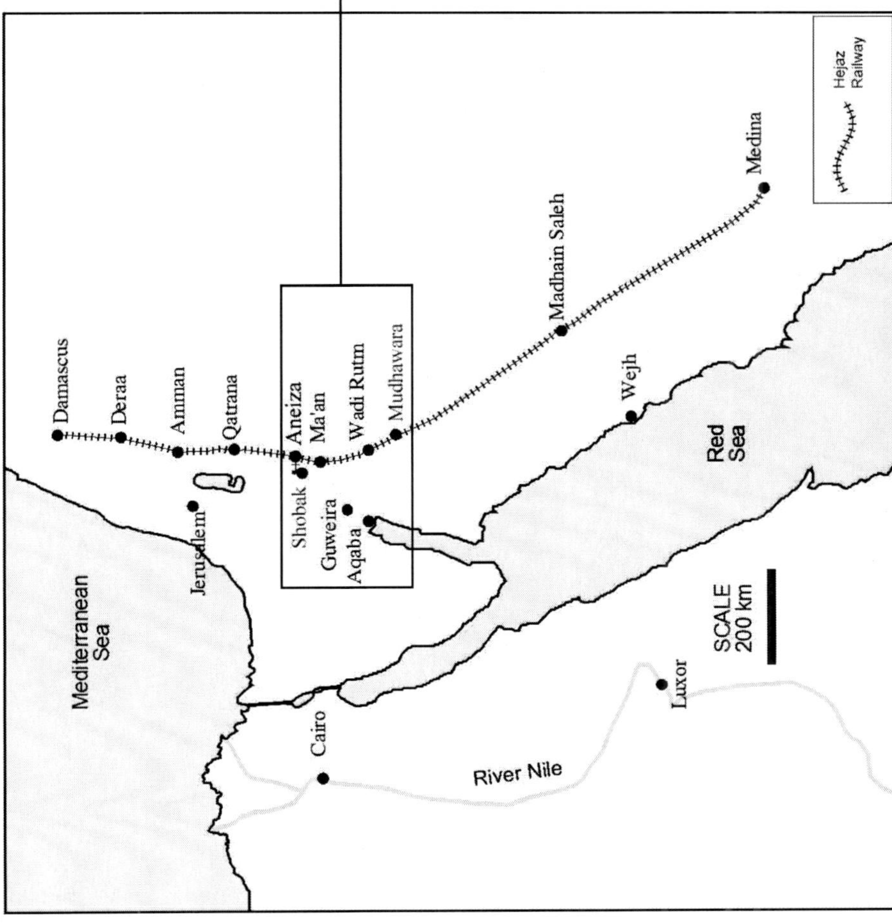

Map of Arabia, 1918

for the night. The next evening they were able to continue as the rain had stopped. They were now moving into dangerous territory and were about to cross the enemy line. Makins went on:

> At 1500 I left El Dosak to cross the line which I did in perfect safety. The cavalry from Sherif Abdul Main brought with them three slabs of gun-cotton which we placed in three different positions along the railway and blew the line up successfully.

They found the remains of the Turkish aeroplane five miles east of Aneiza in a gully. They examined it and found it had made a perfect landing as all the parts were in perfect condition. The machine had been cut up and set fire to by the Arabs who had then used the engine for target practice. They salvaged everything they could. In the afternoon an enemy aeroplane dropped a bomb one and a half miles to their east killing three Bedouins. Lt Makins sent a message to Sherif Oba Abul Tie, leader of the Howeitat tribe of Bedouins (the same Auda abu Tayi who featured in the film *Lawrence of Arabia*), asking him for food, camels and cavalry to carry them back over the line. Oba Abul Tie replied that he could not supply food as they too were very short, but sent a small sack of flour, (this was no doubt the flour Frank had talked about in his letter). During that night a group of Bedouins proceeded over the line towards the Turks and because the Turks thought they were from Lt. Makins' group they mistakenly shot at the Bedouins with rifles and machine guns, 'the further result of which I have no particulars of', Makins reported.

On 25 February at 1100 the cavalry arrived (all three of them) along with four camels from Oba Abul Tie, with the greeting: 'How much are you to pay us to take you across the line?' As the answer was in the negative the cavalry went away but came back later and said they 'would take us across provided they were paid after completing the contract'; this was agreed. At sundown they re-crossed the railway line to El Kannas where they rested for the night. It was raining again.

The entry for 26 February read:

> We started off at dawn and got as far as Odroh where we were overtaken by a very severe snowstorm. At this place two camels died and after removing the baggage, straps etc. and packing them on to remaining camels I arrived at a cave five miles SSW of Odroh when I found it impossible for the whole convoy to go on any further owing to ground being in a very bad state. Being short of food and wood for heating purposes I decided to walk on to Mughaira, taking with me 1/AM Birkinshaw, the interpreter and two guides, leading three camels with bare necessities and leaving instructions with the head camelman and owner to follow on at his earliest opportunity. We arrived at Col. Maloud's Headquarters at 2000 where we stayed for the night and received every comfort.

Shobak castle (from Frank's collection)

El Dosak (from Frank's collection)

Above:
Frank standing on the Hejaz Railway

(Both photos from Frank's collection)

Left:
Frank with the downed Turkish plane

And that for 27 February:

> Arriving at Mughaira at 0900 we continued to walk leading the camels on account of the muddy state of the ground to the bottom of the Nagb where we were able to mount the three camels and arrived at Headquarters El Gueira at 1630.

Lt. Makins and Frank returned to Aqaba to report back to HQ. And all the above was described by Frank as 'ripping fun'. He was in fact awarded two medals for his bravery. One citation, in September 1918 (after Frank had been promoted to corporal) was written by the Captain of the RAF commanding 'X' Flight to the Commanding Officer of the RAF at Abu Lisal. It read:

> Corporal Mechanic Frank Thornton Birkinshaw has shown great ability, cheerfulness and endurance in driving cars for long distances over bad country. He accompanied an officer in crossing the railway, when it was held by the enemy, for the purpose of obtaining parts of a hostile aeroplane and on this occasion showed courage and resource.

I was curious to find out what had become of Makins after the war, and accordingly did some research. I discovered from the RAF Museum at Hendon that Lieutenant (later Captain) Arthur Makins started as a Yeomanry Officer serving in the Westminster Dragoons in Egypt before transferring to the RFC in the Spring of 1917. He joined 'X' Flight in December 1917 a month after Frank. He was Mentioned in Dispatches in October 1918 and received the Distinguished Flying Cross 'for gallant conduct and distinguished services'. In 1920 he received the Order of the Renaissance conferred by the King of the Hejaz. In a report on pilots' performance written in February 1918, Lt. Siddons wrote that 2/Lt. Makins was 'good in the air. Does not land very well. Energetic, capable and reliable. Recommended for promotion.'[8] The RAF Museum told me that Makins had walked in with his medals in 1973, just before he died, and presented them to the museum. They gave me his last known address which was 'The Charterhouse, London EC1'. The Charterhouse was a home for elderly gentlemen and, according to their records, it was where Makins went to live in 1958. He was then seventy and was working for the Inland Revenue with no other means of support. It appeared that he had no family, and he lived there until he died in 1974 aged eighty-six. In his will, which I obtained from the Probate Office, he left just over a thousand pounds to cover his burial in Little Hallingbury, the church associated with The Charterhouse. He also left various bequests to the staff who had looked after him and asked that 'enough sherry and wine for a luncheon for the Brothers [residents] at The Charterhouse' be purchased.

Lieutenant Makins (from Frank's collection)

On 1 April 1918 the RFC was subsumed into the RAF and in the war diary there was a list of all the NCOs and Men of 'X' Flight. There were fifty-one names with ranks and occupations and pay listed. Frank was then an Air Mechanic First Class, which was his rank. His trade was listed as 'driver' and he earned 4/- a day. Chief Mechanics were paid 7/- and a second class private (e.g. the cook) was only paid 1/6d. The trades varied from storeman, armourer, blacksmith, carpenter, coppersmith, electrician, aero-engine fitter, photographer, aeroplane rigger, motor cyclist, to sailmaker.

Frank would have driven personnel, spares, stores, water, bombs and petrol around as and when required and no doubt be roped in to anything else that might need doing, including sometimes working on the planes. An entry in the war diary stated that on 17 April Lawrence arrived by car reporting that the attack on Ma'an had failed, and the following Sunday he arrived by 'Ford' car from Mudhawara. It was very likely that Frank was driving Lawrence around on some of these occasions.[9] In May a Crossley Tender took Lt. Col Lawrence to Nagb and remained the night for him there. Week ending 18 May the diary reported that 'every day during this week either one car or two cars travelled from Aqaba to Decie and back, a distance of one hundred and ten miles and one car did the journey from Decie to Guweira and back – a distance of forty miles'. The car was to leave Guweira daily at 0800 with water for Decie and return at about 1000. It was to remain there until the following day and 'will consequently be available for taking urgent messages to Decie at any time of the day or night'. The roads were very rough and sometimes non-existent so the going would be extremely slow and tedious. The entry for 10 August said that a BE 12A left to bomb Ma'an aerodrome but the hanger was found to be empty and instead a herd of camels was bombed. Also on that day one of the pilots flew Lawrence to El Jafar for a conference. Another entry in August stated 'trying to get aerodrome cleared. Only labour obtainable comes from Sherifian army who are of a very independent nature and only work when it suits them.'

In June 1918 'X' Flight moved nearly thirty miles north from Aqaba to Guweira from where they made occasional bombing raids on Ma'an and Mudhawara. There was a letter in the war diary marked 'secret' from the Lt-Colonel, HQ of the RAF to the Officer Commanding 'X' Flight saying that he had had a report that a message was dropped over the enemy's lines near Ma'an, by someone from 'X' Flight, apologizing for having bombed an enemy Medical Unit by mistake, and the Lt-Colonel demanded that 'an explanation of this report is required'. The Lt-Colonel went on: 'Apart from the fact that a mistake of this sort should not have been admitted, it is absolutely prohibited to correspond in any way with the enemy without sanction from GHQ.' There was also an amusing story in *Winged Promises*[10], which is a history of No 14 Squadron, which related how a German pilot dropped a letter over No 14 Squadron's aerodrome advising the CO that they had captured two English pilots and inviting him 'to drop some clothing and shaving kit over the German aerodrome at Beersheba', which was done. On another occasion a message was dropped by the Germans to say that they had buried a downed Australian pilot with military honours and that another pilot was a prisoner whom they liked so much they were 'showing him the country'.

Another disciplinary matter was brought to everyone's attention later in the year decreeing that 'the habit of cultivating long hair is inadmissible; this applies to all ranks'.

The next letter from Frank also had a page missing, but there were one or two interesting snippets; also no date or place. He talked about the victories of the Hejaz which had now become independent from Turkish rule:

> These small 'local' wars are so very much more interesting than the big ones, where one is merely a unit and knows nothing of what happens until it appears in the papers at home, whereas, in *our* war we all know exactly what is going to happen and what the result will be quite a long time in advance. I am afraid that I mustn't talk any more about wars because this is a 'green envelope' letter.

The whole flight is at present engaged in doing nothing, for the simple reason that there is nothing to do. The nearest Turks are miles and miles away from us, so we spend our time in looking as busy as is reasonably possible – and bathing. The weather is absolutely glorious at present, beautifully warm and yet not too hot, a fresh cool breeze and a few wisps of white cloud in the sky – the first for ages. I think that this is easily the best part of the year out here but in Egypt it is quite cool now and everyone wears serge, but here we all stroll about in shorts and the thinnest of shirts – as usual.

I went down to the 'village' to buy some sugar yesterday and it cost ten piastres, the equivalent of 2/1d per pound and it is grown and manufactured in Egypt. All the shops had 'Hejaz' flags displayed in honour of their great victories, so I suppose they raised their prices for the same reason. There are some awfully interesting things to be bought in the bazaar – praying carpets from Manchester and Mecca, jewelled daggers from Birmingham and from Damascus, tins of condensed milk and gilt bracelets – absolutely anything can be bought for a price. They sell rolls of stuff that looks just like leather, it is called mish-mish and is made of dried apricots and one buys it by the yard; the shopkeeper unrolls it, picks out the dead flies, and asks three times the price that he really thinks he is going to get for it. For instance, he might ask four rupees for it. The intending purchaser tears a piece off, starts eating it and says 'one rupee'. The shopkeeper goes raving mad, swears by Allah and all his prophets, by the grey beard of his father and by all sorts of other nice things, that he is selling it at a loss at three rupees, so the buyer offers two rupees, and everyone is happy. This is undoubtedly a much better method of business than having every article plainly marked.

It is awfully good of you to keep on sending parcels, but please don't send any more eatables unless I ask for them because they must be very difficult for you to get and we are getting plenty of grub at present.

If you got my last letter you will know that I have been made full Corporal – Paid. Will write again very soon.

Your loving Son – Frank

Frank had indeed been promoted to Corporal Mechanic (Paid) on 1 September 1918; he had been appointed to the same rank but unpaid on 1 August 1918. He was now twenty. According to the war diary the effective strength of the unit was about ten officers and fifty-five other ranks.

Dr Orange in *Winged Promises* related that General Sir Edmund Allenby's final offensive began on 19 September 1918 and 'Lawrence asked for, and received, RAF help against German aircraft around Deraa' with the intention of moving towards Damascus. Ma'an was evacuated as Arab forces moved in. On 1 October the triumphant Lawrence swept in to Damascus along with the Arab forces. 'X' Flight, with its work done, went on to Suez where it was disbanded in early October. Later the Flight was reorganised and sent to Haifa for anti-submarine duty. The Major-General commanding the RAF sent a cablegram to the Officer Commanding 'X' Flight which said:

> I am anxious to express my very high appreciation of the admirable services which the Flight has consistently rendered, under most trying conditions, whereby all ranks have earned the gratitude and admiration of the British and Arab forces with whom they have worked in co-operation.

The Armistice was accepted by the Turks on 31 October 1918.

On 5 November Frank was in Cairo and wrote again to his mother from there:

> Since writing my last letter from Luxor we moved back to Cairo, then to Suez and the next day I had to come back to Cairo in charge of a convoy of motor cars which are being changed at Cairo for three new ones. We have been here three or four days now, billeted in a depot on the outskirts of Cairo and having a ripping time, including permanent passes into the town. We have absolutely no work to do and as the new cars are not yet ready for us we have to wait here until they are. We came up by goods train, sleeping in a guard's van, it took us two days and we were awfully glad when the journey was over, but we will have a better time on the way back as I think we are going to drive the cars back to Suez instead of going by rail.
>
> I sent a lot of photos home from Luxor. I do hope you get them, but I expect that most letters will get home now that the submarine campaign has been squashed. There is quite an epidemic of Spanish Flu in Egypt which is rather strange as it has been so dry this year. Down in Luxor there is only twenty minutes' rain every year and occasionally not even that. It was awfully nice down there because there are no troops whatever in the place and we could go out without hats or tunics if we wanted to. Besides as there are so few visitors in the place we five were treated with a most terrific amount of respect, even to the length of being saluted by the Sudanese soldiers. When we left the place we were escorted to the station by the manager of the hotel; the only other guest, an Italian, also came to see us off, as well as our guide and dragoman [interpreter/guide] and his sons. The guide went down on his knees in the railway carriage to our great embarrassment and kissed all our hands, at the same time wishing long life and happiness to ourselves, our sons and our son's sons. The hotel manager also expressed the hope that we would bring our wives there for our honeymoons, and although I

was the only unmarried man in the party, we all promised that we would do our best. I am enclosing a few photos of Cairo, also two of Luxor.

I expect that the war will be over by Xmas so once again I had better express my hope that I will be back again in Hall Green [Birmingham] by next June.

Your loving Son – Frank

According to the war diary Corporal Mechanic Birkinshaw was admitted to hospital on 10 November 1918, the day before the official Armistice Day which commemorated the ending of hostilities between the British and Germans on the Western Front. He was discharged on 31 December 1918, so he must have spent Christmas in hospital. He told his sister Sheona about it in his next letter dated 17 December 1918. His letter was headed 'X' Flight RAF, Suez:

My dear Sheona

I had better start this letter by apologising most abjectly for not writing before, but the unfortunate part of it is that I *did* write about three months ago, and I don't know whether I posted or lost the letter. (As a matter of fact I am almost sure that I forgot to post it). I was awfully pleased to get your parcel and letter the other day, the socks especially will be very useful.

Nearly half the men in our Flight have gone home to England, at least all the men who have had over three years' service in the East. This only applies to 'X' Flight, which, I suppose, has the reputation of being *it.* The rest of the Flight are at present doing practically nothing as regards work, their time being occupied with listening to rumours of demobilization. Anyway I really expect to be home within six months.

I had a ripping leave a month ago – ten days. Five in Cairo, and five days down at Luxor and Thebes. The ruins at Luxor are without doubt the most wonderful in the world. We could have stayed there months instead of days and we really spent quite a strenuous time going round the temples and at nights going up the Nile in sailing boats by moonlight. We had a simply gorgeous time. I am enclosing two small snaps of the temple at Karnak. I wish I had more printed but the man who took them has gone to England and only left me with the two enclosed 'dud' prints.

I have been in hospital the last three weeks with a mosquito bite on my leg that turned septic and Spanish Flu, but will be out very soon now. Am having quite a nice time. I can't write much more because this is the last page on the pad, but anyway things are pretty slow and there isn't much to write about. We are expecting a mail in tomorrow.

> I expect that you will have heard I have got the 'Médaille d'honneur'.
>
> Your loving brother – Frank

The throwaway remark at the end of the letter showed that there certainly was plenty going on in Arabia which was not always reflected in those of Frank's letters that have survived. In 1956 my grandmother Isabel (Frank's mother) wrote to my mother, explaining how Frank had won the Medal. Isabel said Frank always disliked talking about himself but he had told her that he had volunteered to go to the enemy lines which meant certain death if he was captured. Isabel said Frank's Captain had called to see them and said he could not speak too highly of him. The incident for which he was awarded the Medal was the one related earlier which took place in February 1918 when Frank was only nineteen.

The war diary had a note about it under the heading 'Honours and Rewards':

> The President of the French Republic has, with the appoval of His Majesty the King, bestowed the following decorations on the undermentioned, in recognition of distinguished service during the campaign: Médaille d'honneur, Avec Glaives (en Bronze):[11] AM1 (Cpl Mech) Frank Thornton Birkinshaw RAF.

Frank's brother Bill seemed to be the only one who had a version of the story of how Frank had earned the Medal. The story, which Bill related to me in a letter, was slightly different from the official line and more colourful, but interesting nonetheless:

> A Turkish plane had made a forced landing behind the Turkish Lines. Frank said he thought it would be a good idea to help himself to some sparking plugs and this he did. There were some papers in the plane and as an afterthought he stuffed them in his pocket. Then he thought it might be a good idea to set fire to the plane and this he did. Telling the episode to me he said – 'the balloon went up a bit' and the Turks started firing. So he found his way to the French lines. A fairly senior French Officer kissed him on both cheeks; Frank said he took a dim view of that. The Officer awarded him a Médaille d'honneur for his bravery. Frank said to me 'and that because I only wanted some plugs'.

There was another lovely family story about the occasion, unfortunately never verified, on which Frank received his Médaille d'honneur. The story was that Frank had said he received his medal from the Empress Eugénie herself (widow of Napoleon III who was the nephew of Napoleon Bonaparte) and that she had given him a kiss. A reference to this story was made by Frank in one of his series of '*Literary Fringes*'[12] that he wrote while in New Zealand in the 1940s for broadcast on Radio NZ.

Frank was also given the Meritorious Service Medal which was awarded for distinguished service by ground crew, and the London Gazette of 3 June 1919 listed the following:

> His Majesty the King has been graciously pleased to approve of the undermentioned rewards to Officers and other ranks of the Royal Air Force in recognition of distinguished services rendered during the war.
>
> Meritorious Service Medal 21316 Cpl. Mech. Frank Thornton Birkinshaw. (Birmingham) (Egypt).

Another anecdotal story was that Frank had had some flying experience in Arabia, although this was not verified from the official records. Later in life he reported having survived a plane crash so perhaps that episode occurred during his time there. My mother certainly knew Frank had flying experience as she went as far as to take flying lessons herself not long after they met, in order to 'keep up with him'!

An entry in the war diary said that Corporal Birkinshaw went to demobilization camp at Kantara, Egypt, on 10 January 1919; this was after his spell in hospital having recovered from the Spanish flu. Kantara was where Norman Mackenzie, my mother's uncle, was buried in September 1916; he too was part of the Egyptian Expeditionary Forces and would have been there just a year before Frank.

Frank probably returned home to England sometime in early 1919. If his journey home was anything like that related by George Samuel Hynes it would have been fairly horrific. George was also an air mechanic in 'X' Flight, and he kept notes and drawings of his experiences. He and Frank would have known each other and possibly even travelled back to England at the same time. George later wrote a memoir, which his nephew Jim has now transcribed into a book, *Lawrence of Arabia's Secret Air Force.*[13] George described his three-day journey by sea from Egypt to Taranto in Italy. The ship was crowded and the men 'huddled together at night on floors without bedding to ease aching limbs. We had no means of drying our clothes during the three days and nights on board ship as we sailed to Taranto in Italy.' He went on:

> We had arrived in a miserable snowed up country from equatorial hot atmosphere in clothes that were still damp. There was nowhere in Taranto where we could dry them nor anywhere where we could get cash to buy some warm drinks.

They were housed in Nissen huts and George said his feet were wet through the whole time as he was wearing boots with soles that were worn, which he had been wearing for the past four years. The journey by train to Cherbourg was even worse as they travelled 'in railway wagons rather like meat vans' which took ten days to get to their destination, during which journey several of the men died. George continued:

> We travelled in a far from pleasant state of mind as our discomforts were aggravated by snowfalls on the railway tracks. Men were badly smitten by the cold which was hardly eased by occasional cups of weak tea at some railway stops with hardly more encouragement than 'on your way, pals!' and doses of pills to help us in our feverish conditions.

From the train they watched young girls and women begging for food or asking to exchange bottles of wine for bully beef or cheese; everyone was very poor. George was hospitalised when he arrived in Cherbourg, and, for the first time in years, was put into a lovely clean bed; a soldier who was brought in to the hospital at the same time was sadly 'carried out dead the next morning'. When he was due for release George was told to put his uniform back on, only to discover it was full of lice. Another gruelling journey awaited them in the form of a cross channel tramp steamer, packed like cattle with many sick men returning from the muddy trenches in France.

George's story was interesting, as most books about war have been written by officers or politicians and George was from the ranks. Also there was not much information about 'X' Flight because it was kept very secret, as Jim wrote in the preface to his book:

> Little has been written about the contribution made by 'X' Flight, whose aircraft and personnel in its close support operations worked for several years in adverse conditions in advanced desert landing grounds. In particular, the existence and deeds of 'X' Flight were kept so secret that in fact, for most of the time, the Royal Air Force Paymaster received no pay returns, and consequently the airmen who served with the flight received neither back pay nor hardship allowances because no records of their entitlements were kept!

Frank returned to England and went home to his parents in Hall Green, Birmingham. He was still in the RAF reserve so could be called upon at any time to go and fight. However, he was determined to become a doctor and to this end enrolled on a medical degree course at Birmingham University in September 1919.

Above: Men and vehicles in the Desert (from Frank's collection)

Frank, RAF

Aqaba 1917/18

Officer in front row centre - CdrArthur Snagge of HMS Humber, *holding the leash to the ship's mascot 'Orace the oryx'. Next to him is TE Lawrence. Next to him by the oryx is Lt. Colonel Newcombe and then Nesib el Bekri. Frank at centre back with hand over his mouth. (from Frank's collection)*

Chapter Three

The Birkinshaw Ancestors

Frank's father was Herbert Birkinshaw, born on 1 February 1871, the second youngest of ten children. Herbert's father was John Richard Birkinshaw, a well-to-do and much respected Bradford wool merchant and manufacturer. He was also an ardent Baptist and a Liberal. John Richard's parents were John, who was born in 1795, and Elizabeth. (see Tree 1)

In February 1814 John, aged nineteen, wrote a letter from London to his parents, Thomas, a farmer, and Sarah who lived in Pontefract, Yorkshire. John told them that he had 'obtained a Situation, being employed by very respectable men who are Silk and Insurance Brokers'. He also sent them a miniature of himself:

> With this you will receive my miniature. It is a very striking likeness. I desire it may be hung over the chimney piece in the parlour between the two pictures, exactly in the centre on a small bronze nail and then when you are sat round on a Sunday after dinner you will conceive I am playing some of my tricks amongst you.
>
> On Sunday last I had the honour of seeing the Princess Charlotte of Wales in coming from the Chapel Royal in the Palace. I was on the stair case and saw her very distinctly as she passed me. She is very fat.

John wrote another letter to his father later that month:

> I duly received my brother's letter of the 12th instant and was heartily glad to hear you were all well. A few days ago I met Dobinson who told me I was balloted for the Militia which prepared me for the shock. I am told they can't touch me in the City where I now am but of that Mr Trueman will inform you – don't give my address.

John went on to ask his father to try and get him off having to serve in the militia but if necessary to pay the ten pounds needed to achieve these ends. Men were at that time of the Napoleonic Wars balloted to serve in a sort of home guard to be available in case the enemy invaded, but it did mean they were often taken away from their jobs, so to avoid having to serve at all was preferable. His letter continued:

> I am pleased the miniature arrived safe and met your approval. I thank you for your kind hints as to my taking care of myself and in

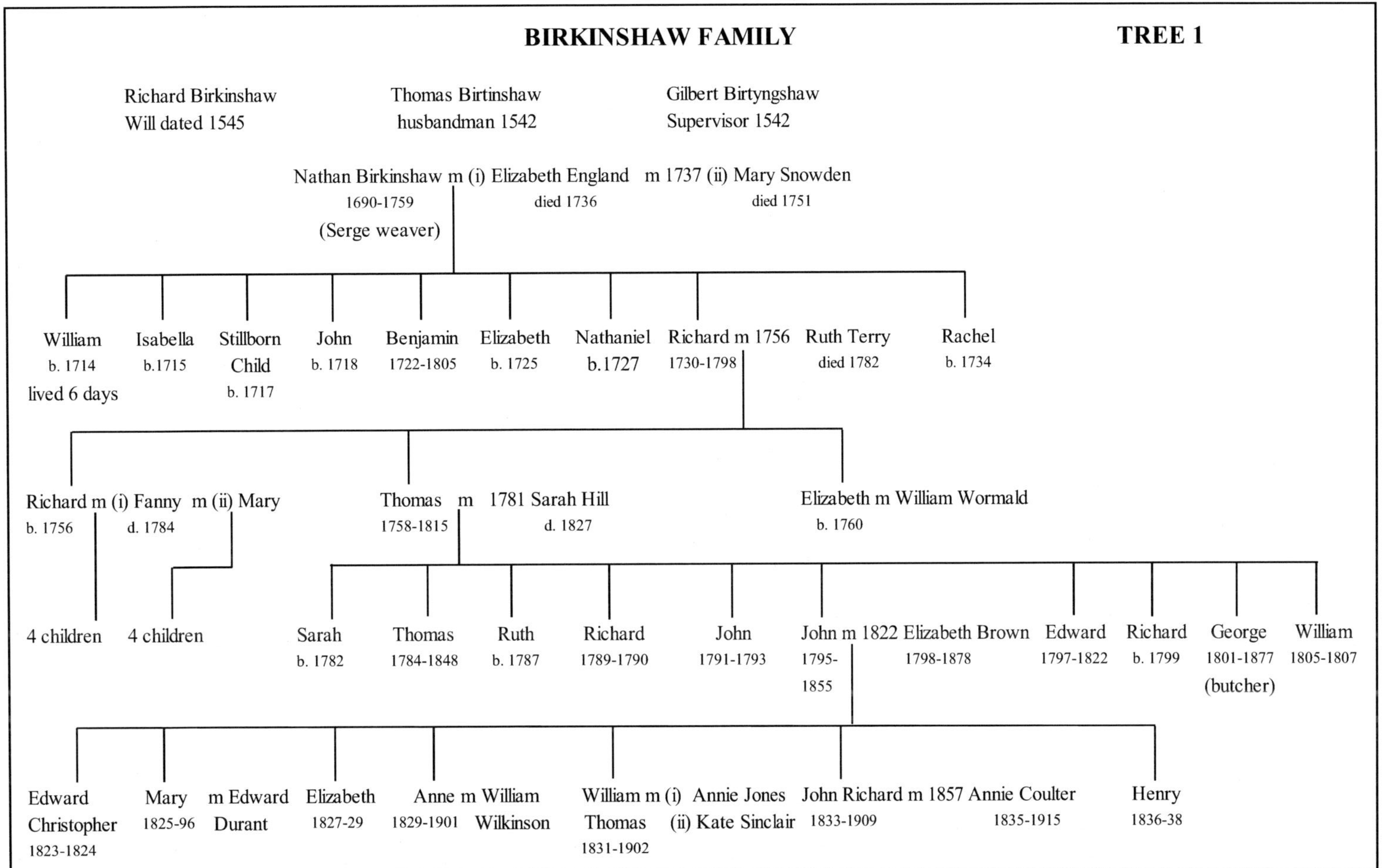
BIRKINSHAW FAMILY
TREE 1
Richard Birkinshaw
Will dated 1545
Thomas Birtinshaw
husbandman 1542
Gilbert Birtyngshaw
Supervisor 1542
Nathan Birkinshaw m (i) Elizabeth England m 1737 (ii) Mary Snowden
1690-1759
died 1736
died 1751
(Serge weaver)
William
b. 1714
lived 6 days
Isabella
b.1715
Stillborn
Child
b. 1717
John
b. 1718
Benjamin
1722-1805
Elizabeth
b. 1725
Nathaniel
b.1727
Richard m 1756 Ruth Terry
1730-1798
died 1782
Rachel
b. 1734
Richard m (i) Fanny m (ii) Mary
b. 1756
d. 1784
Thomas m 1781 Sarah Hill
1758-1815
d. 1827
Elizabeth m William Wormald
b. 1760
4 children
4 children
Sarah
b. 1782
Thomas
1784-1848
Ruth
b. 1787
Richard
1789-1790
John
1791-1793
John m 1822 Elizabeth Brown
1795-
1855
1798-1878
Edward
1797-1822
Richard
b. 1799
George
1801-1877
(butcher)
William
1805-1807
Edward
Christopher
1823-1824
Mary
1825-96
m Edward
Durant
Elizabeth
1827-29
Anne m William
1829-1901
Wilkinson
William m (i) Annie Jones
Thomas
(ii) Kate Sinclair
1831-1902
John Richard m 1857 Annie Coulter
1833-1909
1835-1915
Henry
1836-38

> all respects I will endeavour to obey. I hope my birthday was honoured by you and friends on Tuesday last. I still, when I can find time, go to see Mr Harris and sometimes we keep the game alive to a late hour. Last Friday I took tea with him at eight o'clock in the evening where I met his old intimate friend Mr Berenger who with a few others left Dicky a little groggy about four next morning.
>
> I have not quite so much time on my hands as I had at Pontefract but when I have I make good use of it. Crossland and myself are both hearty as Bucks and join in love to all friends.
>
> I remain dear Father, yours truly.

John, who was one of possibly ten children, became an accountant in Chorlton-upon-Medlock, Manchester. He married Elizabeth Brown in 1822, and had seven children, three of whom died in infancy. John died on 16 June 1855 aged sixty and was buried at Harpurhey Cemetery, Manchester, as was his wife Elizabeth who died in 1878 aged eighty. John's grandfather, Richard, who was a labourer, according to parish records, was one of about nine children. He married Ruth Terry in 1756. Richard's father was Nathan who was a serge weaver born in 1690; he married Elizabeth England. The surname England is Anglo-Saxon and is derived from the old English Engelond which means 'meadow beside a rushing river'. Amongst old family documents[1] I found a small piece of paper with the information: 'Richard Birkinshaw, will dated 29 Dec. 1545. To be buried in church yarde of St Michael of Ardesloe' (near Wakefield, Yorkshire). Also mentioned was Thomas Birtinshaw of Woodhall Calverley (near Bradford), husbandman, will dated 1542, and Gilbert Birtyngshawe, supervisor 1542. It would appear that these were members of the family going back to the 16th century, although there is no information which connects that generation with the 17th century Nathan above. There is a village called Birkenshaw on the outskirts of Bradford from which the name Birkinshaw is supposed to originate, Birken meaning birch wood. [2]

In 1857 John's son, John Richard Birkinshaw (Herbert's father), married Annie Coulter in the York Street Baptist Chapel in Manchester. He was twenty-three and she was twenty-one. John Richard was described as a bookkeeper living in Huddersfield. Annie was born in Ballina, Co. Mayo, Ireland in 1835; her father William Coulter was a wine merchant (see Tree 2). Annie's mother was Eleanor Matthews. There was a family story which has been passed down the generations suggesting that the Coulter family were related to W B Yeats, but the connection is as yet unconfirmed. It was very likely, however, that Herbert met Yeats while staying with family in Sligo; Yeats spent his summer holidays in Sligo. To explore this possible connection I contacted the Yeats Society in Sligo and had a reply from the CEO, Stella Mew. She could not find any connection between the two families, but she did find Coulters and Matthews in the local telephone directory. Eleanor

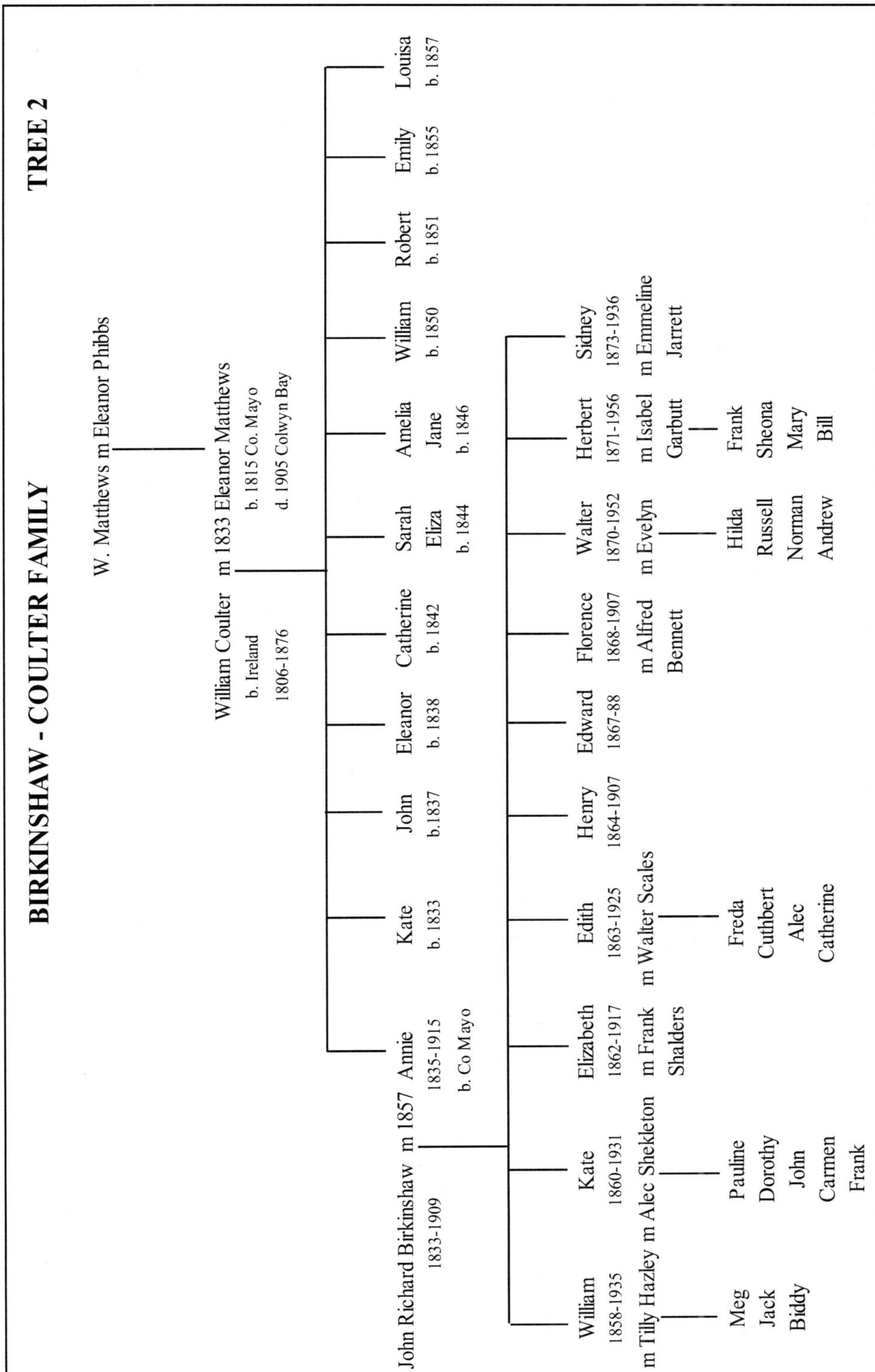
BIRKINSHAW - COULTER FAMILY
TREE 2
W. Matthews m Eleanor Phibbs
William Coulter m 1833 Eleanor Matthews
b. Ireland
1806-1876
b. 1815 Co. Mayo
d. 1905 Colwyn Bay
John Richard Birkinshaw m 1857 Annie
1833-1909
1835-1915
b. Co Mayo
Kate
b. 1833
John
b.1837
Eleanor
b. 1838
Catherine
b. 1842
Sarah
Eliza
b. 1844
Amelia
Jane
b. 1846
William
b. 1850
Robert
b. 1851
Emily
b. 1855
Louisa
b. 1857
William
1858-1935
m Tilly Hazley
Meg
Jack
Biddy
Kate
1860-1931
m Alec Shekleton
Pauline
Dorothy
John
Carmen
Frank
Elizabeth
1862-1917
m Frank
Shalders
Edith
1863-1925
m Walter Scales
Freda
Cuthbert
Alec
Catherine
Henry
1864-1907
Edward
1867-88
Florence
1868-1907
m Alfred
Bennett
Walter
1870-1952
m Evelyn
Hilda
Russell
Norman
Andrew
Herbert
1871-1956
m Isabel
Garbutt
Frank
Sheona
Mary
Bill
Sidney
1873-1936
m Emmeline
Jarrett

Matthews' mother was Eleanor Phibbs; Stella told me that Phibbs was a famous name in Sligo, mainly because of the well-known firm of solicitors, Argue and Phibbs. She said that the name so amused everyone that even today their successors operate from the premises with the title 'formerly Argue and Phibbs'. She told me something about the Phibbs' family estate which is now a ruin:

> The Phibbs family had a large house and estate outside Sligo near Strandhill and the story goes that the house became the abode of a poltergeist, the activities of which were so violent that the family had to seek refuge elsewhere. They finally (though a Protestant family) invited a number of Jesuit priests to stay in the house and to exorcise the poltergeist, but even they failed, and made their escape!

The 1861 census recorded John Richard and Annie living in Leeds with their son William aged two and their daughter Kate aged one year. Also living with them was Annie's sister, Sarah Eliza Coulter aged seventeen; she was born in Manchester. The Coulter parents Eleanor and William, who was described as an agent, were living in Chorlton upon Medlock, Lancashire. They had eight daughters and three sons, of whom four children died young. William Coulter died in 1876 and Eleanor continued to live in Chorlton with her unmarried daughter Kate, where they were registered in the 1891 census. Eleanor died in 1905 in Conway, Wales where her daughter Sarah Eliza lived.

An article[3], written in the church magazine, about John Richard after he retired from teaching at the Sunday School of the Westgate Baptist Church described something of his life. It said he had commenced his Sunday School work in 1854 as a teacher at the Union Chapel in Manchester. He taught in that school until 1861 when he went to Huddersfield. The article continued:

> Here he attended the Baptist School in Bath Buildings, and, joining the teaching staff, became such a power that the first annual meeting after his advent he was elected superintendent. His stay at Huddersfield, though productive of real spiritual good, was short, and he came to Bradford in 1862 and joined Westgate Church. His talents were quickly appreciated, for he soon was elected to the position of Superintendent of the School, which office he filled for thirty years, 1862-92.

The article went on to say that John Richard had been President of the Yorkshire Baptist Association and he had rendered great services as a lay preacher and as a member of the Executive of Rawdon (Baptist) College. The article also indicated that John Richard had been in America[4] and that he was well-loved wherever he went:

> There are hundreds, nay, thousands of men and women in this country and America who remember him with love and reverence.

John Richard lived at 32 Marlborough Road in the suburb of Manningham, Bradford, from 1862 until he died in September 1909. Except for his three eldest children the other seven, including my grandfather Herbert, were born at that address. An obituary dated September 1909 said John Richard's funeral took place at Nab Wood Cemetery, Shipley, near Bradford, with a service held beforehand at Westgate Baptist Chapel just down the road from the Birkinshaw family home. The address was given by the Rev. Ibberson of Ilkley who said he spoke as an old friend:

> It seemed only yesterday that he had met that strong, fascinating personality that was possessed by Mr Birkinshaw, and yet they were mourning the loss of one of the oldest members of the church at Westgate. Their beloved brother had a marvellous power of drawing out the best of every man, and although he could be severe in his criticism of superficialities he would listen with warm interest to the humblest utterance which he believed to be honest and true … Although in the best sense an independent thinker, untrammelled by tradition or church creeds, there was no mistaking his theology. It was not eulogising him too much to say that to know him was to love him. The church at Westgate would miss him beyond description.

The Rawdon College Yearbook of 1910-11 wrote of him that 'he was one of the pillars of the institution and we lovingly think of him as a brother beloved, as a sympathetic and inspiring helper and friend'.

Marlborough Road, Bradford; no.32 is the first door on the left

During a visit to Bradford we found the terraced house at 32 Marlborough Road in the suburb of Manningham. From the outside it appeared quite small and modest, and I wondered how he had managed to accommodate so many children there, although a local estate agent said that many of that type of house had five plus bedrooms including a large cellar. Annie died there in May 1915 aged eighty. She left no will but under Letters of Administration her estate was valued at just over £1,000. Annie was described variously by members of her family; some thought her selfish and others lovely. According to one she had 'taken to her chair at the age of forty and not moved from it'.

Catherine Illingworth, Frank's first cousin, had responded to my letter of October 1979 in which I asked for information about the family. This was after my mother died in 1977 when I started to look for information about my father's family. At that time there were no home computers so it was a matter of visiting the public record office and writing letters by hand; I also discovered that Birkinshaw was not such an unusual name, so my task was quite daunting. By chance I came across someone who was also researching Birkinshaws. She gave me an address for Sir Stephen Henry Gordon Kaye, 3rd Bt, whose grandmother Edith Emily was born a Birkinshaw, and who, she believed, was related to me. I wrote to him and he passed my letter on to his aunt Catherine Illingworth, daughter of Edith; Edith turned out to be an elder sister of my grandfather Herbert, and Sir Stephen was therefore my second cousin. Catherine was very interested and gave me some help with names and dates, particularly of her Birkinshaw aunts and uncles, who were my grandfather Herbert's siblings. Catherine did not give me any information about herself or her immediate family and anyway at that time I was more interested in our antecedents. She did tell me that her mother Edith was born in 1863, the fourth child of John Richard and Annie and that Edith had married Walter Scales, who had inherited his father's wool business in 1875. They had four children, the youngest of whom was Catherine, who married John Illingworth. After receiving two letters from Catherine, the second one in May 1980, I became distracted with bringing up my children, and put the family history research to one side. It was not until nearly thirty years later, in the summer of 2006, that my interest was re-kindled.

I looked over Catherine's letters and realised that she would probably be long dead, so where to go next? Luckily her address was unusual: 'Pantrys, The Square, Shere, Nr Guildford.' Shere was a small pretty village in Surrey and it had a local museum, so I rang them to ask if they knew what had happened to the Illingworth family. I was told they had gone away many years previously and all they knew about the family was that Catherine's daughter had been an actress. As no actress with the name Illingworth registered on my radar I did not pursue it. However, a little later I was emailing my cousin Anne (daughter of Frank's sister Sheona) in the Lake District discussing family history with her and I mentioned in passing that Catherine's daughter was an actress. It just happened that Anne's secretary Ibby was standing next to her reading our exchange of emails and she recognised the name Illingworth as a family she had known as a child. Ibby's father Harry Darbishire had been an old boyfriend of Catherine; they had known her as Bim. Ibby made the suggestion that the actress might be Prunella Scales[5]. 'No', I replied, 'her name was Illingworth'. Undaunted my cousin and Ibby googled Prunella's name and up came the information – 'born Illingworth'. Prunella, who I now realised was my second cousin, had adopted her mother's maiden name.

I wrote to Prunella, via her agent, to ask her if she could fill me in a little with her immediate family history and asked if she had a photograph of her grandmother Edith. She kindly sent me a print of Edith who looked very like my grandfather Herbert. Prunella also put me in touch with her brother Tim who is a retired colonel and he was able to add to the story. He told me that it was Charles Laughton the actor who suggested to Prunella that she changed her name from Illingworth. I also came across the biography about Prunella written by Teresa Ransom[6] which gave me some more insights into the family. Prunella is married to the actor Timothy West and they have two sons, Sam and Joseph.

Catherine had an elder sister Winifred born in 1888; she was known as Freda. My Aunt Sheona, Freda's first cousin, told me that she remembered being chased round the garden by her with a rake saying she was Mr McGregor and Sheona was Peter Rabbit; I think Sheona was somewhat alarmed.

Freda married Henry Gordon Kaye, who became the wealthy Second Baronet Kaye of Huddersfield. He owned a wool mill. The baronetcy was created in 1923 for his father, the textile manufacturer Joseph Kaye. Joseph was also a director of the LMS Railway and Lloyds Bank. Henry Gordon Kaye was a Captain in the Royal Flying Corps during the First World War but had to relinquish his commission in 1918 because of ill-health, according to the war records. Later he joined the King's Own Yorkshire Light Infantry.

Freda and her husband Henry Gordon (or Gorgie as he was known), had three children. The eldest, Stephen, helped his father run the mill and eventually became an actor. He became the Third Baronet on his father's death in 1956. Stephen was the person who put me in contact with Catherine. He never married and after he died in 1983 the baronetcy passed on to his brother David. David became a doctor and was in the Parachute Regiment during the Second War; he married Adelle Thomas who came from Brisbane and where the family now live. David and Adelle had two sons and four daughters. David died in 1994 and the baronetcy passed down to his son, who became the Fifth Baronet – Sir Paul Henry Gordon Kaye of Huddersfield.

Wedding of Freda Scales to Captain Henry Gordon Kaye, 1916
On Freda's left is her brother Alec, mother Edith (seated), sister Catherine (standing), Freda's Aunt Lizzie (seated), with husband Frank Shalders (standing).

The third son of Freda and Gorgie, Brian, had a first class law degree from Oxford and was a fighter pilot in the Battle of Britain. Unfortunately his war experiences affected him and he did not go back to the law. He married Freddie Grisewood's daughter Anne (Freddie was a well-known broadcaster); they had one son. Tragically Brian committed suicide later in life. The three brothers were all my second cousins as are Prunella and her brother Tim. Freda died in 1971.

Catherine's eldest brother was Cuthbert Scales who was born on 15 June 1890. He was also Frank's first cousin. Cuthbert, familiarly known as Cus, qualified as a doctor in Edinburgh and joined the Royal Army Medical Corps. He fought in World Wars I and II, gaining a Military Cross with Bar in the former for his bravery in collecting casualties from the battlefield. He was also awarded the Order of St John. I found the citations for his MCs in the National Archives. They were both for 'conspicuous gallantry and devotion to duty when in charge of stretcher-bearers'. The first one received in July 1918, as listed in the *London Gazette* read:

> He collected and evacuated many wounded under heavy fire and remained at his post until forced by the advance of the enemy to withdraw his collecting post further back. There he continued collecting and evacuating as long as possible, showing a fine example to his men.

The second, dated 11 January 1919, read similarly. Unfortunately, his nephew Tim told me, his medals have gone out of the family and their whereabouts are unknown. Cus was in charge of the hospitals in Malta during the Second World War and rose to the rank of brigadier. In later years he worked at the Millbank Military Hospital and lived in nearby Chelsea. He died unmarried in 1960.

Edith Birkinshaw's Descendants

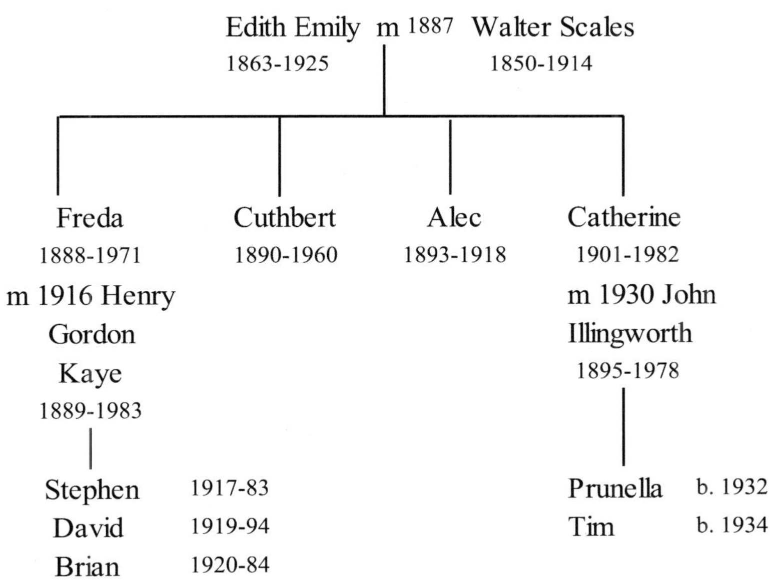

Alec was Catherine's second brother. He was Walter Alexander Scales. He inherited the family wool business after his father died in April 1914 but soon after joined the 6th Battalion, The Prince of Wales Own (West Yorkshire Regiment) in the First World War where he became a captain. He was awarded the MC in March 1916 and the citation from the *London Gazette* read:

> For conspicuous gallantry. During an attack, by his prompt and energetic action he succeeded in getting his platoon through without injury. Later he assisted in the rescue of wounded men from a wrecked dug-out in full view of the enemy. He has repeatedly carried out good patrol work.

He served in France and Belgium and died on 6 January 1918, aged twenty-four, in France. His war record stated that his death was an accident but there was no further information. However, another entry in his war record said that he 'Died in Action' At the time there was no actual fighting going on where he was stationed; his battalion was in Potijze (Belgium) providing working parties to supply stores to front line troops, according to the war diary, which made no mention of his death. The official story was that he died when two planes collided while training. He was buried at Doullens Cemetery in the area of the Somme. His nephew Tim has a presentation case containing Alec's medals which was given to Alec's mother Edith after he died. Also attached to Alec's war record was a thank-you card to everyone for their expressions of sympathy 'from the family and Miss Hepworth'; she was Alec's fiancée. She eventually married someone else and apparently wore the engagement ring Alec had given her throughout her marriage.

Alec was very friendly with his first cousin Jack Birkinshaw, son of Edith's eldest brother William. Cus, Alec and Jack were all first cousins of my father Frank; all four of them fought in France in the First War.

Catherine herself was born on 8 May 1901 and became an actress. She married John Illingworth who was the son of a doctor whose family owned the Illingworth Tobacco factory. John left school at sixteen and three years later in 1914 went off to war and was invalided out after the Battle of Ypres. He was later seconded into the Indian army after which he obtained a job with Tootal the cotton firm, eventually becoming their London Sales Manager. Catherine and John had first Prunella, born in 1932, followed by Timothy who was born in 1934. Prunella went to school on the west side of Lake Windermere in 1942; I was at school on the other side of the lake twelve years later.

Catherine also told me, in one of her letters, that there had been a family photograph of John Richard and Annie's golden wedding in 1907 which her cousin Jack (son of William) had promised to give her, but he had died just before he was able to send it. At that stage of my research I had not located any of William's family and so was not able to ask them if they knew of its whereabouts, so I believed I would never set eyes on what was clearly an important key family photograph. Catherine said she loved her grandparents dearly and she had a portrait of her grandmother Annie whom she described as 'a lovely old lady'. My Uncle Bill did not have such happy memories of 'Grandmother Birkinshaw'. He described her as a very selfish woman.

Tim Illingworth joined the Wiltshire Regiment as a soldier when he left school and was later commissioned into The Royal Irish Fusiliers and served all over the world until retiring in 1986. He had various interesting jobs in the army, including being aide-de-camp to the general in charge of East Africa before independence and an instructor at Sandhurst. He had command of an OTC at Queen's University in Belfast, the British Army Training and Liaison

Team in Kenya, and the Military Corrective Training Centre in Colchester, and was also a military magistrate for two years. He married Kathryn Munro in Kenya in 1964. They have a son who is an army colonel who has served in both Iraq and Afghanistan as a helicopter pilot. They also have a daughter who is a primary school teacher.

Walter Scales died in 1914 while on holiday in the Isle of Wight; the family were living in Manningham, Bradford at the time. Catherine was only twelve. Edith died in Harrogate in December 1925.

Catherine died in 1982 shortly after I first corresponded with her. I was most grateful for her help as without it I would never have been able to trace as many of my grandfather's siblings as I have done. She gave me enough clues about them all to enable me to find most of their families.

John Richard and Annie's eldest son William was born in 1858 in Huddersfield. The young William wrote a letter[7] to his parents while at school in Bradford:

> Midsummer 1867
>
> My dear Parents
>
> I take this opportunity of expressing to you my sincere thanks for having afforded me another quarter's attendance at school. That favour I feel confident in saying has not been bestowed in vain. The subjects to which my attention has been directed have been carefully studied and much progress made accordingly. They are the geography of the British Isles and the continents of Europe, Asia and Africa; in grammar the Parts of Speech, their powers and inflections with examples in parsing. Reduction of money, weights and measures and revision of the four Compound Rules; in British History the Norman line of kings, and Scripture History from chapter XXX to Z with twelve chapters in St John's Gospel, also reading, dictation and elementary book-keeping. The writing may be seen from the letter [and a very find hand he had for a nine year old]. I am anticipating much enjoyment during the coming holidays. I am expecting no small share of sport – it will be all play and no work then, until called upon to resume studies when I intend to make still more diligent application.
>
> With kind love to you I remain
> Your affectionate son – Willie Birkinshaw.

For more information about William I had to search through the records. I discovered that William became a general textile manufacturer's agent; he married Matilda (Tilly) Hazley who was born in Dublin. They lived in Bradford and, Catherine had told me, had three children, Margaret (Meg), John Hazley (known as Jack) and Florence (Biddy). William died in 1935 and Tilly in 1940.

William and Tilly's first child Meg married Lionel Watson and they had two children Ruth and James and lived in Ilkley. Ruth went to school with my first cousin Anne at High Wycombe but unfortunately they had not subsequently kept in touch, and the school had no more information as to what had become of Ruth. I then discovered, from the records, that Ruth had married Michael Beazley, a solicitor, and they had one daughter Alexandra Jane but I could not find any more information about James, and Watson was not an easy surname to research, there being so many of them.

William and Tilly's second child Jack, born 1893, did not marry and became a clerk in a textile mill. He joined the Yorkshire Light Infantry in the First War and then the RAF. My second cousin Tim Illingworth, who knew Jack, described him as a lovely man.

It was Tim's mother Catherine who had told me that Biddy, the youngest of William and Tilly's children had married someone called Whitaker (with one 't') and she didn't mention any children. She said they lived in Huddersfield and were not very well off. Tim said he was very fond of Biddy, describing her as 'delicious' and that one day his mother Catherine had bought her a Spode teapot and Biddy had cried.

I had now come to a frustratingly dead end in finding the descendants of William and Tilly as I had hoped to be able to put together all the pieces of the jigsaw. I knew Ruth and her daughter were out there somewhere but I could not locate them. I put Ruth's daughter Alexandra's name into Google and up came a likely person who had produced and directed documentary-type films, who eventually did turn out to be the right person, but at that time, try as as I might, I could not catch up with her; no one seemed to know where she was. I wrote to Ruth at an address I had come across, but the letter was returned with 'gone away' on it. I could find no trace of Biddy in the records but I found Jack's death certificate and from that I found the address where he had last lived, which was in Ben Rhydding just outside Ilkley in Yorkshire. He died in 1975 aged eighty-two.

We visited Yorkshire in the Spring of 2008 to look at the area where John Richard and his family had lived. We went to Ilkley to see if we could find any trace of the Watson family there who might lead me to Ruth; unfortunately we could not, although we found some of the houses where they had lived. Ironically, I lived in Ilkley and nearby Burley-in-Wharfedale as a child at the time when Meg, Jack and Biddy and their families were living in the area, but we had not known about them.

But where to search next? I looked again at Jack's death certificate and noticed that the person who had been the informant of death was one Sheila Rosemary Watson. I presumed that she was one of the Watson family into which Meg had married. I looked up the name Sheila Watson in the records and found someone who had died in 2003 and who looked as though she might fit the place and timescale. I then went to the Probate Office to check whether she had left a will. It was an extraordinarily long shot, but nonethless I typed her name and date of death in to the Probate Office computer and up she came. Not only had she left a will but there were two beneficiaries listed with their names and addresses and one happened to be – Ruth Beazley, so I knew I was on the right track. There was no telephone number listed in the telephone directory for Ruth but there was one for the other name, so I gave her a call. She told me she had been a great friend of Sheila and was able to tell me a little about the Beazley family and gave me the name and telephone number of someone called Annabel she thought might be able to help me. I duly rang the number and after talking to Annabel for a while I realised she was the daughter of the elusive James, Ruth's brother. Her father James, who

Meg, Jack and Biddy

died in 1968, was my second cousin as was Ruth. Annabel in turn gave me the telephone number of Ruth's daughter Alex who I then called. She was very surprised to hear from me and said that she had asked her great uncle Jack before he died to help her with the family tree and was very interested to know more. She also told me, to *my* great astonishment, that her great-aunt Biddy had married Harry Whittaker (with two 't's) and that they had had a son who was called Jerry. Not only that but she had been speaking to him earlier in the day and she gave me his telephone number. Jerry in turn was quite amazed to hear from a second cousin he knew nothing about and we arranged to meet. At our meeting he was able to identify many of the Birkinshaw family photographs I had and tell me more about some of the people. He told me that his uncle Jack (who was always known as Birky) had joined up to fight in the First War on 4 August 1914, the day war had been declared and just a month before my father (Jack's first cousin) joined up; Jack was five years older than Frank. Jack had also been in France and had been wounded and invalided out of the war with a hole in the head although he did later join the RAF. Jack had eventually worked for the Wool Control Board in Bradford and lived with his sister Meg for many years. Jack's interests were walking and collecting maps and he seemed to have been universally liked and respected by all the family. Jerry has three children and seven grandchildren and lives in Berkhamsted. Ruth, whom I eventually met, is living in a retirement flat in Surrey and her daughter Alex lives in North London with her husband and son.

William Birkinshaw's Descendants

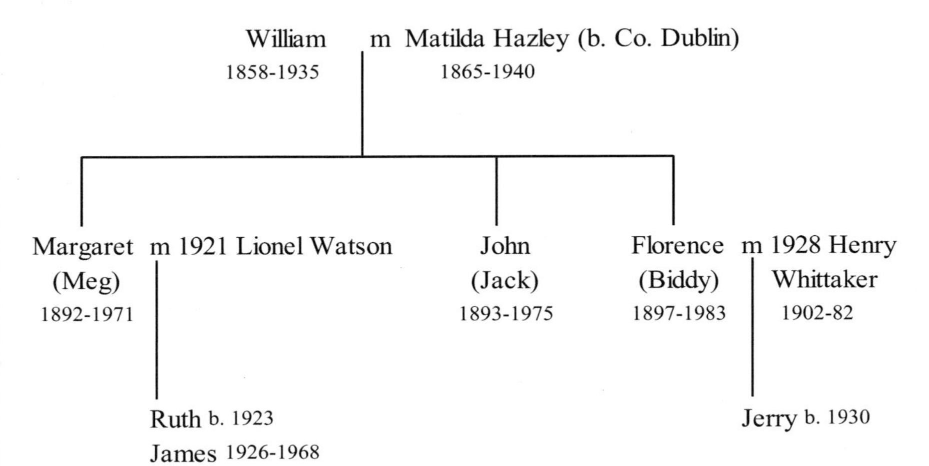

John Richard and Annie's second child was Kate who was born in Huddersfield in 1860. Catherine Illingworth had told me that Kate married Alec Shekleton who was headmaster of Kilkenny College in Ireland. They married in 1883 in St Paul's Anglican Church in Manningham. I found more information from Kilkenny College itself, from where the archivist sent me an obituary and article about Alec from the Irish papers. Alec had previously been a teacher of mathematics and english at Primrose Grange School in Sligo where he was also headmaster; he later became head of Kilkenny College. They had three daughters, Pauline, Dorothy and Carmen and two sons, John and Frank Ross, all of whom were born in Sligo. In May 1904 Alec and Kate, plus one daughter, were invited to a reception given at Kilkenny Castle by the Marquis and Marchioness of Ormonde in honour of a visit by King Edward VII and Queen Alexandra, according to a report in *The Kilkenny People.* Also accompanying the royal couple was their daughter Princess Victoria.[8]

Kate Birkinshaw's Descendants

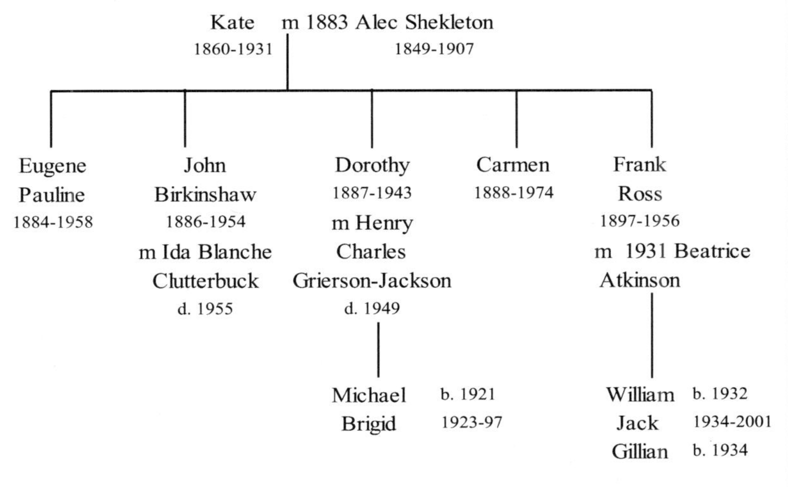

Alec died in February 1907 from a severe attack of influenza at the age of fifty-seven. The *Sligo Independent* carried an obituary which stated:

> For about 28 years the late Mr Shekleton was head master of Primrose Grange School, Sligo. He was a well-known figure in our midst and was universally beloved for the many noble qualities which distinguished his every action through life … the boys who came under his guardianship received the true moral training necessary to make them good men, in addition to the general education they received, and they live to bless his name. He was a man of sterling

> character, kindly disposition, generous to a fault and constant in his willingness to assist every good cause. In Masonic circles his loss is deeply lamented. In this Order Mr Shekleton had attained the highest honours, being a Prince Mason, and it is characteristic of him that he took the deepest interest in all its charities, and the cause of the Boys' and Girls' Orphan Schools had his especial regard and advocacy.

After Alec died, Kate went to live in Colwyn Bay in Wales, probably to stay with her aunt Eliza. In 1909, after her father John Richard died, Kate returned to Yorkshire to live with her mother Annie in the house in Manningham until Annie's death there in 1915. Kate then lived with her brother Walter in Manningham for a time before moving to Harrogate where she died in 1931. Kate left £647 in her will, bequeathing her house (57 St Mary's Terrace, Bradford) to her daughter Carmen and the rest of her estate to her daughters in equal shares. After much searching through records I managed to find out what had happened to Kate's children who were all born in Sligo.

Eugene Pauline, the eldest, born in 1884, trained to be a nurse at St George's Hospital, London. She worked for the Red Cross during the First War and was awarded a medal from the British Red Cross and St John of Jerusalem. She died, unmarried, in Harrogate aged seventy-four.

John Birkinshaw Shekleton, born in 1886, was the second child. He emigrated to Australia and ran a sheep station at Mount Charlotte, Adelaide. According to his war record[9] he joined the Australian army in May 1916 as a gunner in the 6th Field Artillery Battalion and sailed to Plymouth from Melbourne in November 1916, the journey taking just over two months. While in Larkhill Camp on Salisbury Plain (where my father, John's first cousin, had been stationed the previous year) he was fined six days' pay for overstaying his leave. In August 1917 he was sent to fight in France and in December of that year he was fined two days' pay for 'breaking out of camp'. John's war record described his civilian occupation as 'station overseer' and gave his mother Kate, then living in Bradford with her brother Walter, as his next of kin. In his war record I found an amusing memo which was sent from the War Defence Department to the Army Base Record Department querying John's leave without pay in July 1919 'to mind the sheep for Lieutenant Kelly'. However, the reply came that there was nothing in the official records mentioning sheep, but on 7 November 1919 they reported that John 'embarked for return to Australia with stock' so it was assumed that the sheep went with him. I discovered, from googling, a couple of Shekletons (probably very distant relations to John) in Australia who had done some research into their Shekleton family and had discovered that our John married Ida Blanche Clutterbuck in South Australia. John continued to run the sheep station at

Mount Charlotte, part of which he had since bought. This was about ninety miles north of Adelaide. John and Blanche, as she was known, had no children. One of my Australian contacts found a Clutterbuck who was related to Blanche and from him I obtained a little more information, which was that John and Blanche sold their property in 1948 and retired to the coast of South Australia. The migration records[10] showed that they visited England on separate occasions, John in 1950/1 and Blanche in 1954. They both died in Adelaide, John in 1954 and Blanche the following year.

Dorothy was the third child. She was born in 1887 and trained at St Bartholomew's Hospital to be a nurse. She then became matron at King William's College on the Isle of Man. She married Captain Henry Charles Grierson-Jackson at Malew church which was about two miles from the college. Henry was a teacher at Westward Ho Boys' prep school in Devon and had previously been in the Indian Army. They had two children Michael William born in Bideford, Devon in 1920 and Brigid born in 1923. Brigid became a school teacher and married Harry Cousins who was a Lt. Commander in the Fleet Air Arm; after the war he became a civil servant. This information I discovered from their two daughters, Brigid (known as Anne) born in 1949 and Alyson born in 1951, whom, after much searching, I found in the records and have since made contact with; unfortunately their distant family knowledge was limited. Alyson did tell me that Michael, her mother Brigid's brother, went to Oxford sometime during World War II but left with his degree unfinished. He joined the Fleet Air Arm and it was through him that Brigid met her husband Harry. Michael never really recovered from the war and did not complete his studies. He went to Canada for a while and tried working on a whale boat. Alyson told me that he had married, but she did not know whether he had children or what subsequently happened to him, as he and her mother Brigid lost touch with each other. Unfortunately he was the one elusive second cousin I could not trace, even though he had an unusual name. I think somewhere along the line Michael possibly dropped the hyphen in his surname, thus making Jackson too common a name to trace easily. Michael and Brigid's father Henry, who died in 1949, left nearly £1,500 in his will. He left his inscribed bugle to his son and his stamp collection to his daughter, to whom he also gave his property, Michael only receiving half the residue of the estate.

Carmen, born in 1888, was the fourth child of Alec and Kate and, like her sisters, became a nurse, training at St George's Hospital. She was, according to the family that knew her, very short and feisty; she never married. After her sister Dorothy died, Carmen looked after her brother-in-law, Henry. Carmen died in Harrogate aged eighty-six. She left over £8,000 in her will; all her Guinness shares were left to her niece Brigid and her remaining estate to her cousin Andrew's wife, Florence Birkinshaw. Her diamond ring she left to her cousin Biddy Whittaker. Most of the second cousins I have contacted seemed to have met Carmen or at least to know about her. Herbert appeared to have completely lost touch with his siblings' families, and none of my second cousins I came across knew anything about him.

The fifth child and second son of Alec and Kate was Frank Ross who was born in 1897, eight years after Carmen. He was only ten when his father died and he was sent to the Masonic Boys' School in Dublin where he was listed in the 1911 Dublin census. I had difficulty finding Frank in any records until I came across a Ross Shekleton and realised he was the missing cousin; he used Ross as his first name instead of Frank. I eventually managed to contact his grandson, also Ross,[11] and in so doing found another three second cousins. Ross, the grandson, told me that his grandfather went to Trinity College Dublin and met and married Beatrice Atkinson in London. Beatrice was a bespoke seamstress who made clothes for royalty and MPs. She was from Burnley, where she had had a destitute childhood, but went back there with her husband and opened a gown shop. They had three children, Jack and Gill who were twins, and William; they were my second cousins. Ross, the grandfather, died in 1956 just after his sixtieth birthday which he celebrated in hospital having just had his leg amputated. He originally planned to be a priest, according to his grandson, who also told me that his grandfather had been a heavy drinker.

The Shekleton family taking tea at Primrose Grange School, Sligo (Dorothy is not present)

My grandfather Herbert had five brothers. The nearest to him in age was Walter who was just one year older and born in 1870. Catherine Illingworth had provided the next clue for me to work on by telling me that Walter had three sons and a daughter, but that was the only information I had. I started to search through the records of the National Archives to see what I could find.

Walter Coulter Birkinshaw was born in Bradford to John Richard and Annie and became a worsted yarn agent. The 1901 census showed that Walter was married to Evelyn Jane Russell with a daughter Hilda aged four, a son Russell aged two and Norman aged three months.

As Russell was a more unusual name I did a google search for him in the hope that he might have left a son or grandson with the same name. I came across a Russell Birkinshaw living in Auckland, New Zealand, who was in property and who looked a likely candidate, so I sent him an email. I had an immediate reply saying that no, he was not my cousin, but he was very interested in the Birkinshaw family and had procured a document which said that the Birkinshaws had originally come from the Scottish Border Country. I was intrigued as I had always believed them to be Yorkshire folk. Russell forwarded a copy to me and it stated that, according to research of ancient documents, including the Exchequer Rolls of Scotland and the Domesday Book, the first record of the name Birkinshaw was found in Lanarkshire, in Scotland, where the name originated possibly before the Norman Conquest. It stated that 'the family name "Birkinshaw" was probably originally descended from the Strathclyde Britons' who were a mixture of Gaelic/Celts 'whose original territories ranged from Lancashire in the south, northward to the south bank of the River Clyde in Scotland'. In Lanarkshire the Birkinshaws were recorded as a family of great antiquity seated at Birkenshaw (with the slightly different spelling) where the clan held estates. They also held estates in Renfrewshire. And where did my non-cousin Russell find this document? In the Library of the Hall of Names in Selfridges, the large store in London. He paid five pounds for it in the 1960s from a genealogy machine!

However, the estates in Renfrewshire it mentioned did tie in with other information, namely that there was a Birkinshaw Estate in East Renfrewshire. According to the website *Historic Scotland* this estate belonged in the 16th century to the Montgomeries of Eglinton Castle. The estate was developed in the 19th century around two new houses, Birkinshaw Cottage and Birkinshaw House, Birkinshaw meaning 'the birch wood'. In 1858 Alexander Crum acquired the Birkinshaw Estate; the Crum family were involved with the development of the local dye and calico industry. One infamous resident who lived in the cottage was Madeleine Smith; she was accused of poisoning her lover in 1857. Another notable resident was Lord Kelvin the famous Victorian physicist and mathematician. Crum renamed the estate Thornliebank in 1879. The house was eventually demolished in 1963 by which time the estate belonged to the City of Glasgow. It is now called Rouken Glen Park and is open to the public with boating and sports facilities, flower gardens and waterfalls. It comprises some 227 acres and is one of the largest public parks in Scotland.

Having had a bit of a diversion with Russell I searched for a possible will for his father Walter who died in 1952 but he appeared not to have written one. However, I did find one for his wife Evelyn. She died in 1949 aged seventy-seven leaving just over a thousand pounds. Her address was 3 North Park Road, Bradford and she had appointed The Yorkshire Penny Bank Ltd as executor and trustee. She left the income of her capital to her husband for his use during his lifetime, after which both capital and income were to go to her remaining three children, Hilda Tompson, Norman Birkinshaw and Andrew Walter Birkinshaw. (There was no mention of Russell but another son, Andrew, had appeared since the 1901 census.)

In her will Evelyn also asked for her body to be cremated and her ashes to be deposited in the Birkinshaw Vault in Nab Wood Cemetery, Shipley. I located the Nab Wood Cemetery and rang them to ask what they knew of the Birkinshaw family. They told me there was a grave containing Walter, who died aged eighty-two at 28 Westbourne Avenue, Harrogate, his wife Evelyn and their son Russell. Russell had died at the age of twenty-four on 21 November 1922 and their records described him as an invalid who had died in Bedfordshire, although the family home was in Harrogate. Russell's death certificate, which I found later, revealed that he was epileptic and died of pneumonia. The cemetery also informed me that there was still space in the grave if required!

During our visit to Bradford in 2008 we went to visit the Nab Wood Cemetery where we found the grave of John Richard Birkinshaw and family. Buried with John Richard in the vault, underneath a large celtic cross, was his wife Annie, their son William and his wife Tilly, daughter Kate Shekleton, and son Walter with his wife Evelyn and their son Russell.

I started a search through the online death records, from the National Archives, for Andrew and his brother Norman. I eventually found Andrew who had died in the Edenfield Nursing Home in Tewit Well Road, Harrogate aged seventy-eight. Unfortunately the nursing home, which was still there, only kept records for seven years, so that was a dead end.

The search for Norman's death certificate proved more productive. He died in December 1979 in Leicester. The informant named on the certificate was Norman's step-son, Peter Wynn Edwards of Oadby, Leicestershire. I was able to trace the address and telephone number through the BT online phonebook. Peter had died some years before but his widow Renee answered the phone and was able to confirm that Norman was indeed my father's first cousin. Having got over her fluster at my questions and the fact that I had disturbed her during Coronation Street, she was very talkative and helpful. Norman had married Renee's mother-in-law at the age of fifty and he had no children of his own. Renee added that he had come from an affluent family and his father Walter had given him an open cheque book in his youth to spend money as he liked and he had clearly been something of a playboy. Norman inherited the family yarn business, together with his brother Andrew, and the business had obviously been thriving as it stretched from Bradford to Harrogate. Norman had lived in France for a time and also spent seven years living in the Grand Hotel in Leicester. Renee told me that Norman's mother Evelyn was extravagant and there was always the atmosphere of wealth around the family. She said she had been told that Evelyn's hair had turned white overnight when her son Russell died.

Renee also told me that Norman's sister Hilda married Tommy Tompson who had a business in Hong Kong. They only had one child, Ian, who married a wealthy girl and had a nice flat in Leicester. The marriage did not last and they had no children. Andrew, Norman's brother, married and had a daughter. Renee thought the daughter married a doctor and went to live abroad but that was all she could remember. I was soon on her trail.

I already had Andrew's death certificate from the records and knew he had died in 1983 in a nursing home in Harrogate. I decided to ring the funeral director nearest to the home to ask if they would look in their records to see whether they had conducted the funeral. They were very obliging but could find no trace of Andrew. They suggested I try the local cemetery, which I did. They located on their database the grave of Andrew's wife Florence, who had died just five months before him, and were able to tell me that Andrew's ashes had been added to it, and that the next of kin was a daughter who lived in Canada; they had no more information. However, someone did volunteer to walk down to the grave and read the headstone for me. This revealed that they had left behind grandchildren but neither they nor the daughter were mentioned by name. The cemetery gave me the name of another funeral director to try. This time I struck lucky as they had indeed conducted the funerals of Andrew and Florence. Most usefully they were able to give me the address and telephone number of the house where Andrew and Florence had lived in Harrogate. I rang the number on the off-chance there might be someone there who had known the Birkinshaw family twenty-five years ago. The number connected and I found myself talking to the person who had bought the house from them. She was able to give me the phone number of her previous neighbours who had since moved to York, but who, she said, had known the family well.

I rang the number in York and explained my mission. Yes, they had known the Birkinshaws and they told me a little about them. The description of Andrew sounded much like that of Norman. It appeared he had been a great character. He was in the cloth industry and was the middle-man; he would fill orders requested by the shops from the manufacturers. They described his wife Florence as a 'thorough lady'. Apparently Andrew had an amazing memory and could sing the entire score of a musical. He became blind in his later years and would just put his hand up when he crossed the road expecting the traffic to stop. One day it did not and he had a nasty accident. With a bit of prompting they were able to remember the daughter's name was Ann and she had married Alan Meltzer who worked for WHO as a scientist. Ann was a speech therapist and they had two children and yes, they had gone to live in Canada.

Luckily the name Meltzer is not very common so a quick google search on the web revealed Alan had written an article on malaria. I did another google search for Ann and eventually found a work email for her; she ran a stuttering treatment clinic at the Ottawa General Hospital. Within two days I had a response from her; although she had since retired a work colleague had forwarded my email on to her. She confirmed that she was definitely my second cousin, although she was very surprised to hear from me as she had rather thought herself to be the last of the Birkinshaws.

Ann and I soon started up an email correspondence and eventually we met up when she came to London. We discovered we had much in common. We were both born Birkinshaw and have blue eyes, married Jewish men and have a son and a daughter each. Our daughters are in a similar line and have done PhDs and our sons have done MBAs. We both sing in a choir, and when I met her I felt as if I had known her for years. She was also able to provide me with the next valuable clues as to what had happened to the rest of Herbert's siblings.

Walter Birkinshaw and his Descendants

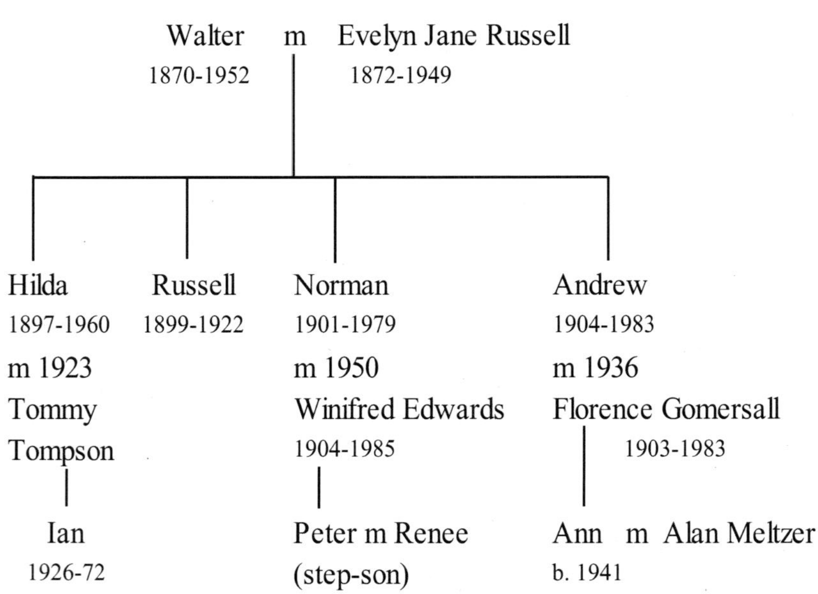

Back row: unknown lady, Tommy Tompson, Norman Birkinshaw, Herbert Shaw, Winnie (Evelyn's sister), Andrew Birkinshaw
Front row: Hilda Tompson, Walter, Evelyn, Ann (later Meltzer), Florence (Ann's mother and wife of Andrew)

At our first meeting in the café at the John Lewis store in Oxford Street in London, Ann produced an old family photograph of John Richard and Annie with all their family around them and said: 'I haven't the slightest idea who all these people are.' *I* knew though, as I immediately realised it was the famous Golden Wedding photo which Catherine Illingworth had told me about and which I thought had long been lost. I could not believe my luck, particularly as it was such a good quality photograph, and there, sitting in the front row, was my father Frank aged nine, and his parents standing at the back holding Mary and Bill. Ann also produced a large album full of Birkinshaw family photos, none of which was labelled. Identifying them has proved quite a challenge but a fascinating one, and between various members of the family we have just about managed it. Ann also had some old family documents which her grandfather Walter had collected and it was from these that I was able to compile the family tree going back to 1690, and with a little gap, even further to the sixteenth century.

Ann was able to fill me in with information about her family. She told me that her cousin Ian, son of Hilda and Tommy Tompson, had a terrible childhood as his mother was an alcoholic and he had to hide his pocket money under the floorboards to stop her from using it to buy gin. His father was away on business in Hong Kong for six months of the year and Ian was sent away to boarding school. Ann had very fond memories of him. Ian, like Ann, was also my second cousin; he died in 1972.

Ann knew Pauline and Carmen Shekleton well, both of whom stayed with her family at various times. Ann's mother Florence nursed Pauline through her last illness. Earlier Ann's grandfather Walter had come to live with them and Carmen helped them to look after Walter, who was her uncle. He went blind with glaucoma as eventually did his two sons Norman and Andrew.

From Ann's documents I was also able to find out what had happened to Herbert's two brothers who went abroad, and their sister Florence who had married an Australian, which information I was given by Catherine Illingworth. Apart from these three, the whole family featured in the Golden Wedding photograph, as I found out later after discussions with my newly found second cousins – between us we worked out who everybody was, and, after some debate, whose grandfather belonged to whom! There was also one missing grandchild – my Aunt Sheona. She would have been about seven at the time, but had been sent to live with her mother's sister.

The third child of John Richard and Annie was Elizabeth (known as Lizzie). She was born in Leeds in 1862. At the age of nine she and her elder sister Kate, aged eleven, went to boarding school in the picturesque market town of Snaith, East Yorkshire, about thirty-seven miles away from their home in Bradford; this according to the 1871 census. They lived in a cottage in a road called Beast Fair with two other boarding students and the school principal and a teacher. The principal's aunt and a servant also lived there.

When she was twenty-five Lizzie married Frank Shalders who was from Norfolk, the son of a silversmith. Frank was a woollen salesman. Catherine Illingworth remembered being looked after by her aunt Lizzie, who had no children of her own. Lizzie died in Manningham aged fifty-five after a bout of pneumonia. Frank died in 1923 aged sixty-four leaving over £30,000 in his will. He left one hundred pounds to each of his wife's Shekleton nieces, Pauline, Dorothy and Carmen; the residue went to Meg Birkinshaw another of Lizzie's nieces.

I now started to search for Herbert's two brothers who went abroad. From the documents that Ann Meltzer had brought me I found their names, dates and places of birth and death. The first was Henry Birkinshaw who was born in Bradford in 1864. He appeared in the 1891 census as a boarder living in Leeds; his occupation was given as 'woollen merchant manager'. Otherwise all that was definitely known of him was that he died in Culebra in Panama in August 1907 aged forty-three. By 1907 building work had started on the Panama Canal which eventually linked the Atlantic Ocean to the Gulf of Panama and the Pacific Ocean, so I assumed that he was working on that in some capacity, and that he either died in an accident or from disease, possibly malaria, as many did at the time. Construction of the Culebra Cut was one of the greatest engineering feats to have been undertaken in its time; six thousand men worked drilling, placing explosives, handling shovels, working on the dirt trains and shifting the tracks as the work progressed. Twice a day work stopped for blasting; sometimes 52,000 pounds of dynamite were used in a single blast. Dozens of dirt trains took the spoil from the steam shovels to the dumps about twelve miles away. At Culebra 160 trainloads of material were hauled away from the Cut which was nine miles long, and a train would come in or out almost every minute. Over five and a half thousand people died between 1904, when the Americans first started work on the canal, having taken over from the French, and its completion in 1914. There was also the climate of Panama to contend with as the temperature was never normally less than 100°F, more often 120-130°F. There were also torrential rains that increased the incidence of mud and rock slides, so it was certainly a dangerous and difficult place to live.[12]

Henry Birkinshaw (photo from Ann Meltzer's album)

I came across an entry on the Ellis Island website for a Harry Birkinshaw in 1906, aged forty. Ellis Island was the entry point for immigration clearance into the USA. Harry was listed as single, English and a civil engineer. His last residence was given as Tampico, Mexico and the boat he arrived on was the *SS Yucatan* from Mexico via Cuba to New York; he was travelling steerage class and arrived in New York in June 1906. The entry indicated that he had been living in New York the previous year. It was quite likely that this was our Henry and he probably did not marry, or the family back home would have known about it. It was quite possible that he worked on the Canal as an engineer, Panama not being that far from Mexico. Also he would have to go to the US to sign up to work in Panama as Panama was under American control at that time.

More web searches discovered the National Archives and Records Administration in Maryland, USA, who hold all the personnel employment cards for everyone who worked on the Panama Canal. They confirmed my suspicions that Harry had worked on the Canal, and found his service record card which they sent me. This said that he had worked in the Engineering Department as a track foreman at Culebra. He signed the oath of employment on 23 October 1906 in the US and reported for work in Panama on 6 November 1906. He was paid $100 a month. He took leave from 21 December to 4 January 1907 and again from 28 February to 7 March. The next entry, on 4 August 1907, simply stated: 'Died.' He was forty-three. I tried to locate a death certificate for him from the US Authorities but without success. The probability was that he died from an accident or disease.

Edward was the other brother who went abroad; he was born in 1867. All that I knew of him was his place and date of death, which I had found from Ann's documents. He died two days after his twenty-first birthday in 1888 in Wollongong in New South Wales, Australia in the Albert Memorial Hospital. I managed to obtain his death certificate from the New South Wales Registry Office on which it said that Edward was a labourer and died from typhoid fever which he had had for five weeks. The name and occupation of his father was recorded as 'not known' nor was it known how long he had been in Australia; altogether a rather bleak picture. He was buried in the Congregational Cemetery, Wollongong, but when I enquired of the cemetery whether they had any record of him they replied in the negative. In any case it would have been unlikely that anyone would have erected a headstone for him, his family being so far away, and all the records were probably lost in the mists of time.

The fourth and last daughter to be born to John Richard and Annie was Florence; she was born in Manningham, Bradford, in September 1868. All that Catherine Illingworth told me about her was that she married an

Australian called Benny who was an eye and ear specialist and they went to live in Australia. From Ann's records I was able to discover what had happened to Florence; she married Dr Alfred Henry Bennett (Benny) in 1892 in Melbourne and she died fifteen years later in 1907 in Adelaide. Again, I was on my own to find out more.

I contacted the State Library of South Australia (SLSA) to see whether they held any information on Florence. From their records they were able to confirm what I had been told, and the fact that Florence and Alfred had no children. Eventually I obtained her death certificate from the Adelaide Registry Office which told me that she died of a duodenal ulcer aged thirty-eight and that she had lived in Buxton Avenue (an upmarket area) in North Adelaide. Dr Bennett then married Elizabeth Florence Garnaut in 1911, but again had no children. The SLSA sent me an article from *The Observer* of 24 April 1926 which outlined Dr Bennett's plans to give some of his Manningham Estate (named after Florence's birth place) over to public use:

> In a most commendable sense of public spiritedness Dr A H Bennett, the well-known specialist and sportsman, has recently constituted a trust and conveyed to the Executor, Trustee and Agency Company, several acres of his beautifully situated and valuable estate at Hampstead for use in perpetuity as a children's playground, for adult recreational purposes, and for the erection of houses for members of certain of the learned professions and their female dependants who may fall on evil times.

More google searches uncovered a memorial (partly instigated by the local Rotary Club) to Alfred and Florence Bennett, and a chance email I sent to the Rotary Club of Australia introduced me to Dr Peter Kreminski in Adelaide who took up the story:

> In 1975 after a three year stay in England, where I worked as a doctor, I moved back to Adelaide and settled in a brand new block of 'semi-detacheds' on NE Road Manningham. Digging around the little yard I found several horseshoes and learnt that there had been stables on that site. The park next door had a children's playground and my infant daughter regularly played there. There was a very modest memorial to Dr Bennett in the park and the Returned Soldiers' League had just finished building a new clubroom. Years later as a member of the Rotary Club of Enfield, and as a GP in the area, I was able to get the Bennett memorial renovated to a much better standard. Only a couple of my older patients remembered the Bennetts by the time I started enquiring (that area of Adelaide had been semi-rural eighty years ago so relatively sparsely populated). One lady complained that the playground promised by the Bennetts

Florence Birkinshaw

(photo from Ann Meltzer's album)

Dr Alfred Bennett

(photo from Ann Meltzer's album)

> was never built until many years later. (It was, after all, the Depression.)
>
> I researched the City of Port Adelaide and Enfield library, viewed the archives of the Library of South Australia where they have old newspaper obituaries and checked the Medical Board registration records. From these three sources plus from a booklet put out by the RSL I composed the inscription on the new memorial. In that booklet was a photo of Dr Bennett – an obviously portly fellow who enjoyed life, and the obituary mentioned horse-racing and fox-hunting.

Peter told me that in 2005 the Memorial was renovated by the City of Port Adelaide, Enfield, on the initiative of, and with a financial contribution from, the Rotary Club of Enfield. This was to mark the 100th Anniversary of the purchase of the land by the Bennetts and the 100th Anniversary of the foundation of Rotary, whose principles, Peter Kreminski said, 'were embodied in Doctor and Mrs Bennett'. There was an opening ceremony attended by the President of the Rotary Club of Enfield and the Mayor of the City of Port Adelaide, Enfield, in the presence of the District Governor and various onlookers. This is what Peter wrote for the opening, calling it 'An Untold Love Story':

> Love is the greatest thing ….
>
> In a small park on the Main North-East Road six kms from the Adelaide city centre in South Australia stands a modest memorial to Florence and Alfred Bennett. Their ashes lie together beneath. In 1907 the 38 year-old wife of this well-known Adelaide ear, nose and throat specialist died. There were no children. They had bought 32 acres of land at Hampstead two years before and established their own home, an extensive garden, and paddocks for several thoroughbred horses. Dr Bennett remarried but again there were no descendants. He died at the age of 62 in 1930 having beforehand willed 1.5 acres of his land, which had been set aside shortly after his first wife's death, to the people of South Australia for a children's playground. The dedication plaque at the memorial states: 'In loving memory of Florence Birkinshaw. Born at Manningham, Bradford, Yorkshire, England on 8th August 1868. Died at Adelaide 27th July 1907, whose gracious influence inspired the dedication of this playground, and in memory of Alfred Henry Bennett, MB Ch.M Aberdeen, husband of the above named Florence Birkinshaw. Born at Moonta, South Australia, 11th October 1867. Died at North Adelaide on 9th August 1930. Their cremated remains repose beneath this fountain.' Thus Adelaide acquired the suburb of Manningham and in this suburb at the

> Bennett Memorial Reserve, Bennett Avenue, Manningham Street and Birkinshaw Avenue.

Peter finished by quoting from Dr Bennett's obituary in *The Advertiser* of 11 August 1930:

> He was known to his many friends as the soul of good humour, and his genial nature made him a favourite with all who had the pleasure of his acquaintance. He took a broad and philosophical view of life and as a medical man encouraged his patients with a spirit of hopefulness which was invaluable to them. He was always ready to help a friend in need and was noted for his friendly and kindly disposition.

As Peter said to me there was little doubt that the love of Alfred Bennett's life was his first wife Florence. In the photo album which Ann had given me there was a signed photograph of Alfred as a young man. I sent Peter a copy and he said he would put it up in his surgery.

Dr Bennett's obituary in *The Advertiser* said that the loss of his first wife was a tragedy to him. It also said he was interested in gardening as well as horseracing and that he had studied medicine at Aberdeen University in Scotland from where he went to London and Vienna. He then returned to Australia where he married Florence.

There is a little postscript to this story in that I located Alfred and Florence's marriage certificate from the Melbourne Archives. This told me they had married on 5 November 1892 by licence in the Melbourne house of the Rev. Alexander Skene a Presbyterian Minister (he also happened to be a Professor of Hebrew). Alfred's address at the time was given as Kapunda,[13] South Australia and Florence's as the *SS Thermopylae*, Port Melbourne. The two witnesses appeared not to be family members. I found Florence's name in the migration lists from the National Archives. She had travelled on the *SS Thermopylae*, a three-masted clipper-bowed steamer, leaving London on 22 September and arriving Melbourne 4 November 1892. The ship sailed via South Africa, where, incidentally, she was wrecked in 1899 just off Table Bay due to fog, luckily with no loss of life. Florence must have arrived in Melbourne, met Alfred who was presumably waiting for her there having organised the wedding, and was married the following day.

As to where they met, that is still a mystery. However, I had a thought to look in the Scottish census records of April 1891 as Alfred was a student at Aberdeen University. To my surprise I found an entry for Alfred H Bennett who was recorded as a visitor in the house of a leather manufacturer who lived with his wife and two servants in Stonehaven, fifteen miles south of Aberdeen. He was described as a Doctor of Medicine, General Practitioner, from South Australia. But guess who was also staying there as a visitor? Florence Birkinshaw!

Memorial to Alfred and Florence Bennett - Adelaide
(with thanks to Peter Kreminski)

Grave of John Richard and family
(Nab Wood Cemetery, Shipley, Yorkshire)

The youngest son of John Richard and Annie was Sidney, born in 1873; he married Emmeline Jarratt in 1906 and they lived in Acton, London. Emmeline's family owned a laundry which Sidney took over and ran. They had no children. Beyond this information which I gleaned from Catherine and Ann, there was not much to find out about Sidney, except a comment my Uncle Bill made in a letter to me saying he did not like him! I discovered from the records that Sidney died in 1936 and left £1,315 in his will to Emmeline. In the event of Emmeline predeceasing him he had made provision in his will for £100 to go to four of his sister Kate's children: Pauline, Carmen, Dorothy and their brother Ross Shekleton. Emmeline spent the war years living with Herbert and Isabel in Birmingham to get away from London and the blitz; she died in 1965.[14] Emmeline's brother was Sir William Smith Jarratt, a barrister and copyright lawyer. He was educated at the Royal College of Science in London and Trinity College, Cambridge and became the Comptroller-General of Patents, Designs and Trade Marks by the time he retired in 1932. He was the best man at Sidney and Emmeline's wedding.[15]

Sidney and Emmeline's wedding, 1906
Annie and John Richard sitting left; Sir William Smith Jarratt standing behind them

John Richard and Annie's Golden Wedding, 1907

1. *Walter Birkinshaw*
2. *Mary Birkinshaw*
3. *Herbert Birkinshaw*
4. *Isabel Birkinshaw*
5. *Bill Birkinshaw*
6. *Emmeline Birkinshaw*
7. *Sidney Birkinshaw*
8. *Pauline Shekleton*
9. *John Shekleton*
10. *William Birkinshaw*
11. *Tilly Birkinshaw*
12. *Frank Shalders*
13. *Cuthbert Scales*
14. *Walter Scales*
15. *Carmen Shekleton*
16. *Dorothy Shekleton*
17. *Meg Birkinshaw*
18. *Freda Scales*
19. *Frank Ross Shekleton*
20. *Biddy Birkinshaw*
21. *Jack Birkinshaw*
22. *Evelyn Birkinshaw*
23. *Kate Shekleton*
24. *John Richard Birkinshaw*
25. *Annie Birkinshaw*
26. *Lizzie Shalders*
27. *Edith Scales*
28. *Andrew Birkinshaw*
29. *Russell Birkinshaw*
30. *Hilda Birkinshaw*
31. *Norman Birkinshaw*
32. *Frank Birkinshaw*
33. *Alec Scales*
34. *Catherine Scales*

My grandfather Herbert[16] was the second youngest of the family. He was born on 1 February 1871. The 1871 census showed Herbert, at the age of two months, staying with his Coulter grandparents in Chorlton on Medlock, Manchester. In the family home were the grandparents William and Eleanor and five of their children. William was a clerk. John Richard and some more of his family were staying in Ilkley on census day; perhaps they were on holiday there or John Richard was on business. John Richard was described as a foreign merchant on the census form.

Nothing much was known about Herbert's childhood except that he was sent to Sligo, either to boarding school there or in his school holidays, probably to stay with his elder sister Kate (she was eleven years older than him and was married in 1883). Herbert went in to the family wool business but did not appear to be very successful at it. He married my grandmother Isabella Garbutt in 1897. My grandmother was always known as Isabel and I was given her name as my second one. The family suspected that Herbert might have had a drink problem as he never appeared to have any money and was always very belligerent towards his children and long-suffering wife.

Of John Richard and Annie's children, two did not marry and three married but had no children. The remaining five produced twenty children, and they in turn had fifteen, who were all my second cousins. I managed to discover what had happened to all but one of them, and of those others, to meet up with five.

John Richard in the garden

Chapter Four

The Mysterious John Thornton

Frank's middle name was Thornton and I often wondered where the name came from. Frank's sister Sheona was christened Jane Thornton Birkinshaw, and their brother Bill was William Thornton Birkinshaw. Sheona was named after her maternal aunt, Jane Thornton Baigent, who later 'adopted' her[1] and Frank was named after his uncle Frank Thornton Garbutt. Sheona continued the tradition by passing the name on to her daughter Anne. The name must have had some important significance to have been passed down the generations. The question was, who had they all been named after?

A visit to my cousin Anne's house in Ambleside, in the Lake District, soon put me on the scent. Anne pulled out drawers filled with papers, documents and photographs, which had belonged to her mother Sheona. Sheona had always been very interested in family matters and to that end we had exchanged many a letter in the 1970s and 80s in which she poured out much of what she knew of the Garbutt/Henderson family history. Garbutt was my grandmother Isabel's family name, and Henderson was Isabel's mother's family name. Anne said that all she knew about the Thornton connection was what her mother had told her. The story was that John Thornton (whose name the family had always believed to be *Frank* Thornton) had lost a leg on the battlefield in the Napoleonic Wars and subsequently had lived in Edinburgh. Anne has his gold watch which he had also supposedly lost on the battlefield; the watch was engraved with his initials (the 'J' on it being mistaken for an 'F') and regiment, the 94th. According to the story the watch had later been found by someone and returned to John Thornton's regiment which in turn sent it to John. It had then been passed down the family. However, whether John Thornton was a relation or family friend, no one seemed to know.

Amongst Sheona's papers we came across a letter dated September 1978 from the Regimental Museum of the Border Regiment in Carlisle. This was in reply to one that Sheona had sent them enquiring about the person she believed to be Frank Thornton who had served in the 94th Regiment. The Museum said they could only find a *John* Thornton who matched the description, and they quoted from *The Connaught Rangers*[2] which listed the careers of all the officers who served in the 94th Regiment. The entry was as follows:

> Thornton John: Appointed Ensign 94th Regiment 27 August 1807; Lieutenant 2nd August 1810; Half-pay 42nd Foot 17th July 1817. Served in the Peninsular War 1810-1814 with the 94th. Military General Service Medal and clasps for Fuentes D'Onor, Cuidad Rodrigo, Badajoz, Salamanca, Vittoria, Pyrenees and Nivelle (dangerously wounded).

John Thornton joined the 94th Foot Regiment in 1807 just as they were finishing their nine years' tour of duty in India. In January 1810 the 970-strong battalion embarked for Portugal and then on to Cadiz in Spain to join Wellington's army.[3]

The French, under Napoleon, had invaded Portugal in 1807 and in 1808 Napoleon declared war on Spain, eventually putting his brother Joseph on the Spanish throne. The British army, at that time under the command of Arthur Wellesley (later to become the Duke of Wellington), arrived in Portugal in August 1808 and defeated the French at Vimiero near Lisbon. In 1809 the British mounted a new campaign in Portugal and Spain.

John Thornton remained in Cadiz until September 1811 in the front line and then sailed to Lisbon after which there was endless marching in terrible conditions. The men's feet stuck in the wet and clayey soil causing them to lose their shoes. At one time they were on half rations and worked six-hour shifts digging trenches at night in the bitter cold and dark.

The Caithness soldier, John Harper, in his *Caithness Archives*[4], gave a vivid description of life in the army, where many recruits were chosen by ballot or by the temptation of a bounty of eleven guineas if they signed up for a lifetime:

> Army life in the early 1800s was somewhat different to today's regime. Discipline was harsh, punishments draconian … Wellington's soldiers, having no access to fresh uniforms, went about in rags … Bad roads and non-existent transport meant that every journey was foot-slog; shoes rapidly wore out, men marched barefoot over flint roads.
>
> In the absence of stores a ready alternative offered itself: after every skirmish or battle the dead and wounded were stripped to the skin of uniforms, weapons, shoes, watches, purses; even false ivory teeth were removed. Any wounded man who resisted this pillage was unceremoniously done to death.

The Caithness Archives also described the grim realities of what happened after the Battle of Badajoz in April 1812, one of the battles in which John Thornton fought, where the British casualties were particularly heavy:

> The victorious Allies took a fearful vengeance on their French enemies, the town being given up to a three-day orgy of drunken looting, rape and murder.

John Thornton's next battle was Salamanca where the Allies lost 5,000 men as opposed to the 15,000 lost by the French. On 12 August 1812 Wellington took Madrid while Napoleon was busy invading Russia.

In November 1812 during the British retreat from Madrid, with the French in hot pursuit, the men marched twelve miles in torrential rain along roads which were knee-deep in water; they were drenched to the skin and many went bare-foot. The wind was cold and they had to sleep in wet blankets. To compound their misery their food had been left behind because of mismanagement and they marched for four days on empty stomachs. Many men fell out and were taken prisoner by the French and many more died.

The website *Historyworld.net* described the outcome of John Thornton's next battle at Vittoria:

> The decisive campaign comes in 1813 when Wellington moves north from Portugal and meets the army of Napoleon's brother Joseph Bonaparte (technically at this stage King of Spain) at Vittoria on 21 June. Wellington captures the entire French artillery train of some 150 guns, and all the baggage – including Joseph's impressive collection of art, which now graces Apsley House (Wellington's residence in London).

The Caithness Archives described the conditions the wounded had to endure, including the Caithness soldier, John Harper, who was himself wounded in the leg:

> In those days battlefield surgery was primitive to say the least and surgeons were duty-bound to attend to officers and NCOs before private soldiers. Anaesthetic was unknown, hygiene non-existent, nursing staff unheard of. No wonder then that so many soldiers died of gangrene, amputation shock, loss of blood or fever as a result of treatment for wounds.

The Battle of Nivelle, on 10 November 1813 took place by the River Nivelle in south-west France and was another success for the British. The French casualties were 4,351, compared to Wellington's 2,450. The commanding officer of the 94th was killed along with ten men; two officers were wounded, one of whom was John Thornton, who was seriously wounded, and probably only survived because he was an officer and was given preferential treatment.

All these battles were violent and bloody and were starkly depicted by Goya in his series of etchings, *Disasters of War*. Napoleon was finally defeated at the Battle of Waterloo in 1815.

Nivelle was the end of John Thornton's fighting career although he stayed with the 94th until July 1817; of the nine hundred who sailed out to Lisbon in 1810 only one hundred and fifty survived. The regiment sailed to Ireland in the middle of 1814 and remained in Ireland until the regiment was disbanded in 1818 which was why John transferred to the 42nd Royal Highland Regiment of Foot, the Black Watch, from whom he drew his pension.

John Thornton received the Military General Service Medal which commemorated the campaigns and battles of the British Army between 1801 and 1814. It had bars, or clasps, which were awarded for each battle fought, with the name of the battle engraved thereon. John had seven clasps on his medal.

A search through the Scottish 1841 census found that John Thornton, aged fifty, was living at Nivelle Cottage, Liberton, in Edinburgh. He had named his cottage after the battle in which he had been wounded! With him were two servants Isabella Anderson, aged thirty-five, and Thomas White, aged fifteen. The three of them appeared in the 1851 census where Isabella's occupation was given as 'house servant' and Thomas as 'coachman', and again in the 1861 census. They continued to look after John until his death on 18 November 1870 aged eighty-one.

I found John Thornton's will, which he had written in 1867, in the Scottish archives. John had appointed his sister Jane Henderson, 'presently residing at Mount Pleasant near Wooler in the County of Northumberland' as his executor. He left a legacy to his housekeeper Isabella Anderson of £130 and one to his manservant Thomas White of £30. The residue of his estate was to go to his sister Jane. The will recorded that John Thornton's pension as an officer wounded in battle was £70 a year, paid by the War Office in Scotland. In addition he received regimental half pay as an officer of 4/6d per day. In 1869 he added a codicil to his will which stated that as his sister Jane had now married Joseph Owen, a banker in Ipswich, he was leaving his furniture, which he had formerly intended to leave to Jane, to his two servants. There was no mention of John's gold watch but perhaps it went with the residue of his estate to his sister Jane. On his death certificate his parents were named as John Thornton (occupation 'merchant') and Ann Davidson.

According to the 1871 census, Thomas and Isabella were still living in Nivelle Cottage. Thomas was described as a market gardener and Isabella the housekeeper and they also employed a servant, Janet. Isabella died there in 1875 aged seventy-four and Janet, who had become the housekeeper, stayed on with Thomas until 1882, according to the local valuation roll.

I was now getting closer to discovering the Thornton connection, as Henderson was the family name of my grandmother Isabel's mother, Mary Elizabeth. The question now was which member of the Henderson family had Jane married? A look at the 1861 census showed Jane Henderson living at Hetton House, Wooler, in Northumberland. Hetton House was the home of my great-great grandfather Richard Henderson, who died there in 1860. According to family history Richard married a fearsome Miss Owen after his first wife Isabella died, although nobody seemed to know her first name; she was always known as Grandma Owen. I pursued the Owen/Henderson connection through the records and discovered from the certificate of Richard Henderson's second marriage that he had actually married - Jane Thornton.

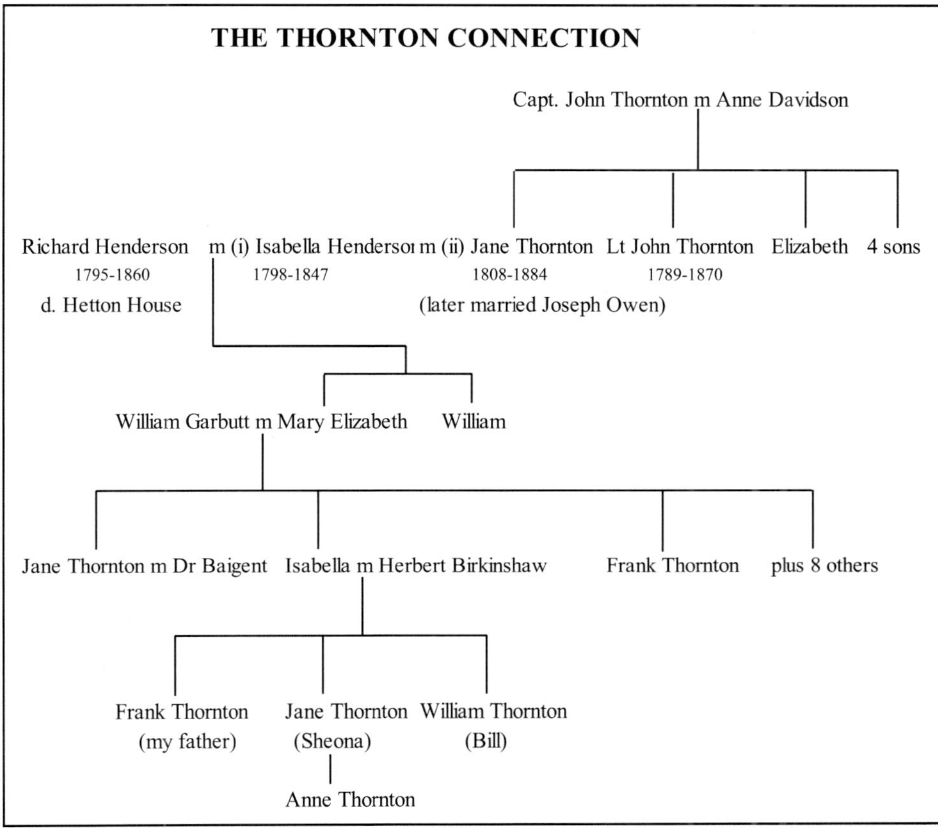

On her marriage she became Jane Henderson and after Richard died she married Joseph Owen, a banker from Ipswich, as John Thornton's will had revealed. Therefore 'Miss Owen', whom the family believed Richard had married as his second wife, and Jane Thornton, were one and the same. Richard and Jane were married for twelve years and after Richard died Jane Thornton/Henderson then went on to become *Mrs* Owen. It was now clear that John Thornton was not a blood relation of the family but obviously had a certain standing amongst them and must have been someone they all looked up to and admired.

More google searches revealed a gravestone in the Liberton Kirk churchyard in Edinburgh with the name John Thornton. I emailed the church with the information I had and asked them if they could let me know whether their John Thornton was the one I was looking for. A local historian from the church, John Rennie, replied that, yes, he was the right one. Fortuitously for me, John Rennie had in the past taken the trouble to list all the names from the gravestones of the people buried in that churchyard and had posted them on the church website and was able to answer my question immediately. The unusually detailed inscription on John Thornton's headstone was as follows:

> In memory of Lieutenant John Thornton, late of Her Majesty's 94th Regiment, born at Wooler, Northumberland on 18 August 1789, died at Nivelle Cottage, Liberton 18 November 1870. Lieutenant Thornton joined the army under the Duke of Wellington in 1807 and remained in it until 1817. He was present and engaged in many great battles of the period, and being dangerously wounded at that of Nivelle he was obliged to retire from active service and during the remainder of his life he chiefly resided in this parish, where he was much respected, and died deeply regretted by all to whom he was known.

The fact that John was born in Wooler was a surprise, but it did make sense given that the Hendersons also lived there. A search of the 1841 census found John's sister Jane Thornton living in Wooler at Mount Pleasant with the Davidson family; this was before she married Richard Henderson. The Davidsons were John and Jane Thornton's mother's family, as John's death certificate stated. The Davidsons in Wooler were probably family friends of the Hendersons which is presumably how Richard and Jane Thornton met. From the census it appeared that Jane was born in 1811 in Haddington, south-east Scotland.

In 2008 we visited Edinburgh and met my contact John Rennie and he showed us John Thornton's headstone in the Liberton churchyard. He then took us to where he believed Nivelle Cottage had been, having researched the area from an old OS map. The cottage, we discovered, had in fact been incorporated into Liberton Hospital, but was plainly visible as an old building subsumed into the modern.

When we told John that Jane Thornton was born in Haddington he told us there was an archive office there which we should visit, to see whether we could find any further information about the Thornton family. Haddington was only a few miles out of Edinburgh so we duly stopped there on our way home. We found a very helpful archivist who soon dug out a copy of *Reminiscenses of the Royal Burgh of Haddington* by John Martine which contained some relevant information about the Thornton family and their reason for living in Haddington. There was also information about the house where they had lived in Fishmarket Wynd (a wynd is a Scottish name for a narrow lane or alley):

> Captain Thornton, who was one of the officers of a regiment which was quartered in the barracks, bought the house, and built a new front to it. He had a number of sons who served their king and country as soldiers and sailors. His oldest son, Lieutenant John Thornton, of the 94th Regiment of Foot, deserves here to be specially mentioned as a hero and brave soldier, having fought in all the great battles of the Peninsula under the Duke of Wellington. He

Lt John Thornton's grave, Liberton Kirk, Edinburgh; April 2008

Below: Lt John Thornton's watch, with initials 'JT' and his Regiment, the 94th, inscribed on the back

Above:
Nivelle Cottage, incorporated into Liberton Hospital; April 2008

Left:
The Thornton house in Haddington, near Edinburgh; April 2008

was dangerously wounded at the battle of Nivelle. Born at Wooler in 1789 but brought up in Haddington, and educated at the grammar school, he entered the army in 1807 and remained in it until 1817, when, on account of his wounds, he was obliged to retire from active service. During the remainder of his life, he resided at Nivelle Cottage, Liberton, much respected. He died in 1870 and was buried in Liberton churchyard, where a handsome tombstone, with an inscription, keeps his name in remembrance.

As the Fishmarket Wynd no longer existed in Haddington our friendly archivist did some more searching and eventually discovered that it was now called Cross Lane. He directed us to it and we found the house as described in John Martine's *Reminiscenses,* the house being on the west side of the original Fishmarket Wynd. The house dated from 1790 or 1800, having been occupied by Dr Richard Somner the principal surgeon in Haddington at that time; it was now a shoe shop. We went in and explained the reason for our visit to the rather bemused sales assistant and she allowed us to look round.

According to the birth records in the archive office, there were six more children, four boys and two girls, born to John and Anne Thornton between 1802 and 1808 following their move to Haddington, East Lothian. Jane's birth was entered as Jean (another form of Jane), born in 1808. Later Jane took the opportunity to knock a few years off her age as she appeared to be much younger on her marriage certificate and on the census returns. There was only one other girl in the family, Elizabeth, born in 1802, who died in December 1806 of fever. It was perhaps because John only had one surviving sister that he took so much interest in her and her family. No further information came to light concerning John and Jane's four brothers. Possibly, the reason John's mother stayed in Wooler for a time with her family was because her husband, Captain Thornton, was away fighting, and that might account for the age gap between John and his siblings.

Recently I was speaking to my cousin Karen about John Thornton and she told me she had a photograph of him. Not believing that could possibly be so, I immediately hopped on a train to go and visit her near Nottingham to see for myself. The photo turned out to be a very old one in an equally old frame, on the back of which Karen's father Bill had written – 'My grandmother Elizabeth Henderson Garbutt, aged eighteen, with her uncle Captain Thornton and her aunt Elizabeth Henderson'. Realising that the labelling could not be correct as 'Captain' Thornton was John's father and Elizabeth Henderson (Jane's stepdaughter) did not become Garbutt until she was twenty-five, I persuaded Karen's husband to take the back off the photo frame to see if there was anything written on the reverse of the photo and, sure enough, it said 'John Thornton and his sister Jane with Elizabeth Henderson'. The young Elizabeth in the photo *was* Bill's grandmother. The Elizabeth that Bill had assumed to be the aunt was in fact Jane Thornton, and the John Thornton in the photo was our hero (and not his father, the Captain). Karen said John did not look as though he had a false leg, but I checked with the Thackray Museum in Leeds who assured me that false legs were sophisticated enough to have a knee bend by 1850. The most exciting thing about the photograph, apart from its existence, was that John was wearing his medals.

That is all the information currently known about John Thornton but I discovered a little more about his sister Jane and the Owen family she later married in to by searching through more records.

Joseph Owen, a banker, was born in 1813 in Yorkshire. He first married Margaret Hall and they had two sons, Joseph and John Smith Owen. They were born in Berwick-on-Tweed, not too far away from Wooler where John Thornton was born, and his mother's family the Davidsons lived, so perhaps that was the family connection to the Owens. They subsequently moved to Ipswich in Suffolk. John Smith Owen became a vicar at the parish of St Matthews in Thorpe Hamlet, Norwich. He married Anna Temple in 1867 in Norwich. John and Anna had seven children between them, one of whom carried on the Thornton name. He was Joseph Thornton Owen, born in 1872 and he became a school master.

After his wife Margaret died in 1865 Joseph Owen married Jane Henderson in 1868 and they lived at 18 Founnereau Road, Ipswich.

Jane Thornton/Henderson/Owen died on 1 August 1884 at Ipswich aged seventy-four. Just before Jane married Joseph in 1868 they made an Indenture of Settlement between themselves and William Henderson, farmer, who was Jane's stepson through her first husband Richard, and also William Davidson Smith from Fife who was a fish curer, no doubt another of Jane's family. This in effect gave her husband absolute control over her affairs. Even so Jane wrote a will in August 1869 and left her husband life entitlement to her stocks and shares and personal effects. After his death she wanted various legacies to take effect, including one of £100 which was to be given to Jane Thornton Garbutt (her step-granddaughter who was only three at the time), the daughter of William and Elizabeth Garbutt of Dunston Lodge, Gateshead. Jane wanted her brother John Thornton to have an annuity of £50; in the event he died before her. The residue of her estate was to go to her stepson John Smith Owen the clergyman. However, it looked as though Joseph was not happy with her will, and because he was the sole executor and her husband he declared her intestate and claimed sole entitlement which he was legally allowed to do. Her estate was worth around £3,000.

Joseph Owen died on the same date and month as Jane, thirteen years later, in 1897. His estate was worth £18,400. He wrote his will in 1893 and left all his property to his son John and various legacies to his grandchildren. He also left the £100 promised by his wife Jane to Jane Thornton Garbutt. Another legacy was left to a friend, interestingly called Owen Thornton Gibb.

Although we now have a pretty good picture of who John Thornton was – definitely a much-respected war hero, perhaps a godfather to some of Elizabeth's children or perhaps a beneficent uncle and great uncle - the mystery is not completely solved.

Jane Thornton (Mrs Henderson), with her stepdaughter Elizabeth Henderson, and Lt John Thornton wearing his medals, 1857

Chapter Five

The Hendersons and the Garbutts

Richard and Isabella Henderson were Frank's maternal great-grandparents. They lived near Wooler, a small stone-built village in Northumberland, now known as the gateway to the Cheviot Hills and the Northumberland National Park. Isabella's family were also Hendersons, rather confusing the family tree (see Tree 1), but it was not clear whether the families were related. Isabella's parents were Alexander and Mary Henderson, and Alexander was the miller at the Wooler Flour Mill which was built in 1783. He and Mary lived just opposite in the mill house where all their five children were born. Little is known about their two eldest sons David and Matthew, but they were followed by a sister Elizabeth who did not marry. After Elizabeth came Alexander who became a surgeon but died young at the age of thirty-seven in the nearby village of Glanton where he had a medical practice. Isabella, who was born in 1798, was the youngest of the five children. Alexander and Mary, their daughter Elizabeth and son Alexander were all buried in a family grave at St Mary's Church, Wooler.

Richard Henderson was the son of William and Elizabeth who were tenant farmers at Langleeford which is about five miles south-west of Wooler. Langleeford is a beautiful remote place nestling at the foot of Cheviot, the highest peak in the Cheviot Hills. The Henderson family had been tenant farmers at Langleeford since 1591, the farm being owned at that time by Sir John Selby. The Haggerston family were the next owners in the 1800s followed by Lady Stanley, then the Leyland family. In 1851 Lady Stanley was supposed to have leapt over a deep gorge at Langleeford on her white horse to escape marauding Scotsmen, in order to save her honour; the gorge is locally known as 'Lady Stanley's Leap'.[1]

Throughout this period of three hundred years our Henderson family continued their unbroken tenancy. Their main source of income was from the valuable wool which the Cheviot sheep provided and they would also have had some cattle. In addition they kept goats which produced milk from which they made cheese, and there was much scope for hunting and fishing. There would be plenty going on round the farm, and sports days for the local lads and lasses were not uncommon. There were also tourists who came past on their way to climb Cheviot.

In 1791 Sir Walter Scott spent several nights at Langleeford. Scott had travelled to Wooler with his uncle, and on arriving in the town they discovered there was nowhere suitable to stay and so were invited to Langleeford by Richard's father William Henderson. Scott's stay there was recorded in a letter[2] which he wrote to William Clerk and he described himself as being:

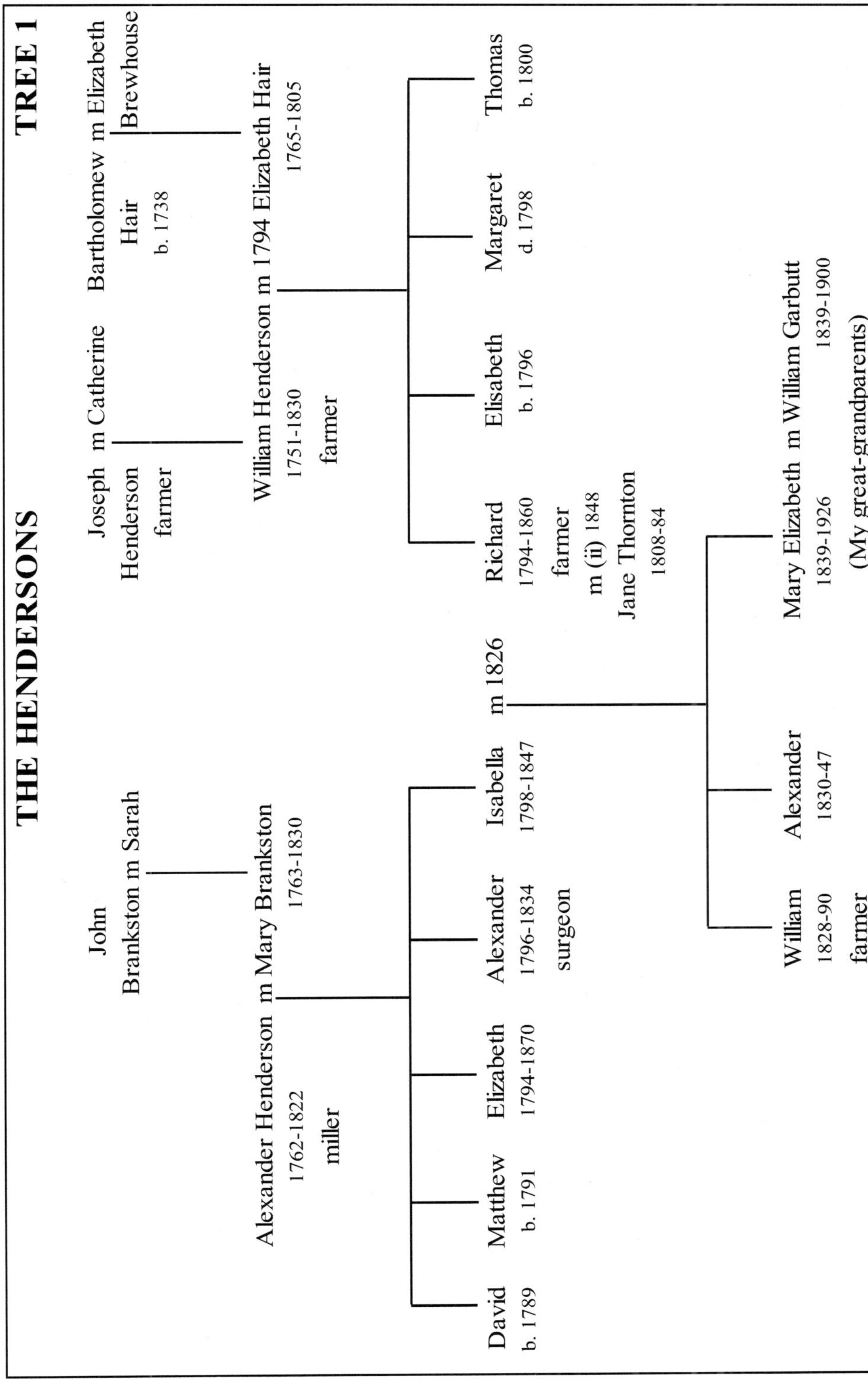
THE HENDERSONS
TREE 1
John Brankston m Sarah
Mary Brankston 1763-1830
Alexander Henderson 1762-1822 miller
Joseph Henderson farmer
m Catherine
William Henderson 1751-1830 farmer
Bartholomew Hair b. 1738
m Elizabeth Brewhouse
m 1794 Elizabeth Hair 1765-1805
David b. 1789
Matthew b. 1791
Elizabeth 1794-1870
Alexander 1796-1834 surgeon
Isabella 1798-1847
m 1826
Richard 1794-1860 farmer
m (ii) 1848 Jane Thornton 1808-84
Elisabeth b. 1796
Margaret d. 1798
Thomas b. 1800
William 1828-90 farmer
Alexander 1830-47
Mary Elizabeth 1839-1926
m William Garbutt 1839-1900
(My great-grandparents)

> Very snugly settled here, in a farmer's house, about six miles from Wooler, in the very centre of the Cheviot hills, in one of the wildest and most romantic situations which your imagination, fertile upon the subject of cottages, ever suggested.

He continued to describe how he and his uncle passed their time at Langleeford:

> My uncle drinks the whey here, as I do ever since I understood it was brought to his bedside every morning at six, by a very pretty dairy-maid. So much for my residence: all the day we shoot, fish, walk and ride; dine and sup upon fish struggling from the stream, and the most delicious heath-fed mutton, barn-door fowls, poys, milk-cheese, &c., all in perfection. So much simplicity resides among these hills, that the pen, which could write at least, was not to be found about the house, though belonging to a considerable farmer, till I shot a crow with whose quill I now write this epistle.

The comment that Scott could not find a quill pen, with which he could write, in the Henderson house does not sit happily with the descendants of the Hendersons who knew quite well that the house would have abounded in pens as they were a very well-educated family!

Langleeford Farm, circa 1900

The old Wooler Mill and Mill House, from a watercolour by local artist Alex Dalziel, 1823

Langleeford Farm, 2008

Hetton House, 2008

Fowberry Mains, 2008

Samuel Donkin wrote about Langleeford and the Hendersons in his *Reminiscences.*[3] He said Langleeford was a household word within the Border Counties because of the unbroken lineage of the Henderson family. Mr Henderson (William 1751-1830), he said, had 'an inexhaustible store of anecdote'. One of those stories was about how he, William, had taken Lord and Lady Clive (of India) to the top of Cheviot. The story went as follows:

> In his youth he had to be a 'guide' to Lord and Lady Clive to the summit of the mountain. The countenance of the *genii* of the mist was far from fascinating – his lordship, who was duly warned of the meteorological forebodings, replied 'don't be afraid, guide, her ladyship has been accustomed to climb the highest mountains in Wales'.
>
> The guide, nettled at an imputation upon his want of pluck, indulged in a monologue. 'Afraid! Not for my own safety, but only for that of Juno in her flight to the clouds with her peacock'. About midway to the mountain's summit, rain fell, his lordship's infirmities taking shelter, with an attendant, under a shelving precipice; her ladyship braving the rain and reaching the top of Cheviot. On returning, his lordship was sitting shivering within a rug, whilst the 'guide', who had been suspected of cowardice, was inwardly enjoying the ludicrous catastrophe.

Richard farmed with his father William at Langleeford and carried on the tenancy after William died in 1830; Richard and his wife Isabella also occupied the rather grand Hetton House on the other side of Wooler. Hetton House was the property of George Culley, Esq., and Richard was his tenant. George Culley and his brother Matthew were great agricultural reformers and improved methods of soil cultivation in the nineteenth century, according to local history. Richard Henderson had a younger brother Thomas, born in 1800, and two sisters: Margaret who died young in 1798, and Elisabeth who was born in 1796. The family always talked about 'the three beautiful Miss Hendersons', they being Isabella, her sister Elizabeth and sister-in-law Elisabeth.

Richard and Isabella had three children, all born at Langleeford. Their firstborn was William who farmed with his father at Langleeford and also at Fowberry Mains which was near Hetton House. Fowberry Mains was the farmhouse of the Fowberry Estate, also owned by the Culley family. William, according to family history, was sporting and scholarly with an extensive library, mostly inherited later from his father. Richard and Isabella's second son Alexander was born in 1830 but only lived to the age of sixteen after contracting tuberculosis; he died at Langleeford.

Mary Elizabeth, always known by her second name, was born in 1839. When Elizabeth was seven her mother died. This was less than four months after Alexander, so it was likely that Isabella also had TB. Her death certificate gave the cause of death as 'diarrhea', which might have been a side effect of TB. (She died in Spittal, which is part of Berwick-upon-Tweed, the nearest town to Langleeford.) Just a year later Elizabeth's father Richard married again. It took a great deal of searching through records to discover that his second wife was Jane Thornton, a spinster aged about forty, who was at the time living with some of her mother's family, the Davidsons, at the house called Mount Pleasant in Wooler. (There was a Christian Davidson present at Isabella's death, according to her death certificate, so there must have been a connection between the Thornton/Davidson family and the Hendersons.) Jane was a formidable woman and not liked at all by Elizabeth who was promptly sent off to boarding school in Edinburgh. Jane was the sister of the somewhat mysterious John Thornton, as mentioned in the previous chapter.

Elizabeth was happy at school and in later life would delight in telling her grand-daughter Sheona (my aunt) stories about her childhood. Sheona mentioned many of these in her autobiography *Swan Feather*.[4] Elizabeth won the Senior English Prize at school and was awarded *The Poems and Plays of Oliver Goldsmith*; apparently she preferred Sir Walter Scott. Elizabeth enjoyed music and dancing lessons, to which she was taken in the holidays always heavily escorted, according to Sheona's reminiscences. Elizabeth said that an escort was very necessary as there was one exciting and romantic episode when one of the girls was accosted by a young man. 'Grandmother spoke of this episode with a little twinkle in her eye,' recounted Sheona. Elizabeth also rode in the holidays and one day she saddled her own horse and went out unattended to follow the hunt. She was not supposed to go riding without a groom and someone happened to mention to her father what a good horsewoman she was; her father was furious.

William Henderson's aunt Elizabeth (the second of the 'beautiful Miss Hendersons') was living at Langleeford with William in 1851 according to the census of that year. Langleeford had 4,500 acres and William employed seven men there. William's father and stepmother Jane continued to live at Hetton House with Elizabeth.

In September 1860, according to family history, Richard broke his neck jumping a five-barred gate at the end of a day's hunting. His death certificate stated that he died of 'fever following concussion from fall with horse after seven days'. He was sixty-five. He was buried at Ilderton churchyard four miles south of Wooler, alongside his first wife Isabella, their son Alexander and Richard's father William.

Jane remained at Hetton House where she was registered in the 1861 census. She had a friend staying and there were two servants with them. Jane later moved back to her mother's family at Mount Pleasant in Wooler until her marriage to the banker Joseph Owen in 1868, after which she moved to

Richard Henderson circa 1855

Family in mourning after Richard's death, 1860

William Henderson (son), Jane Thornton/Henderson (widow), Elizabeth (daughter), Elisabeth (sister)

Suffolk. Jane was thereafter always known as 'Grandma Owen' to Richard's grandchildren. According to his will Richard left about £3,000 which he divided between his children William and Elizabeth, and his wife Jane. Family gossip intimated that Jane took the family jewellery that had belonged to Isabella and which should really have gone to Elizabeth.

The 1861 census showed William Henderson farming at Langleeford and his aunt still living with him, and also his sister Elizabeth now aged twenty-two; she probably preferred her brother's company to that of her step-mother at Hetton House.

Sheona day-dreamed about Hetton House describing it as 'Queen Anne and beautifully proportioned, which is said to have the finest small rough shoot in the whole of Northumberland'. She imagined what it must have been like when her great-grandparents Richard and Isabella, and later Jane, lived there:

> When I saw the dining room I imagined it with candles lit, the spode dessert service on the table, my grandmother (perhaps as a small girl allowed to come down for dessert) with her father benign and dignified (as one sees in the portrait) with his side whiskers and high collar.[5] At the far end of the table his second wife always known as 'Grandma Owen' severe and forbidding in spite of her ringlets. As a step-mother and grandmother she was not a great success though my mother [Jennie Baigent, Sheona's 'adopted' mother] (who prided herself on getting on with difficult people) was quite fond of her.

Sheona mused about the River Till, an English tributary of the Scottish River Tweed at the foot of the garden of Hetton House and about which Sir Walter Scott wrote:

> Said Tweed to Till what gars ye rin sae still?
> Till said to Tweed though ye rin with speed
> And I rin slaw
> Yet where ye droun ae man I droun twa.

We went to stay in Wooler in the Spring of 2008 along with my cousin Anne. She had her mother Sheona's enthusiasm for the Hendersons, their lives and their homes. We saw the very impressive Hetton House, Fowberry Mains and the remote Langleeford where the Hendersons had farmed for so long. We also visited the house called Mount Pleasant in Wooler where John Thornton's family had lived and where later my grandmother Isabel and her sisters stayed when they were young. The owners, with whom I had been in touch prior to our visit, showed us round. I asked them whether they knew where Wooler Mill was or whether it still existed, as I knew from the records that Isabella's Henderson family had lived there. They did not know but

William Henderson
1751-1830
(father of Richard)

Grandma Owen

directed us to an elderly gentleman called Mattie Fairnington, who lived further down the hill, who was something of a local historian. He was able to tell us that the Old Wooler Mill and house were still standing and where they were located. Not only did he give us the information, but when he realised our connection with the mill he very generously gave me a painting he had of the mill, done by a local artist. We found the mill, which had recently been converted to a dwelling, on the other side of the village. The mill house was also there so we decided to go and knock on the door to see if we could glean any further information. A young man opened the door to us. He said that he was up from London visiting his family and, rather surprisingly, was able to tell us about the history of the house. He said his grandmother, whose house it was, used to tell him stories about it when he was a young boy!

Elizabeth Henderson, now twenty-five, married William Garbutt in January 1865 in St Peter's Church, Newcastle. Sheona said she found a letter written to William Garbutt from a friend offering congratulations to him on his marriage to Elizabeth and on 'catching the heiress'. Not only had Elizabeth been left about £1,000 by her father Richard after he died but she also stood to inherit from her brother William, being his nearest relative.

Exactly a month after their wedding William and Elizabeth's first child William was born in February 1865. Elizabeth was by this time an orphan and was perhaps rebelling against her stepmother Jane. According to their marriage certificate, on which William was described as a farmer, William's married sister Isabella Wilkinson was one of the witnesses; the other was not a family member. There was no sign of Elizabeth's brother William or Grandma Owen. Elizabeth had been expected to 'marry into the county', so her marriage probably did not go down too well with her family.

The Garbutts (see Tree 2) were originally Dutch immigrants who came to live in the Tyneside area. The first to arrive was Cornelius Garbutt who was born in 1750. His son, Cornelius II, who was born in 1778, was a builder and built St Edmund's Chapel in Gateshead sometime around 1810. He, his wife Isabella and her father William Gustard are all buried in the Chapel graveyard along with one of Cornelius II's children, William Garbutt and his wife Mary. The original chapel had been demolished and the land from it divided up into plots for private houses, and in 1813 Cornelius II and another builder built four houses on the plot they had acquired. These houses were in what was to become King James's Street, Gateshead, which was throughout the nineteenth century one of the most select streets in the town; this according to information from the Central Library in Gateshead. Cornelius III was born in 1806 and opened a chemist's shop in the middle of Gateshead in 1838 and advertised regularly in the *Gateshead Observer*. He was elected twice to the local council and was later Chairman of the Board of Guardians. This body administered the Poor Law and ran the workhouse. In 1841 the census

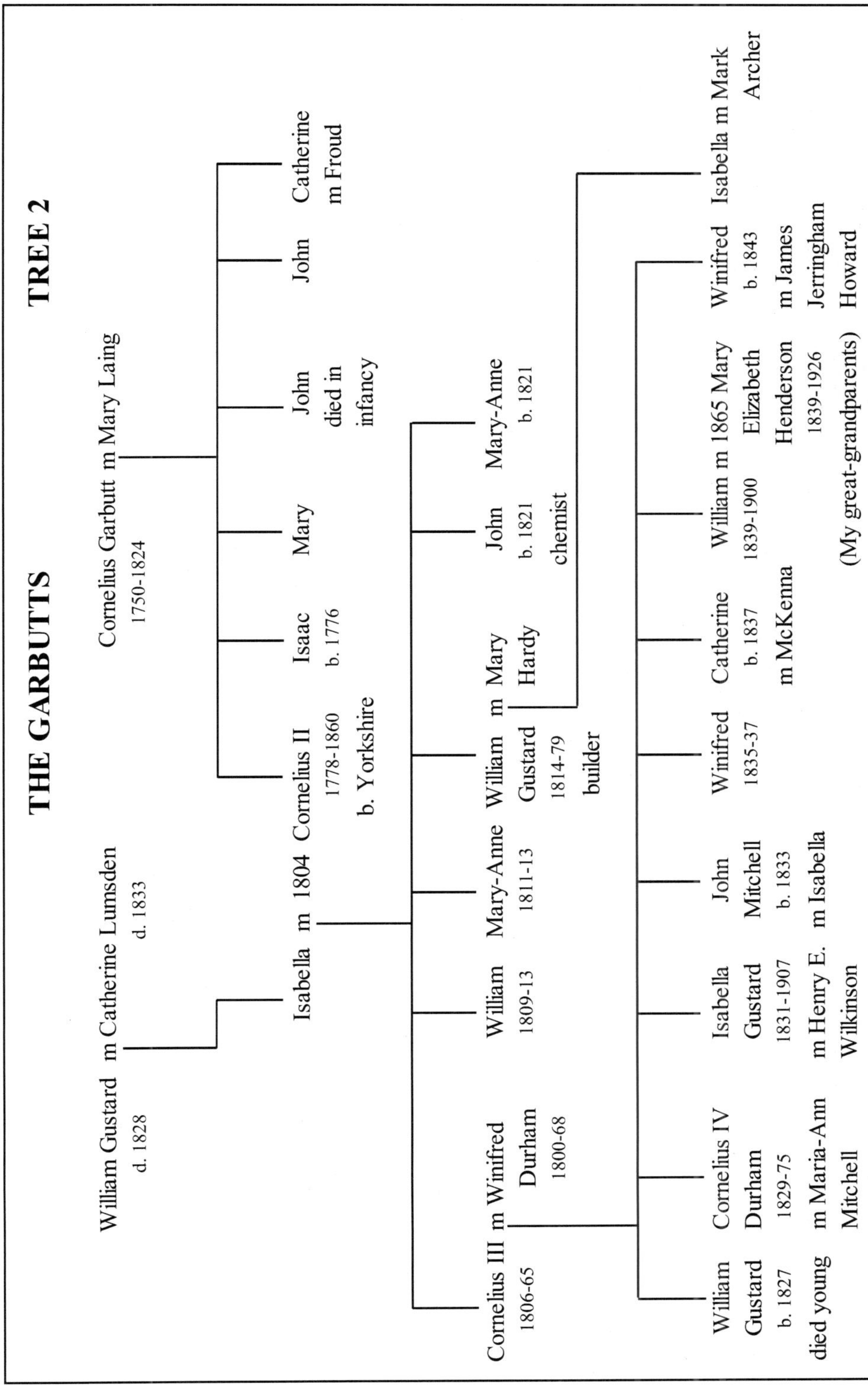
THE GARBUTTS
TREE 2
William Gustard
d. 1828
m Catherine Lumsden
d. 1833
Cornelius Garbutt m Mary Laing
1750-1824
Isabella m 1804 Cornelius II
1778-1860
b. Yorkshire
Isaac
b. 1776
Mary
John
died in
infancy
John
Catherine
m Froud
Cornelius III m Winifred
1806-65
Durham
1800-68
William
1809-13
Mary-Anne
1811-13
William m Mary
Gustard
1814-79
builder
Hardy
John
b. 1821
chemist
Mary-Anne
b. 1821
William
Gustard
b. 1827
died young
Cornelius IV
Durham
1829-75
m Maria-Ann
Mitchell
Isabella
Gustard
1831-1907
m Henry E.
Wilkinson
John
Mitchell
b. 1833
m Isabella
Winifred
1835-37
Catherine
b. 1837
m McKenna
William m 1865 Mary
1839-1900
Elizabeth
Henderson
1839-1926
(My great-grandparents)
Winifred
b. 1843
m James
Jerringham
Howard
Isabella m Mark
Archer

William Garbutt
circa 1865

Elizabeth
Henderson/Garbutt
circa 1865

revealed Cornelius and his wife Winifred and their five children living in Bottle Bank (named after the Saxon word 'botl' meaning settlement), Gateshead. Also living with them were Cornelius's brother, William, twenty-five, a builder, John, who was twenty, a chemist, and their sister Mary-Anne, also aged twenty.

In 1852 Cornelius III inherited a private lunatic asylum. This was Dunston Lodge in Whickham, near Gateshead. Dunston Lodge was originally an old mansion house owned by the well-known Marley family of Tyneside. In 1830 John Etridge Wilkinson leased it from the Marley family and established the asylum. Local history records revealed that in 1851 a male pauper in the asylum bit the arm of Mr Wilkinson. The patient was put in a straight jacket and flogged, after which two of his teeth were removed by a medical attendant. The visiting magistrates held an inquiry which was taken up by the Commissioners for Lunacy; Mr Wilkinson was found guilty 'of the most flagrant cruelty' and his licence revoked. The asylum was then taken over by his friend Cornelius Garbutt whose daughter Isabella later married Mr Wilkinson's son Henry who was a veterinary surgeon in Newcastle. Cornelius II lived with his son at Dunston Lodge and died in 1860.

The 1861 census of Dunston Lodge Asylum showed that Cornelius III was living there with his wife Winifred, his two daughters Catherine and Winifred, his son William, who was the farm manager, and another son John Mitchell Garbutt. John was the asylum physician and his wife Isabella and their two sons also lived there. Cornelius's brother William, the builder, was also living at Dunston Lodge along with his wife Mary and family. There was a matron, nurses and several 'lunatic attendants', various farm hands, a dairy maid, a tailor and shoemaker and some domestic servants. There were one hundred and sixty-eight 'lunatic patients' listed in the census, by initials only, but their occupations were given and also the place where they were born; they were mostly from the local area. Among these were a miller, a miller's wife, an innkeeper, a ladies' maid, two wives of engineers, the wife of a draper, a gentlewoman (from Suffolk), a curate, a landowner, a sergeant major in the Royal Artillery, several farmers, a solicitor, a master mariner (from the Isle of Wight), a chemist, several domestic servants, a weaver's winder, a power loom weaver, a bobbie winder, a schoolmaster and several vagrants.

Cornelius III died in November 1865 at Dunston Lodge and his son William, just married to Elizabeth Henderson, became the proprietor of the asylum. However, William did not exactly inherit the asylum from his father as the family had always believed, as was made clear in Cornelius's will.

In the will, the effects of which were valued at about £8,000, Cornelius III was described as 'Lunatic Asylum Proprietor'. He had appointed his son William and daughter Catherine to be executors and trustees and left his wife Winifred all his 'furniture, plate, linen, china and household effects as she shall choose to have to the value of £250'. William, being a farmer, was to

Above: Dunstan Lodge (with thanks to Gateshead Council, Libraries and Arts)

Below: Dunstan Lodge, circa 1900

have all the farm estate, which Cornelius owned or was the tenant of, which adjoined or was near Dunston Lodge. The houses, shops and businesses Cornelius owned in Gateshead were to be put into a trust. One of these premises was 'now in the occupation of Cornelius Durham Garbutt', his son, and another occupied by William Gustard Garbutt, who was the brother of Cornelius III. (William Gustard was married to Mary and they were the parents of Isabella, who later had a big influence on the family; Isabella married Mark Archer.) The income from the trust was to be for the benefit of Cornelius's wife Winifred, and after her death was to go to his three daughters, namely Isabella the wife of Henry Etridge Wilkinson, Catherine, who was at that time unmarried, and Winifred, who was later to marry James Jerringham Howard. Dunston Lodge and all the other premises nearby in which Cornelius had an interest were to be sold and the proceeds distributed, with two equal fifths going to his sons Cornelius Durham Garbutt, and John Mitchell Garbutt, and the remaining one fifth part to go to his third son William. Until the asylum was sold it was to be managed by his son John Mitchell, who was a doctor, at a salary to be agreed between the three brothers. William and Catherine were bequeathed Cornelius's two life insurance policies in the sum of £1,000 and £600. Any ready money and residual estate was to go to his wife and any residual real estate to William and Catherine. It was not clear how William came to take over and run Dunston Lodge, but perhaps he bought his brothers out.

After the Great Fire in Gateshead in 1854, Cornelius IV had taken over his father's chemist shop and also traded in wines and spirits; he later went bankrupt.[6] Cornelius IV died, aged forty-five, in July 1875 leaving a will of under one hundred pounds. He had written his will, in which he was described as a 'gentleman', in March of that year. There was no mention of his wife Maria-Ann although from the records she appeared not to have died until 1902. He made his two executors guardians of his six children and left the children all his household furniture and effects. However, he left his pictures and his gold watch and chain to William Stobbard, innkeeper, although these items, according to the will, were already in William's possession. Any residue of his estate was also to go to William Stobbard. It would appear that Cornelius had debts which had to be paid to the innkeeper, even at the expense of his own family.

There was a description of Dunston Lodge in this extract from *Echoes of Other Days, Some Leaves of Northern Lore*[7]:

> In its management he [Cornelius III] was ably assisted by his son William, who in 1865 took entire control and up to the time of its closing in 1900 showed the greatest tact and judgement in all matters concerning the working of the institution. So much so that in a printed pamphlet the position of this Asylum was shown to be

> one of the highest throughout the country; and that a large number of the inmates through right and humane treatment, combined with medical skill had been discharged, recovered.

The article continued by saying that the asylum contained 'several members of influential families' and that the 'unfortunate inmates' were familiar figures in the village and because they were harmless and gentle they were both pitied and respected by the people. Every consideration was shown towards the inmates. They even held dances in the ball-room for them, to which they could invite their friends, and there was a cricket XI. The estate consisted of about sixty-five acres which included a farm and gardens. The writer of the article said he had spoken to many of the servants who worked at the asylum and that all 'have spoken in high praise of the Garbutts, who have left quite an honoured name in the district'. There was a rather touching story about one of the inmates:

> One of the best remembered seems to have been a certain lady who was always seen with an umbrella and a bundle as if ready for a journey and who used to walk daily down to the boat-landing and wave farewell to the boats and ships as they passed. It was whispered abroad that a disappointment in marriage had caused her to lose her reason and she was always prepared to go on her marriage journey.

People came from all over the world to visit Dunston Lodge, it having the reputation of being one of the most advanced asylums in England, and its cure rate was well above the results of any other asylum in the country, according to local history.

The 1871 census showed William well-established at Dunston Lodge with his growing family, but a substantially decreasing number of patients, there being only thirty-seven. This probably reflected the fact that public hospitals were taking over more of the general health care, so less people were ending up in mental institutions. William's family now consisted of his wife Elizabeth, son William and daughters Jane, familiarly called Jennie, Winifred, Mary and Isabella, my grandmother, who was always known as Isabel (see Tree 3). John Mitchell Garbutt was no longer the resident physician. There was the same spread of medical staff and attendants but this time the inmates were listed as just 'patients'. These were similar to the type of patient listed in the last census, and also included an army sergeant, a hatter, a ship's captain and a game-keeper from Oxfordshire. Later in 1871 William and Elizabeth's sixth child Augusta Helen (Gus) was born.

Richard Henderson Owen (named after Grandma Owen) Garbutt was born in 1872, the seventh child of William and Elizabeth, and was known as Dick. He became a doctor and lived in Northumberland where he would do his

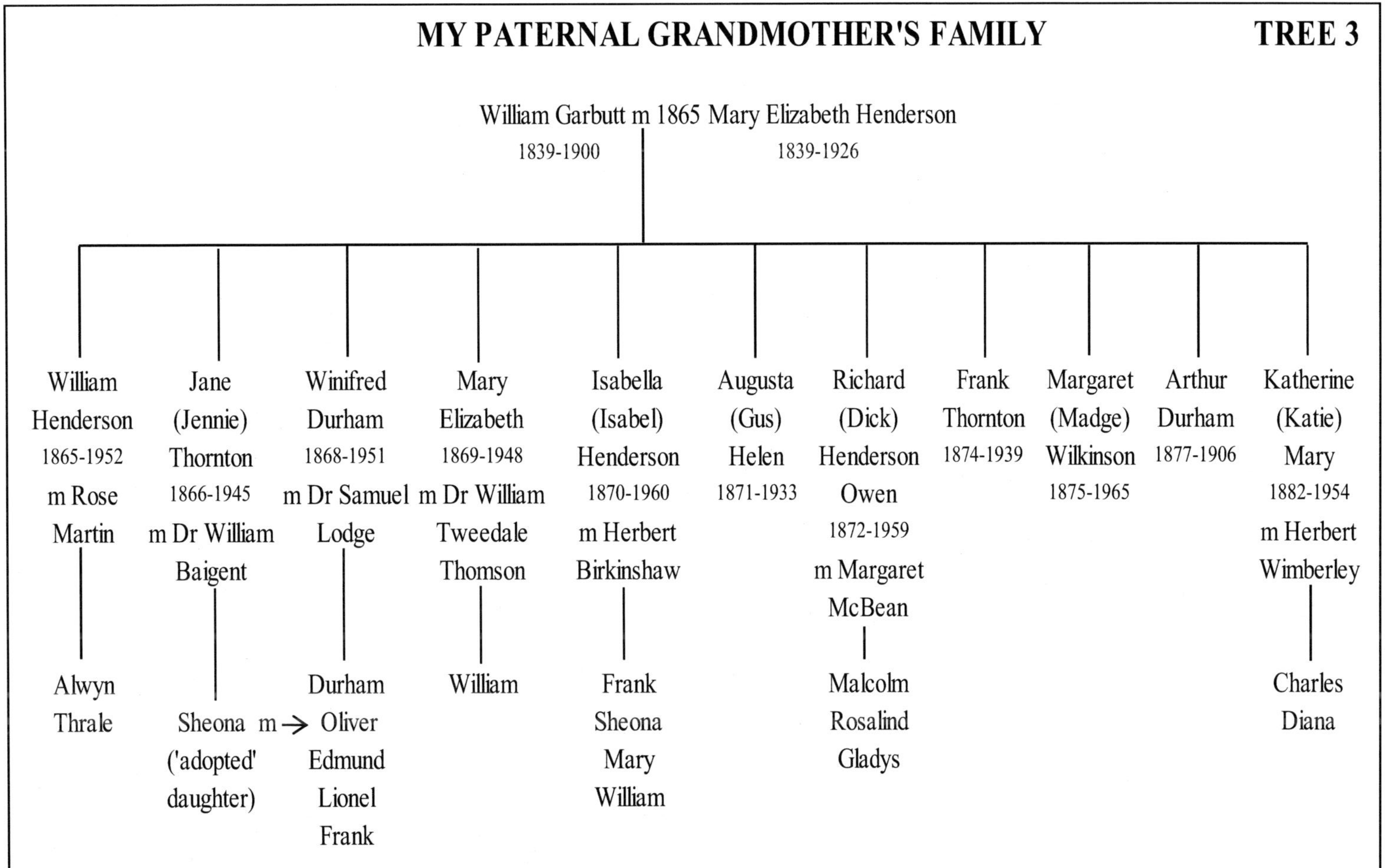
MY PATERNAL GRANDMOTHER'S FAMILY
TREE 3
William Garbutt m 1865 Mary Elizabeth Henderson
1839-1900
1839-1926
William Henderson 1865-1952 m Rose Martin
Alwyn Thrale
Jane (Jennie) Thornton 1866-1945 m Dr William Baigent
Sheona m → ('adopted' daughter)
Winifred Durham 1868-1951 m Dr Samuel Lodge
Durham Oliver Edmund Lionel Frank
Mary Elizabeth 1869-1948 m Dr William Tweedale Thomson
William
Isabella (Isabel) Henderson 1870-1960 m Herbert Birkinshaw
Frank Sheona Mary William
Augusta (Gus) Helen 1871-1933
Richard (Dick) Henderson Owen 1872-1959 m Margaret McBean
Malcolm Rosalind Gladys
Frank Thornton 1874-1939
Margaret (Madge) Wilkinson 1875-1965
Arthur Durham 1877-1906
Katherine (Katie) Mary 1882-1954 m Herbert Wimberley
Charles Diana

medical rounds on horseback. He married Margaret McBean and they had a son and two daughters. His grand-daughter Heather, with whom I got in touch, having found her through the on-line records, knew him well and said how much he cared about his patients whom he would not charge if they could not afford the fee. Consequently he never had much money. Heather told me a rather poignant story about him:

> In the days when he still did his rounds on horseback Dick was called out to a patient some twelve miles away. This man had left his wife who ran a rather lowly drinking establishment in the town and had taken a much younger woman to start a smallholding in the country. His wife told everyone that her husband would be dead soon and she would then inherit his smallholding. Dick knew the old man was dying and gave him some medicine. He realised that when the man died the young woman, who had looked after him for the past twenty years, would be left with nothing. Dick rode back to town and called upon a solicitor to bring his clerk and the three rode back the twelve miles to enable the dying man to draw up a will so that the young woman would be able to continue living in the cottage rather than spend the rest of her life in the workhouse. The solicitor and clerk returned to the town and Dick remained with his patient until he died.

The 1881 census of Dunston Lodge showed forty-one patients, this time referred to as 'boarders'. The occupation of one of the patients was described as 'clergyman without cure of souls'. There was also a solicitor, two captains in the merchant service, a publican, a student of arts, a few farmers, a customs officer, a chemist and a teacher of music. Several of the Garbutt children were living in another building in the grounds along with their governess. By this time another three children had been born, Frank Thornton, Margaret Wilkinson (known as Madge) and Arthur Durham. William and Elizabeth's eleventh and last child Katherine Mary (known as Katie), was born later that year.

In 1884 a journalist, George Herring, spent a day at Dunston Lodge and wrote about his experience there. His pamphlet was titled *A Day in a Private Lunatic Asylum*.[8] William Garbutt had invited him in to counter criticisms which had been levelled at lunatic asylums in general, and Herring was allowed to move freely around and talk to the patients. He was to be introduced to the patients as one of them, and when hinting to William that he didn't feel he looked like a lunatic was 'assured, without any intentional cynicism, that I looked about as mad as many of the patients whose acquaintance I should make'. Herring looked at the books and asked questions and was impressed, especially with the fact that Dunston had nearly twice the rate of recovery over other asylums, giving testimony to the excellence of its management. William told Herring that the Lunacy Commissioners visited twice a year without any warning of their coming, and also magistrates came four times a year accompanied by doctors, who in addition visited twice a year. There were forty-four inmates at the time of his visit of whom nineteen were allowed to go out alone on condition they came back at a given hour. Herring found the rooms 'scrupulously clean, well-ventilated and comfortably furnished'. There were sitting rooms for the patients, a billiard-room where he watched the inmates playing and a ball-room which was decorated for the coming Christmas festivities, where the weekly ball was held. The balls were also often attended by ex-inmates of the Lodge. Everything Herring saw 'demonstrated that even lunatics can be governed by kindness and firmness better than by harsh restraint'. He was told of one case where the attendants were so frightened of one particular man that they did not dare enter his room, even though there were always two of them in attendance. However, William Garbutt would frequently visit the man alone with no problem. Herring sat down to have dinner with the inmates with some trepidation and reported:

> In less than a minute I found myself in a dining-room, seated between two gentlemen who doubtless commiserated my state. But where were the lunatics? They were seated around the table – men and women – waiting quietly to be served with the excellent food provided for them. But the majority of the diners were apparently as sane as diners could possibly be. The minority, however, reminded me that I was dining in Dunston Lodge. My vis-à-vis was a lady suffering from melancholia. When not eating, her eyes were fixed upon the clasped hands which rested on her knees. Once during the meal she covered her face with her hand and from the working of her countenance I assumed that she was weeping. On dropping her hand, however, I caught the traces of a smile which struck one more painfully than tears could have done.

All of William and Elizabeth Garbutt's eleven children, except the eldest, William, were born at Dunston Lodge. Sheona, in her autobiography *Swan Feather*, wrote at length about the Garbutt family and particularly about her grandmother Elizabeth. Each morning Elizabeth had breakfast in bed and her children would be brought in to say good morning to her, by the nurse Jane Jobling who looked after the children. Sheona said her aunts told her that when they went for walks Jane carried the baby in her arms, an under-nurse wheeled another in a pram, two more were in panniers on the pony's back led by a groom, and the rest walked with a governess or a tutor. Sometimes the children would stay with their uncle William Henderson at Fowberry Mains or Langleeford near Wooler. When recovering from measles or whooping cough the children and their nurse would be kept in isolation with William's housekeeper in her cottage at Langleeford; it was a lonely place at the foot of

Cheviot where the children bathed in the stream. Sheona, in her memoirs, described the beauty of the place:

> Even today Langleeford is quite unspoilt and as one climbs Cheviot one sees mile upon mile of coast line with the Farne Islands rising from the sea and the purple heather all around, with not a dwelling in sight, just mountains and sea. It seems completely changeless and just as it was when the aunts, and before them Great Uncle William, and before that his father and grandfather climbed it, negotiating the bog and at each peak wondering if this really was the summit at last.

At Fowberry Mains, which Elizabeth's children found much more interesting, there was a donkey they liked to ride which always waited until it got to a field of nettles before bucking them off.

William Henderson, Elizabeth's brother, died in 1890, unmarried, and was buried in the Ilderton churchyard alongside his family. His death certificate gave the cause of death as Bright's Disease (a kidney condition) and also heart disease. He left his 'fortune', as the family always referred to it, to his sister Elizabeth. This fortune amounted to £17,734 13s 10d. He left several bequests, including ten pounds to each of his four executors. One of these, David Short, who was also a farmer, was bequeathed in addition a hundred pounds 'as a small acknowledgment of the kind services he has rendered to me during the long time I was unwell and unable to attend to my affairs'. He was also left the 'large armchair in morocco in my dining room'. His housekeeper Mary Gray was left two hundred pounds. His friend John Grabham was left 'the water colour sketch by Frederick Taylor of a terrier dog'. His nephew William Henderson Garbutt, the eldest of Elizabeth's children, was bequeathed his bookcase and library of books. Amongst his books, many of which had belonged to his father Richard, was *The History of England* by T. Smollet MD 1825, also *Bacon's Essays*, *The Works of Pope* and *Cook's Voyages*. In 1823 Mr Trevelyan gave William Henderson *A Topographical and Historical Description of the County of Northumberland* and *A Treatise upon Sheep;* William had described the latter as 'nonsense'. William gave Elizabeth 'such of my personal belongings and articles belonging to our family as she shall select', and also the residue of his estate for her lifetime. After her death everything was to go in equal shares to her children. In his will, William directed 'that should my brother-in-law William Garbutt be at my death indebted to me my trustees may allow him time for payment of such debt or make such arrangements with regard to the continuance thereof with or without collateral security as they shall think proper'. William also asked his trustees to pay any life insurance premiums for his brother-in-law if it became necessary. In a codicil to his will William asked that another of his executors, Robert Walker, his doctor, in 'acknowledgment of his kind attention to me' be given 'the two engravings now in my drawing room entitled *The Deer Stalker's Return* and *Bolton Abbey in the Olden Time.*

After William died, his sheep at Langleeford were sold. The *Newcastle Daily Journal* of 11 May 1891 headlined it as:

> Great Border Sheep Sale at Langleeford.
>
> An event of the greatest interest to hill farmers of the Borders and agriculturists generally was the dispersion of the famous Langleeford stock of pure Cheviot-bred sheep … The cause of the sale was the lamented death of Mr William Henderson whose family had been occupiers of the farm for an unbroken period of 300 years … It can be said with truth of the late and last tenant of Langleeford that a more intelligent, clearheaded man or better farmer was not to be met with on the Borders.

The article described William Henderson as being the 'last surviving lineal descendant of the old family save one – his sister'. It reported the fact that Elizabeth had been a spectator at the sale. The article went on to describe Langleeford as a romantic spot in the heart of the Cheviots, 2,670 feet above sea level. It said that the Langleeford Cheviot sheep had never been crossed with any other breed, being at the present day 'as pure in their descent as they were 300 years ago when the late tenant's ancestor took the farm'. Apparently William had been solicited to introduce fresh blood into his breed but had always refused. The Culleys, the local landowners, had introduced Leicesters into the area in 1760, and one day one of the Culley family came to William and said:

> 'The breed of Leicesters will soon be creeping to the top of Cheviot'. 'Ay', retorted the firm believer of the Cheviot race, 'they may creep up but they'll never walk'.

The sheep had to be brought in from the surrounding hills for the sale, and fifty shepherds were brought in to help round up the flocks; the farm covered 4,500 acres. Most of the breeders and agriculturists in the Border area were present and the sale was over within three hours, most of the sheep being sold to the new tenant of Langleeford.

By the time of the 1891 census the number of patients at Dunston Lodge had dwindled to thirty. William and Mary's eldest son, William, now twenty-six, still lived at the Lodge and was working as secretary to a coal company. He later became a company director, married Rose Martin and had two children. Mary, now twenty-two, was the matron of the asylum. My grandmother Isabel, aged twenty-one, was found in the census with three of her younger siblings, Gus, Madge and Katie, living in Ramsey's Lane in

The Garbutt family: Back row: William, Frank, Dick, Isabel Front row: Mary, Jennie, Madge, William, Katie, Winifred, Arthur

Wooler, along with a general servant. Ramsey's Lane was where Grandma Owen had lived with her mother's family before and after her marriage to Richard Henderson, so there must still have been a family connection in Wooler.

Dunston Lodge attracted the best doctors; among them were three gold medal holders from Durham University, each of whom married one of the Garbutt daughters. Dr Samuel Lodge proposed to Jane (Jennie), the eldest daughter, but when rebuffed, asked the next eldest, Winifred, who accepted; they had five sons, one of whom, Oliver, married his first cousin Sheona. Jennie later accepted Dr William Baigent and they 'adopted' Isabel's daughter Sheona. The third daughter Mary Elizabeth married Dr William Tweedale Thomson. They had one son William who became a doctor like his father, and fought in the First World War. William, the son, was Frank's first cousin and they followed similar career paths. William, however, had the advantage of a full education and a commission in the army unlike my father. They both served in France and Belgium. William was two years older than Frank and died three years before him; he too had suffered ill health from his army days. I met his daughter Barbara (my second cousin) for the first time at a family funeral. Not only do we share a name but have many things in common. Barbara sent me some family photographs she had and a letter William Garbutt had written to his future son-in-law congratulating him on his engagement, dated 1 November 1891:

> My dear Thomson
>
> You have my full consent and very best wishes on your engagement to Mary, and when married I trust she will make you a good and loving Wife, as I feel sure as a Husband you will always do your duty by her, and seeing that you both have had every opportunity of seeing and knowing each other no mistake on either side ought to be made.
>
> Wishing you every happiness
>
> I am Sincerely Yours - Wm Garbutt.

Unfortunately there wasn't a doctor for Isabel, and one day on a visit to her elder married sister Winifred she met Herbert Birkinshaw whom she married in 1897.[9]

William Garbutt died at Dunston Lodge in 1900 aged sixty-one. He left many debts, the reason perhaps being because the patient supply had dwindled over the years or, as his brother-in-law William Henderson had realised, he was not good with money. Elizabeth had to pay off his debts but luckily was able to do so with the money her brother left her. Dunston Lodge

My grandmother Isabel; her sisters on opposite page

Jane

Winifred

Mary

Gus

Madge

Katie

was taken over for a time as a market garden before being demolished in the late 1920s.

Elizabeth never talked much to her grand-daughter Sheona about her husband William, but Sheona said her aunts (William and Elizabeth's children) could remember their parents walking hand in hand up and down the lawn, so the family assumed they were very happily married. The aunts also described their father as a kind and gentle man with a brown beard, extremely business-like when it came to other people but not good at managing his own affairs. After William died and Dunston Lodge was closed down and sold, the family lost their home, and the census of 1901 revealed them scattered in different family dwellings round Northumberland. At that time Elizabeth was living in Ovingham near Newcastle with her daughter Isabel, who was now married to Herbert, and their two children Frank and Sheona. Another of Elizabeth's daughters, Madge, was also staying there.

Madge had spent much of her childhood with her father William's first cousin Isabella Garbutt who married Mark Archer; he was a colliery owner. Isabella and Mark lived in the beautiful house called Farnacres, the dower house for Ravensworth Castle, not far from Dunston Lodge; they had no children. Jennie and Dr William Baigent were married there as later were Sheona and her husband Oliver.

Mark Archer died in August 1910 and left over £90,000 in his will. His executors were his wife and his secretary Frederick Kirsopp. Everyone knew that Mark had a mistress and he duly left her a house at Berwick-upon-Tweed. She was Edith Kirsopp, probably Frederick's sister, and to her Mark also left £4,000. He left £500 to Margaret Kirsopp, who was possibly his daughter by Edith. There were legacies to his brothers and everything else was left to his wife Isabella for her lifetime on the condition she did not marry. After Isabella's death the proceeds of the estate were to be divided into four - three parts to his brothers' families and one part to his secretary Frederick.

Isabella Archer loved parties and Sheona remembered Farnacres being at the centre of their family life for many years. She said Farnacres was a fascinating place for children, with a museum, a wonderful collection of butterflies, a superb library, and three carriages in the coachhouse. Isabella had wanted to adopt Madge but Madge preferred to stay with her own family. However, Madge continued to visit her and was living with her in 1930 when Isabella died, aged eighty-seven. Isabella appointed Madge and William Henderson Garbutt, Madge's eldest brother, to be executors. Farnacres Hall and all the land adjoining was left to Madge for her lifetime and at her death it was to go to Thrale Garbutt, William Henderson Garbutt's son. Isabella also bequeathed Madge £1,000. Diana Wimberley, the daughter of Katie, Madge's youngest sister, who was at the time fourteen, received £500, Anne Lodge, who was Sheona and Oliver's daughter, £300 (Isabella was her godmother).

Madge's niece, Gladys Garbutt (daughter of Dr Richard Garbutt), inherited £100 and Joan Drossi (granddaughter of Richard) £50; she was only a baby in 1930. Isabella's gardener received £100 and an Archer relative was bequeathed 'the contents of the two rooms known as the Museum, and also the large silver bowl in the drawing room'. Her books she left to Thrale. Thrale's sister Alwyn inherited the grand piano and the china. The silver went to Jennie Baigent, and the residue of the estate to Madge. Isabella wrote the will on 24 October 1930 and died five days later. The estate was valued at £6,518. Sheona reminisced:

> We laughed at Mrs Archer – at her wigs, at her funny and wildly expensive hats, but we owe her a great deal. We loved going to Farnacres and she gave wonderful parties.

Sheona's daughter Anne, Isabella's goddaughter, remembered Farnacres Hall, long since flattened for development, well. It was imposing and Anne remembered 'suits of armour in the hall like those in the Tower of London, a vast sweep of gravel drive, a ha-ha with sheep and lambs, a walled garden full of fruit and vegetables and more buildings with goats and hens tended by Madge'. Sheona remembered Isabella in her Daimler with her chauffeur Tindall, and her hosting family weddings and christenings. Sheona said that at the Farnacres' sale, things went for ridiculously small sums, but it was the time of the Great Depression. One item, a fabulous candelabra which had belonged to Marie Antoinette, was sold for sixteen pounds. Sheona described Mrs Archer as 'charming and brilliant', although she believed that Elizabeth considered Mrs Archer frivolous. This might have been because Elizabeth's Garbutt relatives were not completely approved of, and that was perhaps why Mrs Archer was never called by her first name among the family. However, Isabella Archer was very popular and much loved by the younger generations.

The 1901 census also revealed that Arthur, Elizabeth's youngest son, aged twenty-three, was staying with the McDougall family who lived next to Dunston Lodge. They were the family of Polly McDougall. Polly had been the laundry maid at Dunston Lodge and the children were all very fond of her.

At the age of about twenty-six Arthur lost a leg in a railway accident. He later became engaged to the nurse who had spent months nursing him back to health after his accident. Unfortunately Arthur's family did not approve of her as she was not considered of sufficient social status. In 1906 Arthur died in suspicious circumstances aged twenty-nine and there was an inquest. He was at the time of his death working as a land and estate agent and lived in Newcastle. He left a will and appointed Frank Foster of Dunston, who was a surgeon, as his sole executor. The estate amounted to over £4,000 and included property. Perhaps Arthur had received compensation for his railway accident as it was quite a large amount of money for a young man to have. He bequeathed everything to Kate Spring Mallett, his fiancée. Further searches by the Newcastle library produced an article in the local *Evening Chronicle* dated 4 July 1906. The article was headed: 'Poisoned by Gas, Newcastle Estate Agent's Sad Death.' According to this article, Kate Mallett, Arthur's fiancée, who was matron at Dr Martin's private hospital in Newcastle, had last seen Arthur alive at 11.40pm on the Saturday night. She said that 'he left her at Dr Martin's house in Saville Row to catch the ten to twelve train to Monkseaton' where Arthur lived with Kate's mother. He had been in good spirits, she said, and they had arranged to meet the following afternoon at 3pm in Monkseaton. However, when she arrived she discovered he was not there, nor had he spent Saturday night there. Kate said that it was not unusual for Arthur to stay at a hotel in Newcastle if he was feeling too tired to make the train journey home, so she was not unduly worried. On Sunday night Kate returned to Newcastle and telephoned two hotels and a friend but there was no trace of him. The following morning she went to his place of work and this is what she found, according to the *Chronicle*:

> She there found deceased lying on the landing outside his office door, fully dressed, with the exception of his collar, which she thought had been loosened by a constable. He was quite unconscious and Dr Livingstone was attending to him. Deceased was removed to Dr Martin's hospital in Saville Row in the police ambulance. He never regained consciousness and died about 4.15 on Monday afternoon.

Kate told the inquest that she had known Arthur for two and a half years and that he was 'very temperate and in good health', and she knew of nothing that would cause him to harm himself as his prospects were very bright. However, she said he was feeling tired and drowsy on Saturday evening after a long day and he had told her he had taken a phenacetin and caffeine powder that morning for a headache. It was the office boy, Charles Wright, who found him on the Monday morning at 9am, and this is what happened:

> He opened the door and saw his master lying back in a chair at the desk, fully dressed. There was a strong smell of gas, and he heard the gas escaping. The gas jet was just above the deceased's head, on the left side, and fixed to the wall … The window, which was generally left open a little, was closed. There were some matches lying about the floor on the left hand of the deceased and the deceased had been vomiting. The matches had not been struck.

Charles thought that Arthur had been trying to strike a match to light the gas but had dropped the matches (about twenty of them) on to the floor. He said Arthur usually kept a box of matches on his desk but he did not notice them that morning. Charles also said that he had been asked to get 'three powders of fourteen grams of phenacetin and one grain of caffeine each' on the Saturday morning 'and the chemist telephoned to the deceased and asked him why he wanted such large doses'. Arthur had apparently replied that 'he had taken them before and knew what he was doing'. The attending surgeon, Dr Stewart, told the coroner that the fifteen grains of powder Arthur had taken was a comparatively large dose and would cause exhaustion and that there was only one powder left on the Monday morning. Dr Stewart summed up what he believed to have happened:

> His opinion was that the deceased, who had only one leg, had not left himself sufficient time to catch his train, and had consequently missed it. Witness knew the deceased's habits well, having had him under his care for an injury to the leg, which was afterwards amputated, and appendicitis, and he was always of a cheerful nature. When he stayed in town he went to an hotel, and witness thought that before doing so on Saturday night he had gone to his office and had taken one of the powders. He had then turned on the gas and attempted to light it, but being exhausted by his run for the train, the powder had quickly taken effect on the heart and he had collapsed in the chair without being able to light the gas.

Arthur's death certificate stated the cause as 'heart failure due to gas poisoning deceased inhaled in his office, but how he came to inhale the gas, there is not sufficient evidence before the jury to show'.

The one member of the family not accounted for in the 1901 census was Frank Thornton Garbutt. In 1896, aged twenty-two, he boarded the *SS Athenian* for Cape Town, a journey of sixty-five days. He went to South Africa to join the British South African Police Force (BSAP) where he fought in the Matabele and Boer Wars. The BSAP was the police force of the British South Africa Company established by Cecil Rhodes, which became the national police force of Southern Rhodesia (now Zimbabwe).

Frank returned occasionally to visit his family in England, the first time in 1897 on board the *SS Gaul*. There were photographs in the family collection of him with his mother and sisters and nieces and nephews on holiday in England. He was in England in 1907 as he was on the passenger list[10] of the *SS Gascon* in August of that year travelling to Cape Town. Frank was a Big Game Hunter and in 1910 sent some animal heads to England. Sheona eventually inherited these and sent them to the Manchester Museum; they were subsequently lost (or perhaps just rotted away). In 1914, according to Sheona, Frank was due for leave and was seen off at Cape Town by several friends. 'See you in Berlin at Christmas Garbutt', they said. 'I'm not thinking of going to Germany', replied Frank. They laughed. War was declared three days later. When he arrived in London Frank went straight to the War Office

Armistice Day parade; Frank Thornton Garbutt, mounted, in charge of men singing the National Anthem, 1922 (as stated on the back of the photograph)

Frank, far left, with troops and machine-gun

and was sent back to German West Africa where he was appointed Special Commissioner of Police at the Caprivi Strip, with the local rank of Captain. The Caprivi Strip, originally part of German West Africa, was captured by the BSAP and occupied by the British in 1914. In 1916 he was appointed Magistrate for N'Gamiland and Kazungula, as he mentioned in a letter to Sheona. He was also still the Special Commissioner at Caprivi and was living at Kavimba, not far from the Victoria Falls.

He wrote several letters to his family back home. One of them was to his mother, dated 15 September 1915, thanking her for sending his medals which he might need to wear on special parades; these were probably medals he had received in the Matabele and Boer wars. In the letter he described something of his life:

> Maun is my Headquarters for N'Gamiland (about 200 miles SW of Kavimba) and there I pay periodical visits to try serious cases. I shall be going to Maun next Tuesday to try a little Masarwa (Bushman) boy for murder – I doubt whether he realized the heinousness of his offence but still he will have to be punished.
>
> My hut overlooks the Chobe River and immediately the sun goes down myriads of mosquitoes commence buzzing round; if it were not that we lived more or less in mosquito proof houses life would be almost unbearable. At night time hippopotami come up and down the river making a peculiar noise and during the day they sleep in huge reed beds.

Frank wrote to his mother in August 1918 to say that he was now in Molepolole in the Bechuanaland Protectorate where he had been sent to quell trouble caused by the son of a local chief, who had recently died. He thought he would remain there until the end of the war. He asked for a transfer from N'Gamiland because he suffered from incessant malaria. He had purchased a Ford vehicle and was able to 'have the occasional run to Mafeking' a distance of one hundred miles over heavy sand rivers, sandy roads and tree stumps.

In 1921 he wrote to his brother-in-law Dr William Baigent. He said he was still living in the Bechuanaland Protectorate in Selika and within twelve months they had transposed bare veldt with no water into 'a police camp with the usual buildings, a well sixty-five feet deep with a windmill, and an ample supply of water'. He was planning to build roads but had very limited labour to do so. He also said that Prince Arthur of Connaught (Governor-general of South Africa and grandson of Queen Victoria) and his wife had visited and he had been presented to them. He talked about life in England after the war:

> I expect it will take years for England to recover from the after effects of the war, especially with regard to the unrest amongst the labouring classes who have not got the savvy to see the only salvation of the country is production and utmost economy.

Frank Thornton Garbutt

Frank with lion cub

Two years later he wrote again from Selika, this time to his mother and told her he had recently returned from a shooting trip accompanying Prince and Princess Arthur of Connaught along the Limpopo river. He had been to Durban to visit them and make the arrangements, and he described the events:

> It was eventually decided to leave everything in my hands to hire motor cars, motor lorries, purchasing shooting ponies, marquees, tents, food supplies, arranging carriers and fixing up roads for motor transport. Everything went off satisfactorily and they were both very pleased, and on saying goodbye they both thanked me for the good time. The Princess alone accounted for 23 head of big game in 25 days. Lions came round their camp on several occasions during the night time and the Prince caught a glimpse of one during the day but he did not get a shot.

In February 1925 Frank wrote to his sister Jennie to say that he was leaving the Service and retiring. He would be awarded a pension of £352 per annum. He outlined what he was planning to do:

> I have entered into partnership with Colonel Daniel in a farm known as the Newcome Estate on the Ramaquabane River, Southern Rhodesia, but the postal address is Francistown. It is a farm of about 6,500 acres and we have about 700 head of cattle. There is still a mortgage of £1,000 due the latter end of this year, after that we will be free from debt. Last month we made £35 sending cream to Johannesburg and this will continue during the summer months, after that we shall have no income unless we sell steers. We have done a lot of improving during the past year, having purchased five

> pedigree bulls and eleven miles of barbed wire fencing from the Rhodesia Government.

He finished by saying that he had spent a few days in Bulawayo before Christmas to see the cricket match 'England XI vs Rhodesia'. Colonel Daniel became Resident Commissioner (one below High Commissioner) to South Africa between 1926 and 1930 but it was not clear what happened to his partnership with Frank.

There was also a postcard dated April 1926 to Madge at Highbury from Durban saying: 'see you in August', so Frank probably made a visit home then. Frank died in 1939, most likely in Durban. According to Sheona he left most of his money to the Matabele warriors and she was the residuary legatee, receiving thirty pounds.

At some stage after William died Elizabeth took a house in Ilkley and eventually went to live at 30 Highbury in West Jesmond, Newcastle, with her unmarried daughters, Gus and Madge. According to Sheona, Granny Elizabeth's room at Highbury was known as the North Pole and there were photographs on the wall of all her eleven children. Sheona said that after lunch Granny and the aunts went to their respective rooms to rest and 'Granny lay on the sofa under her window and read *Black Beauty* to me'. She had a green parrot that had a cage with an ever-open door and it perched on her shoulder at breakfast time; the parrot was often chased by the crows. After Elizabeth died the parrot went to live with Sheona's family.

Elizabeth often talked about her cousin Sir Algernon Borthwick to Sheona. He became Lord Glenesk and owned the *Morning Post.* On one occasion Queen Mary corresponded with him asking his help to suppress a scandal about a young member of the German Royal family who had an affair with a footman.

Sheona said that the only complaint she ever heard her Granny make was 'when I said goodbye'. Sheona's daughter Anne still has Elizabeth's cap, real lace and seed pearls. Sheona, when she was a young girl, remembered Elizabeth wearing a 'black bonnet tied under her chin by wide white satin ribbon. Her silk dress was black, embroidered with beads - it swept the path and had a white frill at the neck. Round her shoulders hung a black mantle.' Her umbrella had a silver handle. Sheona, while out walking with her one day, wanted to pick a flower but there was only gorse growing in the lane. Her Granny bravely picked the prickly furze for her and Sheona related what happened:

> Yellow furze bushes grew on either side of the track. The flowers were beautiful. I couldn't gather them because they were prickly, but Granny did. 'I'll carry them for you', she said, 'we'll put them in water when we get home'. She wore white gloves and I noticed that they were speckled with blood.

Sheona said that twenty-four years later Elizabeth had not changed: 'She was one of the most beautiful women I have ever seen.' Elizabeth could recite Grey's *Elegy* by heart and a good deal of *Marmion* and many verses from the *Book of Isaiah*. Sheona observed that although Elizabeth 'was the mother of eleven remarkably fine handsome healthy children, she was tiny, beautiful, had an air of gentle dignity and authority, and the fragility of Dresden china'. On another occasion Sheona described her as 'the sweetest, gentlest, most adorable woman you could imagine'. Sadly, Elizabeth became almost totally deaf in her old age and had to use an ear trumpet.

Elizabeth died on 30 January 1926 at 30 Highbury, Newcastle, aged eighty-seven. She left only £515 in her will, this perhaps because she had had to pay off her husband William's debts after he died in 1900. She wrote her will in May 1902 while she was living in Ovingham with her daughter Isabel. She appointed her eldest son William and her eldest daughter Jennie as her executors. She left all her household effects to her daughters Gus, Madge and Katie in equal shares. The remainder of her estate was divided among whichever of the three were not married. In effect that was Gus and Madge as Katie had since married Herbert Wimberley.

Katie was twenty when her father died in 1900 and she spent much of her time up to her marriage living with her elder sister Jennie and brother-in-law Dr William Baigent in Northallerton, which was where she met her husband Herbert Wimblerley. He was headmaster of the struggling Northallerton Grammar School. However, the Garbutts did not consider teaching in a struggling school a secure enough occupation on which to support a family, and Herbert was persuaded to apply for a post in the Colonial Service and became a Provincial Inspector of Schools in Nigeria.[11] They had two children, Charles and Diana. (Diana was the mother of my second cousin, Geoffrey Allen, who had already carried out much research into the Garbutt family.)

After their mother died, Madge and Gus lived on at 30 Highbury with their maid May. May had come to the family at the age of fourteen, in 1915. After two weeks she wanted to give in her notice but Elizabeth persuaded her to stay for another month; May ended up staying until Madge died in 1965 at the age of ninety, and was regarded as one of the family. Sheona remembered Aunt Madge had once famously said 'as a family we have always thought rather a lot of ourselves' and after a pause added, 'I can't imagine why'!

Gus died on 8 July 1933, leaving nearly £4,500 in her will. She left bequests mainly to Isabel's children; £25 each to Frank, Mary and Bill, and to Sheona she bequeathed her 'jewellery Chippendale workbox and the choice of twenty of my books'. The remainder of her estate, and also anything she was to receive on her mother Elizabeth's death, she left to her sister Madge for her lifetime. On Madge's death everything she had given to Madge was to be divided up between Isabel's surviving children. Her generosity towards her sister Isabel was probably because Isabel was the most in need in the family.

Madge lived to be nearly ninety and died in 1965, leaving just under £17,000. She left bequests to many, but not all, of her great nieces and nephews. Frank's daughter Jane (my half-sister) received £500. Madge's housekeeper May was left £2,000 and May's sister Doris £300. The residue was to go to Michael Garbutt, who was Dick's grandson, Charles Wimberley, her sister Katie's son, and William Johnson, grandson of Madge's eldest brother William. Her executors also fulfilled her sister Gus's wishes by distributing the money she had left to Madge to Isabel's four children, although Madge had not specifically mentioned this in her will. They each received £650. Frank's second wife Edna (my mother) received his share, as by that time he had already died.

Elizabeth Garbutt

Chapter Six

Becoming a Doctor

In October 1919, at the age of twenty-one, Frank obtained a modified matriculation to Birmingham University and took up his place as a medical student. According to the University records, Birmingham had approved special regulations for students 'having a record of war or national service or detention by the enemy'. Even so, Frank would first have had to satisfy the University that, although he left school at the age of fifteen, he was capable of undertaking a degree course.

The membership fee to join the University was at that time five guineas (five pounds five shillings). Frank would also have had to pay class fees and they amounted to about £158 for the five years' tuition, which was a great deal of money when you had no income. Frank was very likely helped with his finances by his two maiden, and comparatively wealthy, Garbutt aunts, Gus and Madge, who lived in Newcastle, and hopefully his father helped him too. There was a family story which said that he lived mostly off milk and bananas during his student years as he was so impoverished. Frank's first wife Margaret referred to this in a letter[1] she wrote in the 1950s (after Frank had died) to Frank's Aunt Madge, in response to Madge remembering that Frank liked crusts and bananas. Margaret said that Frank went on liking crusts and bananas, and when he visited patients miles out in the New Zealand outback (this was when Frank had a practice in Christchurch) a crust was what he asked for when they offered him a meal!

Birmingham University archives recorded that Frank spent his first three years there and passed all his exams; there appeared to be a blank for the fourth year but he was probably doing a clinical year somewhere else. He completed his fifth and final year at University College Hospital, London.

While at Birmingham University, Frank lived with his family in Selvas Cottage in Alvechurch, near Birmingham. This cottage was built as a nailmakers' cottage in the mid-eighteenth century. Interestingly, in my research I came across one family of Birkinshaws with several generations of nailmakers, but none of them immediately related to my Birkinshaws. According to his brother Bill, on one occasion while their parents were away, he and Frank put the date 1552 on one of the old beams to pretend the cottage was older than it was; as Bill said, they were always up to some mischief.

Frank was involved in founding what became the annual students' carnival in 1921, which began as 'the Birmingham University Hospital Carnival'. The *Birmingham Daily Mail* of 12 December 1921 hailed it as 'A Successful University Rag' with reports on the pageant which took place over the day. The article said it had been organised by students of the Medical Faculty of Birmingham University 'to organise a collection for the General and Queen's

Frank, the student

Hospitals'. This was, of course, before the dawn of the National Health Service which was not founded until 1948.

According to my half-sister Fay[2], it was in 1922 that Frank met Edgar and Frieda Jepson at a nightclub in London. The Jepsons lived at 120 Adelaide Road, Chalk Farm, which was a very large house with twelve bedrooms. Frieda was a concert pianist, a pupil of Clara Schumann; her father was Henry Holmes the violinist. Henry had been a Professor of Violin at the Royal College of Music but eventually 'caused a scandal through his relations with his female pupils in 1893, and was hounded out of the country'.[3] He left London to become Music Director for the city of Berkeley, California. Frieda's mother was the daughter of the artist William Gale. Edgar was a writer, mainly of adventure and detective stories, and hosted literary parties. He opened up a whole new world to Frank, including introducing him to his sixteen-year old daughter Margaret. It was for this reason, no doubt, that Frank transferred his final year medical studies to London.

Margaret Jepson was born on 3 August 1907. She had an older sister Faith who was confined to a mental hospital at the age of seventeen having been 'seduced by her mother's brother, to the destruction of her life but with no apparent difference to his', as Fay wrote in her book. Faith's mother, Frieda, apparently never visited her in the hospital, although Edgar did. Faith died aged twenty-nine of broncho-pneumonia. Margaret and Faith had an elder brother, Selwyn, who, like his father, was also a writer. He was with the Tank Corps in World War I and was a Captain with Special Operations Executive during the Second World War, recruiting women for Intelligence work. Margaret had decided at the age of five that she did not want to go to school and her father Edgar accepted the situation, so she had no formal education apart from two terms at the Slade School of Art; however, she continued the writing tradition of her family and became a novelist. Margaret's father actually considered her to be a better writer than either himself or Selwyn.

In September 1923 Frank was living at 35 Devonshire Street, London and was attending University College Hospital Medical School. He took his final exams in June 1924 but there must have been too many distractions as he did not manage to pass them all and so failed to obtain his degree. However, undaunted he sat for, and passed, the Licence in Medicine, Surgery and Midwifery of the Society of Apothecaries on 22 July 1925. This qualification was often taken to obtain a medical degree when the other route had not been achieved, being thought of as a slightly easier option. The Diploma awarded was just as valid as the MB ChB, and Frank was now a fully qualified doctor. According to the records of the Society of Apothecaries, Frank, when he qualified in 1925, was living at 120 Adelaide Road with Margaret's family.

In October 1926 Frank and Edgar wrote a joint article for the fiction magazine *The Danger Trail* called 'Black Gold'. In July 1927 they wrote another article together for *The Red Magazine* called 'A Tithe of Rubies'.

While I was researching Frank's career I wondered to myself where his medical certificates were, and I suddenly recalled having seen them many years previously at the back of the loft with those belonging to my mother. I dug them out and also came across a framed certificate announcing the fact that Frank had obtained a commission in the Territorial Army, so I contacted the Army Personnel Centre in Glasgow, aptly entitled 'Historical Disclosures', and they sent me some information about his TA career. The documents said that in May 1923 Frank had applied for a commission with the 6th Battalion The Royal Warwickshire Regiment of the Territorial Army (the Royal Warwicks was the regiment in which Frank had served at the start of his World War I career). Frank was appointed to the rank of Second Lieutenant, this appointment being recorded in the *London Gazette*. He would probably have been in charge of two platoons of men and they would attend drills and musketry courses and the annual church parade at St Martin's Church in the Bullring in Birmingham. Annual two-week camps were held in Wiltshire or Wales. They would have been paid a few shillings a day and if called up would have to be available to go and fight for their country. In

August 1925 Frank was promoted to full Lieutenant and this was announced in the *London Gazette* on 18 December 1926. In November 1926 Frank asked for a transfer to London as that was where he was then living and he was transferred to the 167th Field Ambulance, Royal Army Medical Corps. The 167th was also known as the 1st London Field Ambulance and was part of the TA. They were based at Finsbury Barracks, London EC1. His duties would have been varied but again he would have attended two weeks' annual camp at Colchester or Aldershot[4]

Another curious piece of information came to light from an unlikely source. I had asked a librarian in New Zealand to look out any obituaries she could find of Frank, as that was where he died, and she kindly took it upon herself to do some further research and came across an entry in *The Times Archive* online website. In the entry, dated 26 November 1927, the name of Dr F T Birkinshaw, living at 143 Bow Road, London E3, appeared, as posted from the *London Gazette*, in the column headed: 'Receiving Orders – The Bankruptcy Acts 1914 and 1926.' No further information was forthcoming. There were seven names on the London list – five were business people, one a widow, Frank and another doctor. These circumstances were the likely cause for what happened next.

On 7 February 1928, Frank's army records stated, Frank wrote to his Commanding Officer, Lt-Colonel Harwood, RAMC the following letter:

> Sir,
>
> Owing to private circumstances I find that it is very difficult for me to continue with my duties as Lieutenant in the 1st City of London Field Ambulance, and I therefore beg to submit this, my application to resign my Commission.
>
> I am, Sir, Your Obedient servant - F T Birkinshaw.

There was a memo in the file dated 27 February 1928 to the Officer Commanding 167th Field Ambulance from the Colonel Command Paymaster saying that he was 'unaware of any outstanding Public Claims against Lieutenant F T Birkinshaw'. There was also a certificate stating that 'all regimental claims in respect of the above mentioned officer have been paid'. It would appear that Frank had honoured all his army debts but still had paid a high price for appearing in the bankruptcy courts.

On a happier note, on 21 May 1928, Frank, aged twenty-nine, married Margaret Jepson, who was then aged twenty, in the Parish Church of St Bride in the City of London. St Bride's was then, and still is, known as 'the Journalists' Church', so it was a very appropriate place for our two budding writers to get married. Frank's residence was given on the marriage certificate as 16 Bride Lane, EC4 and his father Herbert's profession listed as 'Gentleman'. The register was signed by Margaret's mother Frieda and one G Fowler Wright. This was Gilbert Wright, a journalist friend of Frank and presumably his best man. It was not clear how many family members attended, but Margaret's brother Selwyn was not happy with the match; perhaps he was concerned about his sister marrying an impoverished doctor nearly ten years older than herself. St Bride's Lane and the Church were destroyed by an incendiary bomb during the Second World War, although the Church was later rebuilt.

Frank and Margaret went to France for their honeymoon, leaving immediately after their wedding. Frank's passport showed that he arrived in France (the port is illegible) on 21 May and left on 25 May from Dunkirk.

Margaret's father Edgar died in 1938, leaving his mistress Lois with a young child. An obituary in the *Telegraph* described him as 'a distinctive craftsman of remarkable personality, whose many friends included practically all the literary men of any note during the past half-century'.

Margaret around the time of her marriage

Chapter Seven

Shipwreck

It was Tuesday 21 August 1928 and the main headlines on the front page of *The Star*, the London daily paper, which at that time sold for just one penny, proclaimed: 'London Yacht Party's Adventure ... Rescues from yacht off Essex coast. London Doctor and his Brother wrecked on Sandbank in Gale. Narrow Escapes from Death. Swept by Huge Seas for two hours before help came in sight.' The text read:

> A thrilling story of shipwreck and narrow escape from death in the Thames Estuary was told to *The Star* today by a London yachtsman, Dr F T Birkinshaw, of 13 King's Bench Walk, EC.

The article went on to tell how Frank and his brother Bill came to be shipwrecked and nearly lost their lives in the process. There was a gale blowing at sea and Bill, at that time a dental student at Birmingham University, and Frank had gone out in the yacht *Kestrel* and inadvertently struck the Barrow Sands several miles below Southend. They were out of sight of land and the yacht was being pounded on the hard sand, its sails blown away and the dinghy smashed. The two yachtsmen were in grave danger and they raised the red ensign upside down as a distress signal and waved a pair of pyjamas to try and attract attention. The story continued, describing the rescue attempt:

> At last the Trinity House steamer *Alert* came in sight, but it was a long while before she was able to effect her rescue. She sent off a boat with a crew of eight wearing lifebelts but this boat touched the sandbank before reaching the yacht and had to find another route by which to approach.

Eventually they were able to rescue Frank and Bill; the *Kestrel* was refloated and towed ignominiously to Southend.

The day had started calmly enough. Frank had chartered the six-ton *Kestrel* from Greenwich earlier in the week to take Margaret, his wife of three months, and his brother out for a cruise. They had sailed up the Medway around the Kent coast and dropped Margaret off at Burnham-on-Crouch. Margaret was three months pregnant at the time so, luckily as it turned out, perhaps she had not felt up to a sea voyage. Frank and Bill spent the night on the boat and the next morning set sail for Southend. *The Star* continued: 'Dr Birkinshaw mistook the Barrow Lightship for the Swin Middle Lightship, as the latter has recently been removed, and unwittingly steered straight for

Barrow Sands which are exposed at low water.' They struck the sandbank and were pounded by the waves which swamped the boat; they could see biscuits floating round the cabin and could hear crockery and bottles smashing. Frank continued the story:

> For two hours our distress signal met with no response. We began to get water-logged so we manned the pump. One worked the pump and the other clung to the mast, holding at arm's length a suit of pyjamas in order to attract attention to our plight. We were cold and wet and hungry. We started from Burnham on a biscuit or two and intended to get breakfast on the way.

Frank went on to describe to *The Star* reporter how they saw the steamer *Alert* coming their way, but it could not get within two and a half miles of them. A jolly-boat (rescue boat) with sailors in lifebelts was launched but it ran aground and when the sailors managed to push themselves off the sandbank they had to return to their own ship much to the dismay of Frank and Bill who became even more anxious:

> That was a fearful moment and we shouted and waved pyjamas more wildly. After a time we saw them go about and begin to come towards us by another route. We could see a sailor with a boathook taking soundings all the time. At last they reached us and took us on board the *Alert*, when our physical troubles ceased.

Not only had the *Alert* launched one jolly-boat to go to the rescue, they also had launched a second in case the first got into trouble, as the weather was so atrocious and the sands so dangerous. Frank again:

> We were only just rescued in time, and when the jolly-boat came alongside we were pumping up sand as well as water, which showed that the planks of the vessel were beginning to give way. They told us when we got into the jolly-boat that it was difficult to make out, even by telescope, if anyone was on board the *Kestrel* and in fact, they did not think it possible that any of the crew could possibly retain their hold against the huge sweeping seas.

It was only when the crew told Frank and Bill that the captain's idea at first was to stay in the area on the chance that 'they might pick up any dead bodies', that they realised what grave danger they had been in. *The Star* was the first paper to pick up the story which took up most of the front page; it was next to an article announcing the death of W H Coats, the thread magnate millionaire in Glasgow.

They were not the only boat to get into difficulties that day as the *Daily Chronicle* of the next day stated: 'Thrilling stories of the rescue of yachtsmen and the crews of various other craft during the gale on Monday are reported from various parts of the coast.' In reporting the *Kestrel's* adventure they said that Frank had recounted how they had put out distress signals and that they were 'soaked to the skin'. Frank, described as a 'keen and experienced yachtsman', had praised the seamanship of the officer in charge of the rescue boat.

The Daily Telegraph and *The Times* of 22 August ran with the story as did *The Daily Mail*, saying that Frank and Bill 'owe their lives to the vigilance of the captain of the Trinity House steamer *Alert'*.

The *Morning Post* described Frank as wanting to 'make light of his unpleasant experience', more wishing to express his 'admiration for the work of his rescuers than to describe his own plight … Dr Birkinshaw laughingly put it: "Fifteen miles is rather too far to swim in a sea like that".' The *Daily Express* also had the story with the headline 'Pyjama Signal'. As Bill was living in Birmingham at the time and was President of the Guild of Undergraduates at Birmingham University, the local papers there took up the story. The *Birmingham Gazette* had the headline 'Laughing at Death', and went on: 'Two men faced death on a wrecked sea-swept yacht stranded on a dangerous sandbank in the Thames estuary on Monday and laughed at their peril, while taking photographs of each other.'

There is a family story which said that there was only one lifebelt on the *Kestrel* and Frank, who couldn't swim, said to Bill, who could, 'I'm going to throw it overboard as I know you will insist I have the lifebelt as you can swim and I can't; this therefore gives us an equal chance'.

Frank apparently told a friend, when relating the tale of his shipwreck, 'now I think the only real thrill I haven't experienced is an earthquake'. Little was he to know what a prescient statement that was.

The *Sunday Mercury* picked up the story with the headlines shouting: 'SHIPWRECKED YACHTSMEN NEARLY ARRESTED! Policeman waiting for them on the Pier. TWO DARING BROTHERS.' It recounted the story and added that when Frank and Bill returned to the harbour they found two policemen waiting to arrest them.

The long *Sunday Mercury* article was written by Gilbert F. Wright, a journalist, and best man at Frank and Margaret's wedding. Gilbert went on to explain that Frank and Bill had arrived at his flat after their rescue because they were locked out of their own flat, probably because the door-key had gone overboard, and they related the adventure of their shipwreck to him. Frank and Bill had omitted (probably on purpose) to tell the other reporters from the daily papers the fact that there had been a policeman awaiting them, so Gilbert and the *Sunday Mercury* got the scoop. Apparently a yacht had been missing from its moorings and when a constable saw the battered yacht being towed in to the harbour he assumed it was the missing one. The police were 'eventually satisfied that they were not criminals and left them in peace'.

Another peculiar incident had also come to light when Margaret heard what had happened. She told Gilbert that when they were sailing down the estuary earlier in the week she 'had noticed the Swin Lightship moored at Gravesend but had not thought the observation of any particular interest or worth comment'. If they had only known the Swin had been moved to Gravesend for repairs and replaced by a buoy they would have realised that what they took to be Swin Middle was in fact the Barrow Lightship and they would have been alerted to the danger.

The next headline in *The Mercury* was 'LIFE OF THRILLS, Birmingham Scaffold Dance' and went on to say that their readers were to be 'allowed a more intimate glimpse of the men who gambled with fate and snapped each other while the cruel seas were pounding over their staunch little craft':

> The thousands of people who saw Mr W Birkinshaw do his ballet dance on top of some scaffolding in New Street, Birmingham, on carnival day last year, would hardly expect him to be unnerved by a mere shipwreck. His brother too has had plenty of thrills from life, having been right through the Great War in the army in France and Air Force in Arabia. He was mentioned in despatches and has a fine row of decorations to his credit. He has been in a serious motor smash, a train crash and an aeroplane accident, and now having been in a shipwreck, as he remarked to me: 'There does not seem to be much left to do.'

Family history did not have the story of Frank's motor or aeroplane accidents. The train crash referred to his time in Italy when he was in the RFC and he was thrown from the rack on which he was sleeping on to the less fortunate soldiers who were trying to sleep on the seats and the floor below.

Gilbert, reporting in *The Mercury,* went on to say that Frank appeared to be 'one of those people to whom things always seem to be happening'. He told a story of Frank's days at Birmingham University when he, Gilbert, accompanied him to a fête. Frank won a 'hideous blue vase' on the hoop-la stall. Frank persuaded the girl on the stall to keep the vase and 'a moment later he received a severe blow on the back of the head – it was half a bad coconut which had been discarded by a disgusted winner'. On another occasion Gilbert said that Frank 'absent-mindedly dropped a cigarette end into a waste ticket box on a Birmingham tram "causing endless fun" as he put it to me afterwards'.

Another incident Gilbert described in his article was, as he headlined it 'A CLOSE SHAVE'. Gilbert and Frank were on board the *Kestrel* earlier in the week, before it was shipwrecked, and there was a strong headwind. It was two o'clock in the morning and Frank was asleep in the cabin. Gilbert was on watch and recounted: 'Not being familiar with night traffic, to my horror, I suddenly discovered that a large tramp steamer coming upstream was practically on top of me.' He described the scene:

> I called to Birkinshaw for assistance, but before I had roused him we had passed right under the bows of the steamer. The moment we had cleared her safely I heard a voice yelling down at me from the deck of the boat towering above. 'What did he say?' said Dr Birkinshaw, who had just reached the cockpit. 'I don't know,' I replied 'but he must have been English – his language was so wonderful'.

Gilbert's next headline in the *Mercury* article read: 'STOP ME AND GET ON!' This gave an insight into some of Bill's exploits. Bill volunteered to drive locomotives for the LMS during the Great Strike of 1926, as did many students. At first he drove the 'banker' engines that assisted trains to get up the incline from Bromsgrove to Blackwell. Because the strikers 'objected to him going into a hotel outside the station to get food' he was told to buy his meals at Blackwell which meant taking the engine up the incline. Gilbert continued:

> During his [Bill's] waits on the sidings he did a little arithmetic and calculated that every time he went to Blackwell to buy sandwiches he used over £2 worth of the company's coal.

Bill's next job was to 'drive a passenger train between Birmingham and Derby'. He did not have the schedule of stations where he was supposed to stop so he 'decided to stop at alternate ones, and if he saw any signs of passengers gesticulating, either on the platforms or from the windows of carriages as he passed intermediate stations, he pulled up and shunted back'!

Margaret, friend, Frank & Gilbert Wright on board Kestrel

Group on board the Kestrel

Frank up the mast before the storm

Frank waving pyjamas during the storm

Chapter Eight

Italy

Jane Felicity Birkinshaw was born on 19 February 1929 to Margaret and Frank in Alvechurch, which is just south of Birmingham, where Frank's parents Herbert and Isabel were living. Frank was working in London but Margaret must have gone to Alvechurch to be near Frank's parents for the birth; Frank was, at the time, living at 1 Mitre Court Buildings, Temple, London. Jane was later to become my half-sister.

On 30 March of that year Frank took his little family, including his mother-in-law Frieda, to Italy for a holiday. They travelled from Southampton on the ship *Christiaan Huygens,* which was bound for Jakarta, and disembarked at Genoa in Italy on 4 April.

A few weeks later Frank's sister Sheona, who was at that time living in Yorkshire, received a surprise in the post. It was a letter from Frank from the steamer *M/N Puccini* telling her that Jane had been christened and that Sheona was to be the godmother. The event had already taken place, but no doubt Sheona knew her brother well enough not to be offended at not having been asked first. Frank gave his address as The British Club, Alassio, Liguria, Italy. The letter read:

> My dear Sheona
>
> We had the baby christened the day before yesterday in St Paul's Cathedral, Malta. We met a clergyman on the ship who was going there and he very kindly offered to christen her. As it is necessary to have two god-mothers and one god-father Margaret acted as proxy for you and the clergyman's wife acted as proxy for Mary. In other words you are baby's other god-mother! I hope you don't mind!

He told her that the other godmother was to be their sister Mary and the godfather was to be Arthur Machen.

Arthur Machen was a well-known Welsh author born in 1863, best known in his early years for his supernatural horror fiction and later as a 'champion of the mysticism of spirituality and dedicated opponent of the prevailing climate of economic and scientific materialism'. He joined the 'Hermetic Order of the Golden Dawn, the fashionable ritual magic group which also counted Yeats and Aleister Crowley among its members', according to the Friends of Arthur Machen website.[1] Machen was probably best known for the fictitious piece he wrote for the *Evening News* about the Angels of Mons in 1914. These were supposedly a group of angels who protected members of the British army at the Battle of Mons and were phantom bowmen summoned from the Battle of Agincourt to help the British. Many people believed the story to be true.

Arthur was a friend of Edgar Jepson, Margaret's father, and moved in the same literary circles. There was an interesting comment on the Machen website which said that during the 1920s Arthur and his wife lived in St John's Wood and 'were renowned for their parties where the day's "celebs" would rub shoulders with the notorious as well as literary and spiritual seekers after truth'. It went on to say that Arthur spent money whenever he had it and 'it was probably lucky for him that he had collected a coterie of younger men around him who were prepared to wheel and deal for him in order to keep him in some kind of comfort in his old age'. He died in 1947 aged eighty-four.

My brother has a book written by Aleister Crowley which belonged to our father. Crowley was a well-known occultist writer and poet and was often referred to as 'the wickedest man in the world'. Apparently one time when Crowley was ill, Frank saved his life and was given the book by way of a thank you.

Frank's letter to Sheona went on to explain what they were doing in Malta:

> In case you wonder what the deuce we are doing in Malta, Margaret and I are on a very small steamer going from Genoa to Venice. We called at Livorno, Naples, Sicily, Malta, Catania and we are now on our way to the Adriatic and the Dalmatian Islands.
>
> The weather is wonderful. Jane Felicity is growing up to be a very good-looking child. She was incredibly ugly when she was born but every day and in every way she is getting better and better. She likes the boat very much and sleeps on deck all day long. The captain spends a lot of his spare time by her side watching her. I will send you a photo of her when we land. I do hope that you will be her godmother.

Margaret added a PS to the letter saying she too hoped that Sheona would be Jane's godmother and that she would not mind 'being chosen for this position without consent'!

Frank wrote about his visit to Italy in the form of a diary; unfortunately only fragments remain, but some are worth quoting.[2] The diary started from when they were in Genoa, and mentioned their visit to Livorno, from where they visited Pisa, Naples, and Pompeii, then continued with a visit to Palermo and Messina in Sicily, Malta, and finally Catania in Sicily. The cruise started in Genoa, and on 4 May Frank wrote:

> The palaces of Genoa are not a myth, white-flowering bushes shine against the sky along the marble balconies above the streets, and waterfalls stream from rocky pinnacles in verdant gardens. A

> pleasant and a grandiose city. Returning to the boat we watch her being loaded with bales and hides and barrels, and speculate on the length of life of the derrick cable which is frayed to a single strand, and the probable longevity of the gentleman of the dramatic gestures who stands beneath it.
>
> We are due to sail at eight o'clock. We do not sail until ten. The American tramp in front of us moves out, and a tug takes us in her wake. It is dark. The harbour lights wink red and white, the port is spangled with the lights of ships and all the hills of Genoa are lighted to the inky skies. At the bar the little tug drops us, the pilot jumps to her from the ship and she sheers away into the night. In a still sea we chug outward and the lights of Genoa fade.

He described what they saw the next day:

> In a faint coloured, misty noon we pass between the Isle of Ischia and the mainland. The mountains of this island rise with softened outlines against a tender sky, fishing boats drift with idle sails across the pearly shining water; the wake of our ship fans out behind in shining ridges, wavering away in lucid ripples never breaking into foam. There is a thin veil of cloud across the sky which presently breaks into spaces of blue, so that the shining mirror of the water becomes opalescent, and the mainland takes on hues of green and amber; and as the mist thins the mountain of Vesuvius appears, smoking white vapour, and the little white specks of houses can be seen along the further shore, like a scene discovered by a lifted curtain.

Frank wrote about the clergyman they had met on the boat who christened Jane:

> We have discovered a clergyman on board. Since the boat started he has been in his cabin – seasick. But now he is quite well. He has two passions, sciatica and Garibaldi. He is on the boat for these two reasons. He has been told that a certain cure for sciatica is to dangle ones leg over the crater at Mount Vesuvius and expose it to the sulphur fumes; and he wishes to see the spot where Garibaldi landed at Sicily. The Chief Officer is very pessimistic about both Garibaldi and sciatica. He says that it is better to be dead than to suffer with sciatica, and he says that Garibaldi was little more than a common thief. The Chief Officer also told us that there is a wonderful cemetery in Naples, and that we are on no account to miss seeing Pompeii where thousands of Romans were buried alive by the advancing lava. At half past two we will be in Naples. I think we shall go to the crater of Mount Vesuvius with the clergyman and take a photograph of him dangling his leg over the crater.

On 6 May Frank said what he thought about Naples:

> We are steaming out of Naples – The Pearl of the Tyrrhenian Sea. If Naples is a pearl, it must be of the kind that is cast before swine. Never have I seen filthier streets, lousier people, dirtier shops, houses, tramcars, and docks than I have in Naples. The inhabitants of Naples would be a sore to the scum of Port Said, for rapaciousness they would put a wart-hog to shame. On one side of the town are the docks, whose waters can scarce be seen for the thick layer of rotting bread, smelling and decaying vegetation, and dead dogs; and on the other side is the largest chimney stack in the world. It costs three hundred lire to visit this monstrosity, and Mr Cook has built a funicular railway up its slopes.

And he told a good story about his experiences at Pompeii:

> But apart from what I've just said above, Naples was rather amusing. We were immediately collared on landing by a tout, who spoke English with a magnificent Scottish accent. He told me that he had lived in Glasgow for many years, that his two brothers and he had the largest ice-cream factory in that city, and that the family would still be there were it not that seven customers died in one week. The health authorities said it was the ice cream – so the brothers returned to their native shores. Our tout made easy money; he collected three hundred lire from us for the excursion to Pompeii, escorted us to a motor car, gave the driver two hundred lire, and departed in search for some more fool-English for another hundred lire profit.
>
> When we reached Pompeii, it cost us fifteen lire to enter the ruins. We were set upon by a swarm of guides. A notice board said that the charge for a guide was thirty- five lire. The guides told us that the charge was seventy five lire! When we asked how they accounted for the discrepancy of forty lire they explained that they would take round English people and talk Italian to them for thirty five lire, and that they would take Italians round and talk to them in English for the same amount. But if the English wanted to be guided in English, or the Italians in Italian, then it would cost seventy-five lire. We were beaten and the guides knew it. We paid our seventy-five lire. At Pompeii there are small chairs mounted on a pair of poles, and one is carried along in sedan chair fashion for another fifty lire. A degrading occupation, but a paying one.

On 7 May they arrived at Palermo in Sicily:

> In the bright pale morning it approaches, the shadowy outline of a mountainous land. Slowly, with only the faintest steady tremor of

her engines, the ship slides gently through the pellucid water, as though across the surface of a mirror towards its painted rim; the rim, as she progresses, growing clearer and more brightly coloured, showing a noble height of mountains above the minute white city on the sea's edge. Pellegrino rises on its northern extremity, while to the south lies a plain more fertile and more lovely than any in the world. Here the turned soil is the colour of chocolate, and no less rich. Here are green grasslands planted with ancient olive trees; upstanding olive trees of a gnarled and twisted height, set squarely and strongly in rows for miles and miles, well spaced, allowing a wide view of the smooth grassland between their noble stems. Here the lovely gardens of the Favorita, walled, with a splendid gateway, enclosing mile on mile of lemon groves, low trees with shining leaves, and yellow fruit, gleaming in sun and shadow, the air heavy with an overpowering scent of lemon blossom. The whole place is very, very beautiful; every garden is a scent factory with roses for walls. A cool breeze blows in from the amethyst-blue and purple Mediterranean; brilliantly-coloured lizards bask in the sunshine and vanish with a flick of the tail.

It is difficult to believe that peace has but recently fallen on this country after the disruption and strife of centuries; difficult to believe that a dozen nations have fought and bickered over her as dogs do over a bone. But the cathedral of Palermo shows the architecture of north and south, of Moor and Christian, of Roman, Norman, Byzantine and Bourbon, combined in one preposterous whole. The faces of the saints and bishops who stand above the quadrangle are serene enough and appear unabashed by the mixture of creeds. If, in the silence of the night, they abandon their post of contentment and, coming to life, embark on angry arguments, they show no signs of it by day.

No doubt these little painted carts pulled by brightly-plumed horses, have trotted in day by day with farm produce from the mountain valleys since the beginning of history. No doubt until the end of history they will go on doing so, for the plant springs and the fruit tree bears, regardless of political discussion.

By 9 May, they had reached Malta:

As we approached the harbour of Valetta, we passed the *Royal Oak*, of Bandmaster Barnacle fame.[3] Then we steamed past the *Royal Sovereign*, the *Barham*, the *London*, and some others whose names were undistinguishable. After that battleships became like chickens out of an incubator, clucking in and out in their hundreds, aimlessly. Malta itself is rather like Aldershot. The streets are filled with bluejackets, tommies, air-force men and their wives and children. Being a British possession, the food was of very poor quality. In Italy, and even in Sicily, in even the poorer restaurants the most

> luscious ices were obtainable, but in Malta, the ices were of the quality that one obtains at the vicar's garden party.

The last entry in the diary which survives described what Frank thought about Catania, which they reached on 10 May:

> A most unpleasant looking harbour, with the menacing Mount Etna in the background. Etna was smoking furiously, but the inhabitants do not seem to mind. The whole town is built on and with lava. The monuments are lava, the ancient Greek and Roman theatres are lava, and the food served in the restaurants is apparently made of the same substance. The chief industries are fishing and lemon growing. A strange thing is that although the town is filled with carts packed with lemons and all the surrounding country is filled with lemon groves, yet it is almost impossible to buy a lemon in the town. And even then they are much more expensive than they are in England.
>
> As we left the harbour on our way to the Gulf of Taranto [where Frank had been during the War] the smoke from Etna was blown by the wind into the form of a menacing giant, overhanging the whole town of Catania. And a fine lava dust was settling over all the countryside.

Frank, Margaret and Jane returned to England in July 1929 on the Dutch ship *SS Slamat*, travelling from Marseilles via Tangier to Southampton. Margaret's mother Frieda had returned earlier to England. However, as her marriage had broken down she left England in October 1930 from Manchester, on board the *SS Pacific Reliance*, to live with her widowed mother in San Francisco.

At some stage Frank and Margaret decided to emigrate to New Zealand. My mother told me that Frank had been advised to live in a warm climate because he had suffered with rheumatic fever after being in the trenches in the war and his health had been compromised, and perhaps that is why he chose to go. Fay said that he had the choice of a job in New Zealand or a job in California, and chose the former because it was a progressive country and they were doing lots of work in public health in which he was interested. Frank and his family were only home for a brief period from Italy before finally emigrating. They left England in December of that year, arriving in Wellington on 13 January 1930, according to Frank's passport stamp. Frank must have got a job as the ship's doctor as neither he nor his family appeared in the ship's passenger list; crew and their family were not recorded with the ordinary passengers.[4]

After arriving in Wellington, Frank, Margaret and Jane moved on to Napier in the North Island of New Zealand, where they were to face yet more adventure.

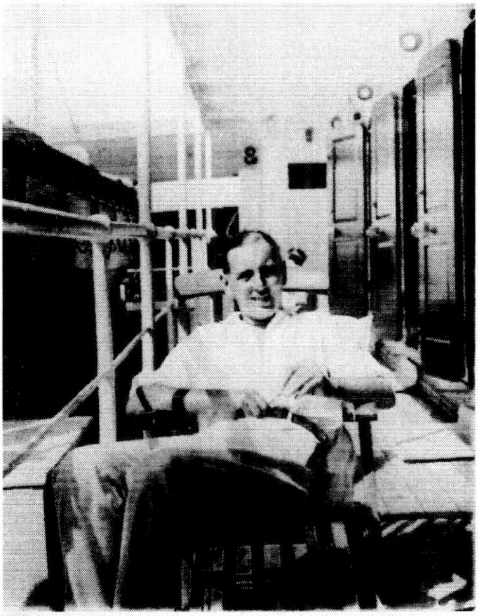

Top left: Margaret and Jane in Alassio
Top right: Frank on board SS Slamat
Centre:Frank in Alassio
Left: Frank on mule

Chapter Nine

Earthquake

Frank and Margaret and their small daughter Jane settled into life in Napier. Napier was a prosperous and peaceful seaside resort, similar to Brighton in the UK, in a wine-producing area in Hawke's Bay on the east coast of New Zealand.

Frank had a medical practice in fashionable Clive Square and was Honorary Physician to the Napier Hospital.[1] They had a nice house and everything was going well. On 27 July 1930 Frank wrote home to his mother saying that he had not heard from them for some weeks but that there were three boats due the next week from England so he was hoping to receive several letters from them.

In his letter[2] he said 'nothing much is happening just at present; we went to a dance last Saturday, to a bridge party on Tuesday and last night got up a theatre party to see *Love Lies'*. He went on to say that they had good 'talkie' shows and that the *Vagabond King* was on that week. He also said that it was snowing in Napier which event had not been seen there for thirty-five years. He went on:

> England got beaten at Auckland in the third test match yesterday, much to everyone's joy and our secret sorrow.
>
> Jane Felicity is well and happy. She holds her head under the water when she has a bath and seemingly likes to be half drowned. I think also that she is getting much better looking.
>
> The only thing I miss in New Zealand is books. When I see the *Sunday Times* and read the book lists and realise that it will be months and months before even a twentieth of them reach here, it is very depressing. Will you ask Pater to send the *Daily Mail* (London) or the *Evening News* out here occasionally when he thinks of it?
>
> Margaret sends her love to all of you. Love – Frank.

Frank enclosed a newspaper cutting about the recent party they went to which was a farewell to a friend who was leaving for England. The ladies who were present were listed first and their attire described: Mrs Birkinshaw was wearing a 'dainty frock of white satin'.

Tuesday 3rd February 1931 in Napier started like any other day, but shortly before 11.00 am the earthquake struck. It measured 7.8 on the Richter Scale and lasted for just over two minutes. Fire broke out and the flames spread out of control. Communications collapsed as did the water supply and the fire station was destroyed so firemen were left helpless. As luck would have it, *HMS Veronica* was moored in the harbour, it having docked only three hours previously, and the Captain was able to alert the outside world to the situation by ship's radio and to send in help themselves. The whole of the Hawke's Bay area was affected and shocks were felt throughout most of the North Island. There were one hundred and fifty aftershocks in the following twenty-four hours and over five hundred during the next two weeks. It was the worst earthquake in New Zealand's history and claimed two hundred and fifty-six lives with many more injured; one hundred and sixty-one of the dead lived in Napier. Twelve nurses died when the nurses' home collapsed; it had only been built the previous year. Many people ran on to the beach and more out on to the streets, although many were then killed by falling masonry. After the earthquake five thousand people were evacuated from their houses as there were no sewage facilities and there was the concern of disease spreading. The floor of the sea just off Hawke's Bay was lifted 2.7 metres and the Ahuriri lagoon was drained; a new airport was later built on this land.[3]

Margaret managed to get a letter out to the family. It was dated Friday 6 February and addressed to her mother-in-law.[4]

> My dear Bella
>
> As I expect you read in the papers there has been a nasty earthquake and both Napier and Hastings have been practically wiped. Fortunately Frank was at home at the time – 11 am - and we all three got out of the house without a scratch. All the furniture came down and the chimneys. The car was in the garage and was pitched out into the road, where the Midland Hotel fell on it and it was filled with bricks.
>
> I stayed in somebody's garden on the Hill all Tuesday night while Frank was working with the casualties. The hospital was a pile of rubble and seven hundred beds were put out on the Napier Park Racecourse. The shocks went on all day and all night and we are still having them every two hours or so.
>
> Frank brought me up here with the baby, to the Ensors' sheep station – about thirty-five miles out of Napier. We are living out of doors because of the continued shocks. They are very kind to me. Frank is still down in Napier and I haven't seen him since Wednesday morning. He has been so hard at work. It would be easier if we were free to look out for ourselves and get a few clothes etc. out of the house, but of course he has to go on with his job.
>
> They say that they are going to demolish the rest of the town. The whole of the shopping and business quarters were burnt to the ground including every bank in the place. In about a fortnight's time they are going to wipe out what is left by gunfire from the sea. The women and children and casualties are already on their way to Wellington. We have about 4/6d in the world and a roofless car. But we're not worrying. It means a move on, that is all, and thank

> goodness there is a comfortable living to be made by a doctor at any time, anywhere. It is a great pity though, because Frank was just going to reap the benefits of a year's hard work.
>
> He took £100 in cash alone last month, apart from the great amount that he would naturally put on the books and we were going well ahead paying off the overdraft he had to keep us going while he was pulling the practice together, and every other doctor in the town was going about groaning over the slackness of things. It's hard, but we've had a very good time while we've been here – and we must just start over again.
>
> I won't try to describe the earthquake itself to you. It looked, smelled and sounded more utterly vile than any nightmare that can possibly be imagined.
>
> However, we are all three without a scratch. Wherever one goes one is absolutely certain of help of every kind and at a time like this doctors are important people. No one in Hawke's Bay has any money, so no one really needs it.
>
> I do hope that you didn't have an anxious time and that the cable got through. Frank gave it to a man who was going to Waipukurau where the wires are still intact, asking him to take it to any doctor in the town to send off. I am sure it would be done if he got through. But that was the best we could do.
>
> It's no use writing yet, because I've no notion how long we shall be here. I will cable an address when I can. Please don't worry – because so long as we are none of us hurt, everything else is absolutely trivial.
>
> With love to you all – Margaret.

The Times of London carried the story on 6 February. It said that the aftershocks were still continuing, and it commented on the reports of the 'great endurance and courage of the survivors'. Six nurses were pulled alive from the nurses' home by some naval men using crowbars and sledgehammers. An old woman 'was pinned under the wreckage of the cathedral when the building caught fire. It was impossible to rescue her and a doctor entered the blazing ruins to administer morphia and give her merciful oblivion'. Even the prisoners from the gaol 'behaved heroically'; they were released on parole to help. 'One clambered up the face of a tilted three-storey private hospital and lowered an imprisoned patient.' Twenty students had died when the technical school fell on them – others had a lucky escape: '200 at another school had just paraded in the school-ground when the shock brought the building down.' Several cars and their occupants were buried under a cliff and many people trapped under fallen buildings. The rescuers, the newspaper article commented, 'laboured 24 hours without cessation in rescuing and aiding the injured, although such work is highly perilous when the renewed tremors may bring down suddenly walls already weakened'.

However, it seemed that everyone rallied round. Money came pouring in for the relief fund and *The Times* reported that 'stocks of food, clothing, blankets and tents have become immediately available for the devastated region' and people outside the area opened up their homes to the refugees.

One of the local Birmingham papers picked up the story and had a photograph of Frank with the caption:

> Dr F T Birkinshaw, late of Birmingham, who, it is believed, hacked his way into a chemist's shop to secure things to help the injured in the New Zealand earthquake.

The *Sunday Mercury,* a Birmingham newspaper, ran the story on the front page, mentioning Frank, with the headline 'Doctor in Earthquake. Midland Medico completes his Stock of Thrills':

> It will come as a surprise to many of his old friends in Birmingham to learn that one of the most recent arrivals in Napier, the centre of the New Zealand earthquake, was Dr F T Birkinshaw ('the Dare-devil Doctor', as he is called by those who know him), who until a few years ago lived at Alvechurch (near Birmingham). He is now an honorary physician of Napier Hospital, which suffered very badly in the earthquake, so doubtless he has had little time yet to send word to his friends at home.

The 'stock of thrills' referred to the fact that after his 1928 shipwreck in the Thames Frank had made the comment: 'Now I think the only real thrill I haven't experienced is an earthquake!' The article continued:

> Dr Birkinshaw went right through the Great War, joining up when he was 16. First in the Army, he was transferred later to the Air Force and he fought in France, Italy and Arabia. In the last-named country he was captured by some Bedouin tribesmen who prepared to put him to death because he had no gold with which to buy his release. Then he had a sudden brain-wave. Writing paper having been short when he started out, he had thrust into his pocket the best substitute available at the moment – a quantity of jam-jar labels impressively printed with illustrations of the numerous medals won by the manufacturers. After a little persuasion the Bedouins accepted the bundle as ransom, and set him free.

Frank wrote several radio plays, short stories and articles in the 1930s and 40s, and one rather light-hearted article was about earthquakes. It began:

> When in 1930 I decided to go to New Zealand, I had no clear conception of the Islands in my mind. One thing I did know, and that was that there had been 678 earthquakes during the year 1929. So to my equipment of tropical wear and two text-books on the

> Maori language, I added a motor-cyclist's crash-proof helmet for the purpose of protecting my head from falling masonry.

He described his five week voyage to Wellington during which time he talked to the New Zealanders on board, who described the country as the 'new Garden of Eden' with a death-rate the lowest in the world. They told him it was 'a Paradise of Pacific life consisting of football, going to the races, sun-bathing, and bathing in a warm and sharkless sea'. The New Zealanders said the scare stories about earthquakes were those put about by 'malicious and wicked tales of jealous Australians'! His story continued:

> I had been a few weeks in New Zealand before I encountered my first quake. It was night, and I was sleeping on the top floor of an hotel in Wellington. Suddenly the concrete building gave a sickening jolt. I felt the bed under me jump out of its position against the wall, advance towards the middle of the room, then spring back again. I switched on the light, and the bulb at the end of the cord was swinging wildly to and fro. I rushed out into the corridor. There was silence, broken only by the sound of snoring from the next room. I went down the stairs. 'Quake?' said a sleepy night porter in the foyer. 'I didn't feel any quake.'

Frank then went on to write about what happened in the Napier earthquake:

> A year later I was in my bathroom one morning at Napier, in the North Island, when the floor began to dance. There was a noise, a deep rumbling from the bowels of the earth. The rumbling deepened to a roar; it was as though a thousand express trains were dashing over the points at the one time. The whole house began to jump in the air, and I was flung from corner to corner of the bathroom, as though being shaken up in a box. The door tore itself off its hinges, the bath pulled itself free from its mooring of water-pipes and disappeared through a hole in the floor. I was propelled through the doorway and shot to the bottom of the stairs. And then, suddenly, the roaring and jolting ceased; everything was terribly quiet; and then one heard the screams of the people of Napier. I was lying on the floor, bruised in every bone. On top of me was the front door and the hall-stand – and my crash-helmet. I staggered into the street, the crash-helmet on my head. I knew now that there really were earthquakes in New Zealand!
>
> Outside the streets were filled with the twisted bodies of the dead and dying. Buildings were razed to the ground; men and women wandered through them, dazedly, with the unreality of figures in an expressionist film. When you breathed you felt the dust from bricks and masonry thick and gritty in your mouth and nostrils.

Frank concluded the article by describing an injured and bewildered man in the street who asked him what had happened. When Frank told him there had been an earthquake the man roared with laughter and said 'that's all right, mate, I'd had four whiskies and I thought I was seeing things. First everything fell down and then you appeared in that hat!' Frank said that after several years he managed to 'acquire the New Zealander's casual attitude to earthquakes which he does his best to deny exist'.

After Frank had done everything he could to help the victims and with his livelihood and house in ruins, he and Jane and Margaret, now two months pregnant, left Napier to start their life over again.

As for Napier, it rose like a phoenix from the ashes and was completely rebuilt. Art Deco was popular at the time and the city was reconstructed in that style and completed in just under two years. The architecture of Napier is regarded as being one of the finest examples of Art Deco anywhere in the world.

We visited Napier when we were on our New Zealand tour in 1998. It is an unusual and lovely city. By coincidence a new Earthquake Museum had just opened and we were able to visit it. I had brought some photos to show them that Frank had taken of the damage to the town but was told the curator was in an important meeting and did not wish to be disturbed. However, someone must have told her I had some interesting items because within minutes she was down and looking at the photos and Margaret's letter with great excitement and interest. She thanked me profusely and said she was very pleased to have her meeting interrupted in order to meet us and said she would add my collection to the Museum archives.

Above: Napier Hospital pre-earthquake
Right: post-earthquake

(Napier photographs from Frank's collection)

Top:
The remains of Frank & Margaret's house

Middle:
General view of the ruins of Napier

Left: Emerson Street, Napier

Chapter Ten

New Zealand 1930s

After the earthquake in Napier, Margaret's father Edgar sent her the fare so she could return to England; he was concerned about her having no home, with a child to look after and a baby on the way. Margaret decided to go as the future looked so uncertain, taking Jane with her. She and Jane took a boat from Auckland to Sydney from where they boarded the P&O liner *SS Mongolia* on 12 June 1931. The voyage took them via Colombo and the Suez Canal, and they arrived in London on 24 July.[1]

Edgar was now living with his new wife Lois, who was also expecting a baby, at the family home in Adelaide Road in London; Margaret's mother had already gone to live in California to be with her own mother. Margaret therefore decided to go and stay with Frank's parents who were living in Alvechurch, near Birmingham, and have her baby there. Frank stayed behind in New Zealand to re-establish himself, having lost everything in the earthquake.

Frank and Margaret's second child was born on 22 September 1931. Margaret called her new daughter Franklin, but on their return to New Zealand Frank said he did not like the name and she was thereafter known as Fay. She was to become my second half-sister. Margaret, with Jane and Fay, left London on 27 November 1931, again on the *SS Mongolia,* spending Christmas of that year at sea. Jane was two and Fay was just two months old. They arrived in Sydney on 7 January 1932 and then continued on to Auckland.

Frank had found a job as a physician in March 1931 at the hospital in Hawera, on the west coast of the North Island of New Zealand. Some of the staff at the Hawera hospital had gone to Napier, on the east coast, just after the earthquake (which they had felt in Hawera some two hundred miles away) to offer their help. The hospital then offered accommodation for thirty of the injured, the rest being 'accommodated' in an emergency hospital which had been established on the showgrounds of Palmerston North, a town a little further south. Frank was lucky to find a job as the effects of the world-wide depression were beginning to be felt even in New Zealand. Just after he started working at Hawera there was a ten per cent cut in everyone's wages.[2]

In April 1932 the family moved to the South Island and Frank established a medical practice in Amberley near Christchurch, and later in Christchurch itself. Fay and Jane's childhood in New Zealand, with all its trials and tribulations and adventures, is well documented and colourfully told in Fay's own autobiography.[3]

Frank had an interest in radio and formed the New Zealand Radio Institute (also called the Air Institute of New Zealand) in Christchurch and tried,

Jane in England, 1931

unsuccessfully, to get air time for it on the main city stations which were then non-commercial and privately owned; these were the precursors to National Radio. Instead, he was given an hour's slot every Sunday night on a B class station on which he was able to produce a succession of plays, most of them by New Zealand authors; Margaret too wrote plays for it. Frank had different themes each week and one night he broadcast a 'sea theme' which included an SOS. This caused consternation as the life boat rescue service thought a real ship was sending out distress signals.[4]

Frank also wrote a regular column for a Christchurch daily paper on the subject of broadcasting. After Frank's death the *Auckland Star* wrote an obituary about him and commented on his column, saying that much of the stuff Frank put out, even though often wrong, 'was psychologically tops; it made folks sit up and take notice at a time when that was needed'. The *Star* continued saying that Frank thought that radio plays needed their own writing technique: 'He also thought the average radio actor, used to stage work, hepped things up too much.' One of the people who was roped in to help Frank was Geoff Alley, who had played for the All Blacks and was a leading literary figure. He became New Zealand's first National Librarian. Geoff said in the *Star* article:

> I got roped in as a sort of utility man. I'd be given a handful of character parts to put over in the one show. Making funny sounds in different dialects into the mike's dead blank pan used to addle me a bit. Do you wonder that our arty plays often got a bit scrambled?

Geoff then related an amusing story concerning George Bernard Shaw:

> G B Shaw, visiting N.Zed, heard one of these [Frank's plays]. Frank Birkinshaw had not only kidded him into listening, but also wrung consent for us to put on *Androcles and the Lion*, free of royalties. No other playwright has a longer nose for royalties than GBS, but Frank Birkinshaw had a sort of intellectual toehold on the old master … I nearly blew my tonsils and a radio valve in the dual roles of the lion in the name part, and the equally noisy gladiator, Feruvius. Shaw's comment on the play was that the lion had sounded very hungry.

Frank approached GBS again, just as the great man was leaving New Zealand, to ask whether he would allow him to broadcast his *The Shewing Up of Blanco Posnet* as a radio play. (The play had been banned in London in 1909 by the Lord Chancellor for alleged blasphemy.) Shaw replied to Frank:

> I see no objection to this; but I do not know whether the A I of NZ is a radio concern or part of the Aviation Forces. I have no agent

nearer than Melbourne and have no notion of the fees paid for broadcasting. You can go ahead this time; but in the case of further operations you must really give me some information.

G Bernard Shaw
On the way home – 25/4/34

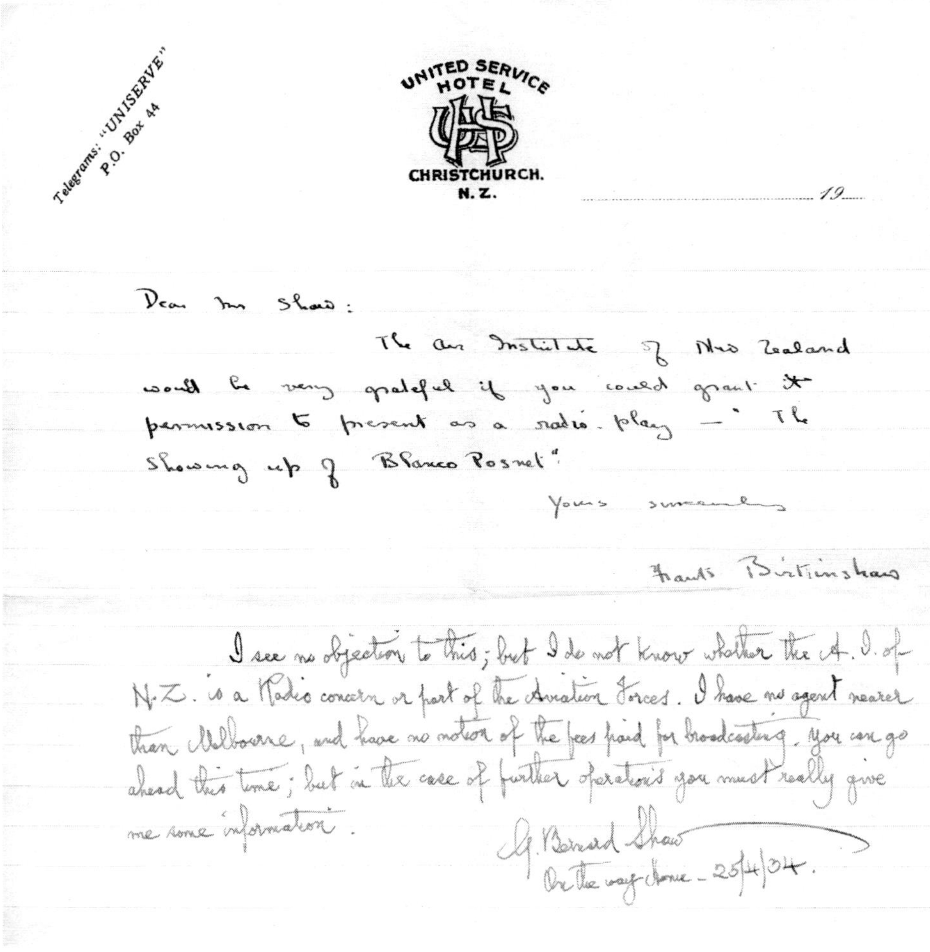
Telegrams: "UNISERVE"
P.O. Box 44

UNITED SERVICE HOTEL
CHRISTCHURCH.
N.Z.

19

Dear Mr Shaw:

The Air Institute of New Zealand would be very grateful if you could grant it permission to present as a radio play – "The Showing up of Blanco Posnet".

Yours sincerely

Frank Birkinshaw

I see no objection to this; but I do not know whether the A.I. of N.Z. is a Radio concern or part of the Aviation Forces. I have no agent nearer than Melbourne, and have no notion of the fees paid for broadcasting. You can go ahead this time; but in the case of further operations you must really give me some information.

G. Bernard Shaw
On the way home – 25/4/34.

Letters to and from George Bernard Shaw

Margaret wrote a book called *Via Panama*[5] which was published in 1934 under her maiden name, and although the book was 'published both in England and the US to critical acclaim', as Fay said in her autobiography, it was not welcomed in New Zealand, being seen as a criticism of the provincial way of New Zealand life. Frank was planning to become involved in politics at that time and felt that Margaret's writing was not helpful to him.

Picnic, Amberley, 1933
Frank with Jane on his knee; Margaret at far right with Fay beside her

Frank in Christchurch

There had been a coalition government in New Zealand since 1931, put in place to try and alleviate the hardships the country was suffering during the Great Depression. Frank persuaded the poet and writer Denis Glover, who was a literary friend of his, to approach the Labour Representation Committee (LRC) with him, with a view to setting up a central Christchurch branch of the party for the coming 1935 election. Frank believed a Labour Government would be the answer to the country's problems and the only hope for society. Denis Glover was one of New Zealand's foremost poets. He was also a printer and publisher, according to Gordon Ogilvie who wrote a biography of Glover.[6] In this he said that another friend of Frank and Glover, the poet Rex Fairburn, believed that the only remedy for the 'joint leader of the hapless coalition government trying to rescue New Zealand from the Depression was to "beat him all over with a stocking-full of hot shit".'

Frank and Glover duly approached the LRC and Glover described the meeting:

> I thought this was a great idea until we did appear before the LRC. The LRC as a body is not noted for its sense of humour … We were listened to with polite attention and then the questions started. It was quite clear that we were white collar. It was quite clear that, with the one a doctor and the other a student, we were the class enemy – no doubt indoctrinated with Marxism and seeking by this audacious spoof to white-ant the whole Labour Movement.

Eventually Frank and Glover realised the whole idea was a non-starter, but in due course the LRC wrote to them, as Glover said, 'proving that after all the LRC can have a sense of humour'. They had been offered not Christchurch but the 'non-existent Fendalton branch'. Unfortunately Fendalton was a Conservative stronghold and would have been political suicide for them.

In his autobiography *Hot Water Sailor*[7], Denis Glover described Frank as 'a mad merry doctor, politically minded, greatly concerned with writing, greatly concerned with stirring up trouble in a boyish mischievous way'.

In 1934 a radical publication emerged in Christchurch called *Tomorrow.* It was started by Kennaway Henderson, a 'Christchurch radical', as Gordon Ogilvie wrote in his biography of Glover. He said that *Tomorrow* was established as an 'open forum', but 'radical tendencies were apparent from the outset' and attracted New Zealand's 'emerging writers and poets' who were by any standards 'a remarkable group, and included a large number of the intellectual, artistic and political elite of New Zealand'. *Tomorrow* soon 'became colonised by left-wing writers', and although it only lasted for six years it was 'probably the most influential independent periodical in our country's history', wrote Ogilvie. Frank was one of its contributors and one of his articles was entitled 'Some Social Aspects of Broadcasting'. Another of

Frank's contributions was his 'A National Health Plan for New Zealand' which was serialised in five parts over three months in late 1936. At that time there was no National Insurance scheme in New Zealand but there was a voluntary system conducted by the Friendly Societies and known as the Lodge System. This system, though admirable in conception, as Frank said, suffered one major disadvantage in that a medical examination was necessary before a person was allowed to become a member. That requirement ensured that those suffering from serious complaints were barred from joining the Lodges, and hence ensured that the very people in need of medical or surgical attention were unable to obtain it. Another disadvantage was that since the payments were voluntary there was nothing to compel the subscriber to continue with his subscriptions.

Frank's plan consisted of four proposals:-

- A central research organisation, to develop modern methods for improving the health of infants, school children and adults.
- The organisation of a National Health Insurance Scheme, which would ensure adequate medical treatment for every employed person over the age of sixteen and earning less than a stated sum yearly.
- The nationalisation of the Plunket Society, which provided support services for the development, health and well-being of children under the age of five. The aim would be to bring the Society under the direct control of the Minister for Health, and to ensure close co -operation between the Society and the School Medical Service.
- The organisation of a National Youth Health Movement, which would care for the health of the young adult of both sexes through summer camps, physical culture classes etc.

Denis Glover co-founded the Caxton Press in 1935 to give voice to the 'burgeoning literary renaissance' that was taking place in New Zealand at that time, as Ogilvie said. He also said that one of Glover's customers and 'literary friends' was Frank who commissioned Glover and the Caxton Press to publish his 'National Health Plan' in 1937. Whether the relevant authorities ever took any notice of it was unclear, but presumably it was published in order for them to at least consider it. Frank was described in Ogilvie's book as 'the visionary Frank Birkinshaw'. The current Managing Director of the Caxton Press, with whom I made contact, said that Frank must have been a colourful character if he was a friend of Glover. He also said that Glover was 'booted out' of The Caxton Press in 1951 even though he was a co-founder; Glover had been 'drinking the company profits'!

Another friend of Glover was A R D (Rex) Fairburn, one of New Zealand's first major poets, who also contributed to *Tomorrow*. Fairburn was quoted in *The Letters of A R D Fairburn*[8], as saying that he 'set up a meeting with Frank in 1937 in an Auckland pub which Frank didn't get to'. He wrote:

> I had a ring from Birkinshaw when he was in Auckland. He made an appointment, which I kept religiously (although it was at a pub) and he not at all. I waited for him for over half an hour and then chucked it. Is he like that much?

And a footnote to that comment read: 'Dr Frank Birkinshaw, a notable wit and author of medical notes in *Tomorrow*. He invented the Birkinshaw breathing apparatus.' Unfortunately, I could not find any more information about Frank's breathing invention!

It was some time after their move to Christchurch that, as Fay put it, 'things fell apart'. Although Frank and Margaret now had a nice house and Frank a thriving medical practice, they were not happy. Margaret said she was fed up with Frank's debts and his infidelities and she once more determined to return to England.

Frank and Margaret agreed to separate and before Margaret left for England they drew up an Agreement of Separation on 31 October 1936.[9] This stated that they would 'live separate and apart as from this day'. Margaret agreed she would maintain herself and not make any claim on Frank for maintenance. Frank was to have sole custody of the children and would maintain them, and Margaret was to have reasonable access. They both signed the Agreement in the presence of a solicitor.

Margaret travelled on her own to England on the cargo ship *Port Fremantle,* which arrived in London on 7 December 1936. There were only two other passengers on board, a thirty-seven year old hostess secretary and a twenty-three year old male student. Margaret gave her address in England as care of Gilbert Wright, who had been best man at her wedding. She had been offered a job in London which she took up on arrival and also found herself somewhere to live. Her plan was to send for the children when she became settled. Fay said that after only a short time Margaret's plans were thwarted when a letter arrived from Frank to say that Fay had polio. He advised her to return immediately 'before it was too late'. Margaret duly gave up her job and her flat and left London on 4 March 1937 on board the *RMS Rangitane*. The journey took thirty-five days and went via Panama; Margaret did not know what she would return to.

However, no sooner had Margaret arrived back in New Zealand, finding that Fay had recovered, than Frank declared that *he* was now going to England. He wanted to work in London and add to his medical qualifications. Frank left New Zealand for England in June 1937, not to return for nearly two years.[10]

Chapter Eleven

Frank and Edna

It was while he was in London that Frank met and fell in love with Edna. The early story of Edna's life and that of her family is told in *Many Journeys*, Part One of this trilogy.

Edna Mackenzie was born in Scotland in 1904 at Dundonnell, a highland estate in Wester Ross. Her family had owned Dundonnell since 1834 and her great-grandfather, Dr Kenneth Mackenzie, sailed to Australia in 1836, having been given money by his father Murdo to buy up land and seek his fortune there. Dr Kenneth prospered, married and had five children who in turn produced thirty-one grandchildren for him. He eventually returned to Dundonnell where he spent the last few years of his life. Edna's parents, Jack and Florence, who were both born in Australia, lived at Dundonnell after they were married. Their two daughters Edna and Mavis were born there and shortly after that time the family went to live in Australia. Tony, their son, was born in Queensland in 1912; Florence died in 1920. Edna obtained her medical degree at Sydney University and then travelled to London where she had been working since 1929.

When Frank arrived in London he worked mostly in University College Hospital, which was where he and Edna met in 1937. He also gained the extra medical qualifications he was seeking. During his stay in London, Frank took the opportunity to give a lecture on New Zealand to the Brentwood Congregational Literary Society. He was living in Upminster at the time. The lecture, described as a 'pleasure trip to New Zealand' was reported in the local paper and the article read:

> The lecturer gave a short account of New Zealand and its early inhabitants, and then by the aid of colourful slides the audience was taken through the Panama Canal to Auckland in the North Island. After visiting the hot springs, the party travelled south through marvellous scenery and the most notable towns on the way, finishing up at Christchurch in the South Island. Dr Birkinshaw was then kept busy for some time answering questions after which the meeting accorded him thanks for his lecture.

Frank went to Barnt Green, near Birmingham, to visit his parents whom he had not seen for nearly eight years. He did not take Edna to visit them, although she did meet his siblings, Sheona, Mary and Bill. Frank and Edna went on holiday together to Holland in July 1938 for ten days and when Frank asked Edna to come back to New Zealand and marry him, she agreed, even though they would have to wait over another year for his divorce to come through.

To that end on 16 February 1939 Frank and Edna left Liverpool on board the *MV Imperial Star*. Frank was employed as the ship's surgeon,[1] and Edna travelled as a passenger.[2] Edna disembarked at Sydney on 30 March in order to spend some time with her family, whom she had not seen for ten years, and Frank continued on to Wellington, arriving on 26 April.

Frank went first to visit his children Jane and Fay in Christchurch in the South Island, and then returned to the North Island and took a job as Superintendent of the hospital in Coromandel. When Edna arrived in New Zealand she went to work for the Health Department in Hamilton, also in the North Island, but some one hundred and twenty miles away from Frank. They would visit each other whenever they could until they were able to marry.

Edna playing the piano, New Zealand, circa 1940

Frank, circa 1940

Chapter Twelve

New Zealand 1940s

A letter[1] arrived for Isabel at their house in Barnt Green, Birmingham, early in the New Year of 1940. It was from Frank in Coromandel. He told his mother that he was expecting Jane and Fay to come up and stay with him for the Christmas holidays. He described Coromandel as 'only a small country place, and as dull as ditchwater, but in war time that doesn't matter much'. He described his garden as 'looking rather beautiful now' with a strawberry patch, roses, hydrangeas, carnations and gladioli, no doubt tended by Edna on her weekend visits. He said that the war was not affecting them at the moment and there was plenty of food for everyone, although he reckoned that imported goods would soon be unobtainable. Frank suggested that if Isabel and Herbert found England unpleasant because of the war, they could 'go to Italy and get an Italian ship to Sydney, and then tranship over here with fairly complete safety, I imagine'. He also offered to help them with the fare. He asked if they could send a Sunday paper over to him occasionally. He went on:

> I don't suppose I'll join the army – not at present anyway, although there's the possibility of joining the RAMC some time later. But since my operation my tummy hasn't been very first rate, so I don't suppose I'd go abroad in any case.
>
> I wonder if you would ask Bill and Mary to write and let me know what is happening to them and how they are. I wish Bill had come out here. Of course the war may only last a short time, if so I'll be coming back to England. But at present of course it's quite impossible.

Coromandel, the town and the peninsula, were named in 1820 after the ship of that name. Timber was its first industry until gold was discovered in 1852. The town boomed during the 1870s and in 1898 the hospital, accommodating twenty beds, was built. By the time Frank arrived the gold rush was over and an agricultural industry had grown up in the area. The Superintendent's house where Frank lived was built in the 1890s, originally as a mine manager's house.[2]

It was to here that Jane and Fay would come during their summer holidays to spend time with Frank, and this became an annual event, as Fay told in her autobiography.[3] Their mother Margaret would take them on the ferry from Lyttleton (the port of Christchurch) to Wellington and from there they would travel alone on the night train to Auckland. Frank would meet them at Auckland railway station from where it was about five hours to Coromandel by car. Fay described the journey from Auckland to Coromandel along the flat, straight road through the mangrove swamps and then in to the hills:

> As we went further north the landscape changed: now we were in sub-tropical bush, and soon the only way forward was along the winding, unmade-up road which skirted the coast. Red pohutukawa trees leaned down from the cliffs to meet the rocky sea-line, where cormorants shrieked and dived, past rough shacks where Maoris, brown, beautiful, glistening, lived and fished, and on to Coromandel bay, and the ghost town of Coromandel itself. And even then as a child I knew how privileged I was, to be in that place, at that time, in the Golden Age.

Fay also talked about their idyllic summers and the freedom they enjoyed and how well they were respected as 'the doctor's children', and how Frank loved the people of Coromandel 'as they loved him'.

Coromandel Hospital, 1940

Frank was also responsible for the small hospital at Mercury Bay on the other side of the Coromandel peninsula which he would visit every Wednesday afternoon. He could also be called out at any time of the day or night which could be very time-consuming as the roads were only made of shingle. The nurses at the hospital would look after Jane and Fay while Frank was working, but when he was called out at night he would bundle the girls in to his car with their blankets and pillows and take them along with him. Fay told me that Frank was a most caring father and always looked after them with great gentleness, particularly when they were ill.

Fay and Jane, Coromandel

In January 1940 Frank petitioned the New Zealand Supreme Court in Nelson for a divorce from Margaret on the grounds that they had had an Agreement of Separation for more than three years. Margaret made no objection and the Decree Absolute was granted on 16 July 1940. Custody of the children was given to Margaret with Frank allowed reasonable access and temporary custody for two periods a year each totalling not more than ten weeks. Margaret was not allowed to remove the children further than two thousand miles from Christchurch without Frank's written consent; Frank was to pay five pounds per month for each child until Fay was eighteen.[4]

Frank and Edna were married on 25 July 1940 in St Andrew's Presbyterian Church in Hamilton. My mother told me that there was no one to walk her down the aisle so the minister 'did the honours'. Their friends the Brooks acted as witnesses. Maurice Brook was also their lawyer. After their marriage Edna went to live with Frank in the Coromandel house and worked as school doctor in the nearby town of Thames.

In May 1941 Frank wrote to his mother saying how happy he and Edna were in Coromandel. (Isabel had kept the letter and gave it to Edna many years later.) He told his mother that Edna was now a part-time school medical officer and also gave anaesthetics at the hospital for him. He said she was very keen on gardening and that they had roses, gladioli, some asters and chrysanthemums out even though it was winter. Jane and Fay were back at school in Christchurch and would soon be coming up again to visit. He said that the girls' grandmother, Mrs Jepson, had arrived from America and they were all moving into a new house with a large garden with cherry and peach trees. Frank also said in the letter that he had heard that the British Museum had been hit by incendiary bombs; he had been bad tempered ever since and declared 'I liked the British Museum'. He said more about Edna whom his mother had never met:

> It's nearly midnight now and Edna is in the next room tapping away on her typewriter. As we each have our own jobs we have all sorts of things in duplicate. She has her own car, and we have a radio each in them so that we can get the news when we're away from home. She has her own typewriter and I have mine. In our work room, where we do our writing and see patients and things like that, we each have our own desk. It's rather fun.
>
> I think you'd like her. In fact I'm *sure* you'd like her. She's rather like you. And she amazes me all the time, even though I've known her for four years nearly now. Besides knowing a lot about medicine she can garden and cook, and knows all about horses, and how to make butter, and she plays the piano. Altogether I never knew what happiness was until I met her.
>
> So that's that. Goodbye for now.
>
> All my love to you and Pater.

Jane and Fay, on their visits to Frank, came to accept Edna as their stepmother. Fay described her as a 'tall, elegant, rather brusque woman … an extremely kind and helpful person who laid the table and sat us down to proper cooked meals, instead of the sandwiches my father favoured.'

One day Nell Barrett came knocking at Frank and Edna's door. She was looking for work as her man had gone off to war leaving her pregnant. Frank and Edna took her in and she helped them round the house until her son Johnnie was born. Nell and Johnnie remained with them for the next nine years.

In 1943 Frank wrote to Margaret[5] in response to a letter from her asking for more maintenance for the children. He agreed to increase it to fifteen pounds a month as he realised that prices had shot up. He continued:

> From a point of view of interest … I'm not really amassing a fortune in Coromandel. I paid income tax in 1942 on just over £900. Tax on this amount was £140, social security tax about £110,

> leaving a net income of £650. I could make more than this if I started general practice in a town but I don't believe that general practice of this type is worth doing, either morally or mentally.

He went on to say that he and Edna would be starting a practice in Auckland very shortly but that they intended to commence a clinic on the group practice principle. However, he had not been able to find a satisfactory successor at Coromandel as yet, although he was hopeful one would be found.

In June 1943 Frank wrote to his mother saying he had not heard from them for a month or so, whereas beforehand letters were coming more regularly. He commented on the war and then went on to talk about 'the little world of Coromandel' and what was happening there. It was the middle of winter and cold and wet and he said 'we're just beginning to feel that the war's been lasting an infernal time'. Most food was still cheap with plenty of bread, meat, butter and cheese but fruit was difficult to find, although there were plenty of apples, and they had orange and persimmon trees in the garden. 'Tinned fruit seems to be a thing of the past and we get about an egg a week', he said, and cigarettes were difficult to get hold of costing a penny each and 'are made of most peculiar kinds of tobacco. However, we smoke them when we can get them.' Clothes, tea and sugar were rationed and household goods were slowly vanishing from the shops. He said that most people were very thankful that everything was as good as it was. Books and magazines were expensive and hard to come by but he had managed to find a second-hand *Encyclopaedia Britannica* and *Oxford Dictionary*, and even *Groves Dictionary of Music* in five volumes (which I still have in my possession). He added 'so I have enough to read for the next few years, even if I don't buy another book'. Frank also said it was amazing that the *British Medical Journal* and *The Lancet* arrived from England regularly every week. He mentioned that the Coromandel hospital had about twenty patients at the present time. Edna, he said, was fine and that she was 'at the piano in the next room playing Bach's *Jesu, Joy of Man's Desiring*'.

In September 1943 Frank put a proposal to the Coromandel Rehabilitation Committee. His suggestions were outlined in the local newspaper, the *Hauraki Plains Gazette.* The message Frank was trying to get across was that Coromandel 'would remain essentially a New Zealand backblock unless certain positive steps were taken or unless gold was rediscovered'. Frank's scheme was 'to declare the whole of Coromandel County as a scenic reserve … State purchase of all pieces of land likely to be of use as government hostels or motor camps … the building of a motor road encircling the peninsula … the re-afforestation of all hilly country in the peninsula which may be suitable.' He also suggested that the peninsula be electrified and a pulp factory built near the wharf at Coromandel. All this would prevent a period of otherwise inevitable unemployment after the war. The article ended using Frank's words:

> If this scheme is accepted by the local rehabilitation committee, preliminary work should include the inspection of suitable areas by forestry experts, and the building up of an advertising campaign stressing the scenic beauties of a more or less generally unknown area less than 20 minutes by air from Auckland.

History did not relate how his proposals were received but the newspaper was impressed enough to publish Frank's forward-thinking scheme.

Margaret wrote to her mother-in-law Isabel in Barnt Green in December 1943 from Christchurch saying she and the children and her mother had moved house to a very nice neighbourhood with many trees and beautiful gardens and added 'it is a most respectable place in a most respectable neighbourhood, within a stone's throw of the Governor General's Christchurch residence'. They were letting one room to a woman tenant who was 'very pleasant and quiet'. Margaret said she was running a small advertising agency while her mother Nona (Frieda) helped with the children and round the house, and she said that Nona had also taken up playing the piano again. Margaret said of the children that they were 'very good and extraordinarily sweet-tempered'. Jane was class leader at the High School and Fay was going to High School a year early. Of Frank she said 'I believe he is starting a clinic in Auckland and it must keep him very busy as he is still in the post at Coromandel'.

However, leaving Coromandel proved to be quite difficult for Frank. The *Hauraki Plains Gazette* dated early 1944 ran a headline: 'Doctor's Resignation Not Accepted.' The Thames Hospital Board had considered Frank's resignation but was not willing to accept it. Frank had asked to resign on medical grounds as he had a kidney stone which was giving him trouble. He said he had found a locum who was able to do the next two months, but the Board was concerned that after that period the area might be without a doctor and therefore they would retain the right to recall him if they could not find a permanent replacement.

There was a further, undated, article in the same paper some weeks later headed: 'Coromandel Doctor leaving the district.' It went on to say that Frank and Edna had intimated some months previously that they would shortly be leaving and that 'Dr Frank Birkinshaw has been medical superintendent at the Coromandel and Mercury Bay hospitals for the past five years'. It stated that during that time the number of patients at the Coromandel hospital had risen by over one hundred per cent, and an attractive children's ward had been added. It said also that patient numbers at the Mercury Bay hospital had risen by over two hundred per cent. The article went on:

> Despite war conditions and shortage of labour the Coromandel hospital has seen extensive changes. During the doctor's term of office a new maternity block, an X-ray plant, extensive alterations to the operating theatre and a steady improvement in the hospital grounds have been carried out.

Frank and Edna finally moved to Auckland in April 1944, taking Nell and Johnnie with them. Their new home in Lucerne Road in Remuera, an upmarket suburb of Auckland, was a two-storey brick house built in 1936. It overlooked the City of Auckland and the Orakei Basin, now a waterskiers' paradise. Edna bought it with money left to her by her mother who had died when Edna was only sixteen. Fay described the house as being 'large, new, grand and dull' but with a spectacular view overlooking the harbour 'and every evening at around five the flying-boat from Sydney would land down below in a flurry of white foam'.

On 15 June 1944 Frank and Edna's son was born; he was named Alan Frank Mackenzie Birkinshaw. He was baptised on 30 July by the former Archbishop of New Zealand at St Philip's Anglican Church in St Heliers, a residential suburb of Auckland. My godmother Poppy, as she told me in a letter, remembered going to the party afterwards, describing it as 'delirious'!

Edna

Frank on steps of Coromandel Hospital

Edna in the garden of their house, Coromandel

Edna and Alan
Lucerne Road,
Auckland

Poppy, who was a pathologist, first met Edna at Sydney University and they had by chance bumped into each other in London when they were both working there in the 1930s. Again, by chance, Edna had noticed Poppy's name on the passenger list of the flying boat which went between Sydney and Auckland and had got in touch with her. Poppy was now married and living in Auckland. After that they saw a great deal of each other. Poppy told me that she remembered being left to look after Alan; she described him as a Devil with a capital 'D'. On one occasion she was trying to feed him his lunch and, she said 'he *never* sat still for one moment. I followed him all around the place till he finally settled for having it in a large marquee that Frank had hired as a possible shelter for the car.'

Frank wrote to Margaret in response to a letter from her concerning Jane taking her matriculation.[6] Frank said he would like to see Jane pass it or her University entrance so she could at least have the option of an academic education. Frank said he was not so keen on her getting an advanced education as a means of making money 'but more so that she can at least have a handle of some kind to give her a lift if necessary'. He said that Jane would probably get married and confound them both; prescient words indeed. He agreed with Margaret that 'to be a school teacher in New Zealand would be a rather dreadful living death'. He felt that if Fay took up medicine she would definitely be assured of a decent livelihood. Frank said he gathered from Margaret's letter that she had 'vague intentions of going to England' but he imagined that would be impossible for the next two years because of the war, but offered to look after the girls if she wished to go on her own. He went on to praise her good mothering and ended on a very personal note:

> I think you have looked after them very well. They are two extremely nice and well behaved girls, and I don't want to interfere in any way, excepting so far as I feel naturally that I have a duty towards them both, and I want to see them both get their matrics at least. This is to some extent personal, as I have had to struggle for a number of years against an educational 'second best' so far as I myself was concerned.

In December 1945 Frank wrote to his sister Mary to tell her that Margaret had been left a legacy of six hundred pounds and would like to return to England with the children. Frank wanted Mary's advice as to whether it would be a good idea for the children to be in England. He was particularly concerned about their education and the situation in London. He was quite happy for them to go if it would be to their advantage. He thought that Fay was quite keen on taking a medical course and Jane was better than average at English. Frank told Mary about the family: 'Alan Frank is growing to be a young man with a very decided will of his own, and is a likeable, strong child.' He said that he and Edna were working hard in their 'semi-consultant practice' and that Edna also had a hospital job and was doing paediatrics. They had had a week's holiday at Rotorua and 'saw the geysers and boiling pools, then went by car to Whakatane and saw the active volcano at White Island steaming in the bay some forty miles away'. They saw another volcano on their way back called Ruapehu which, he said, 'has suddenly decided to erupt furiously, pouring out boulders and throwing them some hundreds of feet in the air; the columns of smoke and steam go as far as 20,000 feet high with fine ash being deposited on the countryside as far as 100 miles away'. He said it was the first time in six years that they were able to get petrol for a holiday although tyres were still a problem, but there were plans to manufacture them in New Zealand. He said ships from England were coming out to New Zealand and returning with butter, meat, cheese and wool. He ended the letter by saying 'if you and Michael decide to come out to New Zealand for a look at the ideal bureaucracy, we'll be able to give you a bed'!

Frank also wrote to Margaret[7] on 26 December telling her that he had written to Mary to ask her to check on the situation in London before giving his consent. He was particularly concerned about the educational facilities there and outlined his feelings:

> The situation now is like this: I would like you to go home to England if you want to. I will give my consent for the children to go, but not if they are to live in an apartment or boarding house in London or any other similar place. My reasons are this: (a) I don't like their education being interrupted, (b) I don't like the idea of their living in squalid and crowded conditions, (c) there is a surplus of women in England at present and unless they are considerably more clever than the average English girls they have scant hopes of competing either in the marriage market, the labour market, or the professional market, (d) I have some hopes of Fay taking up medicine in New Zealand, but have my doubts about her doing the same thing in England.

Frank said that Mary was 'exceptionally unbiased and honest' and that he would be happy to abide by her decision. He finished by reassuring Margaret:

> I hope you will understand that I don't want to thwart you in any way. My plans for the children are not very grandiose, but I do want them to be able to earn their own living comfortably, so that they will not have to marry just in order to get away from home or to have some one to keep them. I enclose cheque and will send on a further one during January. I hope you had a good holiday. I will meet the children on the train on the morning of 5 January.
>
> Yours Frank.

There was a PS to the letter to say that he and Edna were going to Wellington for seven days on 1 February and that they could bring the children back with them as far as Wellington; alternatively the children could stay longer in Coromandel, whichever they preferred.

Shortly afterwards Mary received a letter from Margaret asking for advice. Margaret said she was pleased they had been in New Zealand during the war but felt that England would give the children more stimulation and a better education. As for herself she said 'there is no literary market here and I have no academic qualifications for a job in the Government service'. She had a dependent mother who was not entitled to a pension in New Zealand and no family around. She felt she could get a good job 'in advertising, publishing, making movies or writing fiction; or even, if Providence were willing, doing something useful'. As an alternative to coming to England Margaret said she would start an eating house in New Zealand, if Mary felt the children were better off staying put. She said she had no support from Frank except the money awarded from the court, which Frank had raised to fifteen pounds a month and he had also agreed to pay for some of the children's clothes. Margaret continued to paint a picture of their future lives:

> Jane and Fay have nothing to look forward to here but a fifth-rate university in which all the students, who are not members of Church communities, spend their leisure drowning their frustration in beer and promiscuity … Jane and Fay will be as comfortable as the rest here, but they will remain fundamentally unused. They are not at home among New Zealanders and the longer they stay here the more difficult will it be for them to feel at home in England.

Margaret ended the letter by saying:

> Please don't on any account alter your opinion because you think I would be happier in England. It is in the nature of things that I can be well off only where the children are well off. The horrors of England at the present time may be beyond anything I have conceived.

Eventually it was agreed that Margaret would return to England with her mother Nona, and Jane and Fay. Fay wrote poignantly in her autobiography:

> I waved goodbye for ever to my father from the bow of the ferry out of Wellington which would take us back to Christchurch. He'd never come with us so far south before. He was crying. I watched his figure on the dock grow smaller and smaller, and I knew quite well I would never see him again, and knew he knew it too.

Before they left Frank wrote again to Margaret[8] in August 1946 to say he was sorry not to be able to come down to Christchurch and see them off. He enclosed a cheque for fifteen pounds and asked for an address in England to which he could send further money. He wrote:

> Will you please see that the children write and let me know what is happening. I hope you have a pleasant trip … I also hope you find the happiness you deserve in England. I'm afraid you've had an intellectually lean time in this country, but you *can* write and you should be able to keep on doing so with ever growing success in England. I don't know anything of your plans, whether you intend to marry, whether you hope to keep on writing, or what? As you know I feel vaguely disturbed about the children's future, but you have always been such an excellent mother that I don't think I need worry overmuch. I don't want to see them caught in the working metropolitan maelstrom and become members of the monstrous regiment of working women taking the tube from Ealing or Acton to the City six times a week and wearing galoshes to keep their feet dry. I would like an academic career for them if possible!
>
> All luck and happiness to you - Frank

Margaret managed to procure a passage on the *RMS Rangitiki*. They went via Panama and then up to Halifax, Nova Scotia, to pick up passengers. Amongst the passengers was an entire football team from the north of England, who were returning home, and two Welsh stowaways.[9] Fay said that the ship had been used as a troop carrier in the war and had not been converted back to civilian use so the journey was very uncomfortable and crowded. She described the wonderful sight of porpoises and swordfish in the sea but contrasted it with the outbreak on board of conjunctivitis and dysentery and lice. The *Rangitiki* docked in London on 22 September 1946, Fay's fifteenth birthday. They returned to war-ravaged London and rationing.

Their first winter back in London was spent in a rented single room in Belsize Park where the three of them had to 'live, cook, eat and sleep and use a communal bathroom down the corridor' as Fay wrote. Margaret's mother went to stay with her son Selwyn. Fay said that Selwyn had offered to buy them a house but Margaret had not wanted to be indebted to anyone and refused. It was the coldest winter for decades and they had to stay in bed to keep warm.

Margaret then managed to find accommodation for herself and the children in St John's Wood and in March 1947 wrote to Isabel to tell her about it. She was employed as housekeeper to the owners, a professor and his violinist wife. She said the children were well and happy. Fay, in her book, appeared to disagree saying 'how long ago the golden age of Coromandel seemed'.

Margaret found a new job and moved again, this time to a flat in Victoria which they shared with a bachelor teacher who really liked Margaret, but for whom she had no time. Mary wrote in her diary that when she visited them at the Victoria flat, Margaret's mother told her (when Margaret was answering the phone) that Margaret had received an offer of marriage.

Meanwhile, back in Auckland life continued for Frank and Edna and on 14 August 1946 Alan acquired a little sister. Edna proudly described my birth in a letter dated September 1946 to Isabel. She wrote:

> My dear Mamma Isabel
>
> Well, the pretty little girl arrived safely and weighed 7 lbs 4oz. She is to be named Barbara Isabel, which I hope she will like. She looks as though she may have gingery hair, though it is much too early to tell yet. Her eyes are dark blue and she has a very fair skin. She is full of fun and gave me a proper smile before she was four weeks old, so is a very bold little girl. Alan loves his little sister and of course has to be restrained from pulling her fingers and toes and worshipping her generally. He doesn't show any sign of jealously, but of course we were prepared for that and haven't let him have his nose put out of joint in any way.

Edna went on to say that she hoped they would be able to bring the children over to see them before long and that she wanted to meet Isabel herself. Edna continued, saying that she would not like to make a long trip without the children as 'they are too charming to leave'. She said they were planning to go for a weekend's fishing on the shores of Lake Taupo as Frank had the use of 'a very fine fishing rod'. Edna said how much they were missing Jane and Fay who used to spend their summer holidays with them. They had done this for the last several years during which time Frank and Edna had watched them 'grow into very nice girls'. Edna thought that Isabel would like them very much as 'they have charming manners and are very thoughtful for others'. She said that Frank had been producing Ibsen's *Ghosts* for a small amateur dramatic society. (This was The Phoenix Society of Auckland; the production was later also put on in Hamilton.)

Previously Frank had produced *Peer Gynt* for the Auckland University Dramatic Club in June 1946, 'complete with ballet and scenery'. It was a massive undertaking and, according to the critics, pretty successful. My mother kept the scrap book full of pictures and reviews. The *New Zealand Listener* of 28 June printed a review, which said that several years ago a group of enthusiasts in Christchurch were thinking about producing *Peer Gynt* and went as far as casting the play before giving up. Since then, it said, 'no one had come near to producing Ibsen's fantasy in New Zealand until this month'. The reviewer went on to say that it had opened on a wet June night and the hall was only half-full but that it ran for another six nights to full houses, and that the last night was very well received, even, as an independent observer had reported to him, 'to the overflowing audience hanging from the rafters'. He continued:

> Whatever may be said in criticism of this production only praise may be said of the courage shown by those responsible for attempting it. It was explained to me that cold water, hail, snow and ice were all thrown on the idea of tackling such a producer's nightmare, and that finally the work of producing it was wished on to Dr Frank Birkinshaw, who had first suggested the idea.

According to the *New Zealand Listener*, Frank said 'it seemed to me it was time a group like the University Drama Club produced a mature play, and that's just how I regard *Peer Gynt*'. Frank was quoted further:

> But the important thing is to put it on straight without a lot of mumbo-jumbo and straining after-effects, in fact without approaching Ibsen with held breath as if he's a god or some strange and awesome being. It doesn't matter a fig whether it's a morality play or a social conscience play or a romantic fantasy or what it is; the thing is to put it on and put it on fast and with as much liveliness and as little reverence as possible. I'm sick to death of this attitude of reverence and breath-holding towards Shakespeare and Ibsen and Eugene O'Neill. Let's get on with the plays, and the dramatists and demi-gods can look after themselves.

The reviewer had spent some time before the opening night looking at the scene-painting operations and talking to the wardrobe mistress and had attended one of the rehearsals, and realised the hard work involved in producing the play, which had in the end even made a profit. He watched the stage manager at work and Frank told him:

> My stage manager is a really magnificent organiser. Of course some things take longer than others to organise. Some properties have taken about 18 days and others, cushions and things like that, have taken about 18 hours. But I announced that we needed a keg of beer or a beer keg for the wedding scene and the response was quite marvellous. That keg of beer was not only organised but actually present on the stage in exactly 18 minutes. Oh no, not a beer keg, a keg of beer, all present and correct for the meantime.

The reviewer said that he heard some of the audience 'grumbling about the bicycle, complaining that this was an unwarranted liberty to take with Ibsen, who instructs that Peer and the Woman in Green shall ride off the stage on a gigantic pig'. However, he rationalised that a 'bicycle built for two may be just about the 1946 equivalent of a gigantic pig with a rope on its neck in

1867'. It also gave the undergraduates some fun and then 'removed them from the stage with envious speed'. He finished by saying that the production stood, 'whatever criticisms may be made of details, as an important event in drama in New Zealand'. He said that the significant thing was not that it was a pretty successful venture, but that it was a venture at all.

The New Zealand Observer also carried a review which ended by saying 'the whole production bore the marks of thought and care, and one's primary thought must be to welcome the presentation of serious drama of this kind in Auckland, where Heaven knows it is badly needed'.

Frank continued to do radio broadcasting in Auckland, as he had earlier done in Christchurch in the 1930s, and I managed to obtain from Radio New Zealand, from their sound archives, two recordings Frank had made. One was a series of the Brains Trust, with Rex Fairburn, the poet, Vernon Brown, the architect and Professor Musgrove, an actor and English lecturer at Auckland University. The second recording was Frank relating stories of the Coromandel. It was quite extraordinary to hear his voice.

Frank on right in a radio recording studio, Auckland, 1940s

Frank also drew up a proposal to solve the traffic problem in Auckland which he called The Birkinshaw Plan. The problem, he pointed out, was due to a lack of foresight twenty years previously and he suggested that long term planning was now essential.[10]

My christening took place at the Whenuapai Air Base Chapel on the outskirts of Auckland and my godmother Poppy, who attended the occasion, told me in a letter many years later that she remembered the padre as being a delightful rebel. Poppy also told me something of my parents' lives in New Zealand. She said what a wonderful thing my parents had done in looking after Nell and her son Johnnie. She said that they had continued to live with us for a few years until they returned to Coromandel to be with Nell's family. Poppy called Frank and Edna 'a wonderful pair of people' and said how lovely they were together and that they were both very good doctors, Edna more wrapped up in her medicine than Frank who had many non-medical interests. She said they were the type of medical practitioner that has vanished and that 'their patients were far more important than the fees'. She called them both unconventional and said:

> Some of their parties were marvellous – all sorts, all creeds, but all delightful. I am sorry that you were not able to enjoy their life. They were darlings and speaking with the people who remember them, you find in every one a love of the memories of them.

Edna wrote to Isabel in July 1947 thanking her for some table napkin rings she had sent them which were just in time for their seventh wedding anniversary which was the following week. She said they were trying to organise a short trip to Australia as they had not had a proper holiday for about four years. She went on:

> Alan is just three and at the age of thrills and excitement with every new thing, so would enjoy a trip on a boat, though I think he would be somewhat terrified at going on board, he is always chary of new experiences, but usually likes them in the end. Barbara will be a year on 14 August so won't be much trouble to take about, she is a good wee thing and is now crawling about and cutting her fifth tooth.

Edna said they had had a spate of concerts recently and some good films so there was plenty going on. They were still sending food parcels to Isabel, as she finished the letter by saying another one would soon be on its way.

Frank sent two letters[11] to Margaret in England in August 1947. The first was to explain he was having technical difficulties with the bank sending her money but had telegraphed her twenty pounds that day. He told her that he would continue sending money so long as the children needed it and would also try and help with their academic fees if he could manage it. He said 'if Jane shows any particular bent for any occupation such as potting or anything else, so long as it is not escapism, I'll be equally happy to carry on'. He still hoped Fay would do medicine. He said he had been overworking and had not been very well and not had a holiday for a long time, and that although he was working as hard as was possible, rising prices and taxation kept him down to the same level'. He said he hoped to get away for four weeks at the end of the year. He continued:

> I hope you are getting plenty to eat! I imagine you are. At least you seem to be in comfortable quarters, and I suppose monotony of diet is compensated for by the somewhat higher intellectual level of companionship you are likely to find in England. It should all be very good for the children to realise that New Zealand is a very ponderous country.
>
> The general feeling here is that there is going to be a financial bust-up some time in 1948 and we all feel sad at the recent English newsprint cuts. The days when the *Sunday Times* and *Observer* had some 24 pages or more, seem very long ago.
>
> The cutting down of newsprint has weakened the government in New Zealand eyes. One would imagine that a stopping of football pools would release more potential production.

He finished by telling Margaret about the family:

> The two infants do well. Alan is a nice little boy, thin and wiry; the baby is nearly a year and a very healthy child. They both appear remarkably average. Edna is getting together a specialist paediatric practice.

The second letter,[12] in response to one from Margaret, said how pleased Frank was to hear that Jane had passed her matric. He said he and Jane had an agreement that once she passed her exam he would 'not try and exercise any more moral control over her actions'. If, however, she would take advice from him he would like her to go to university and take some professional course. Frank commented:

> You appear to have handled Jane's affair with great tact. I'm quite sure that you're likely to frown on too-early marriages. I'm sorry for her. Please tell her that she'll find that satisfactory loves are so much more satisfactory than unsatisfactory ones.

Frank said he had sent off a food parcel containing 'five pounds of honey, dripping, chocolate and various other things' and that he had sent a similar one to his parents in Barnt Green.

Jane did in fact get married soon after to Reuben (John) Dodd, much to the dismay of her family. She was by this time nineteen. However, she returned home after only eight weeks and said she wanted a divorce.

Frank and Edna managed to get to Australia for Christmas and stayed at Callandoon in Queensland with Edna's father and sister Mavis. By that time Edna's brother Tony was also living at Callandoon with his wife Olive and their daughter Gillie. Tony and Olive had married in August 1942. Edna and family travelled to Australia by ship, the voyage taking about three and a half days. The ship was the *Wanganella* and I still remember the ship's label on one of our old trunks. On one occasion we travelled on a flying boat which took about ten hours. The flying boats only took a handful of passengers who would usually dress up for the occasion as it was considered a luxurious mode of travel. My brother remembered one journey on the flying boat when it had to return to New Zealand after developing an engine problem half way through the flight. It took off again after about six hours and after another ten hours of flying time came in to land in Sydney harbour in the dark; he remembers to this day that view being the most spectacular he had ever seen, before or since, of the lights over the famous bridge and the harbour, through the spray of the water on the windows.

Barbara at Callandoon, Christmas 1947

Right:
Frank and Edna
Christmas 1947

Below:
Barbara and Alan at
Callandoon

Frank sent a letter to his mother sometime towards the end of 1948 which gave her the latest news:

> My dear Mother
>
> I'm sorry I haven't written before this. Everything goes on smoothly here; Edna is working hard and so am I. Edna, I think I told you, is on the Auckland Hospital staff now as Paediatrician and is also on the staff of the Karitane Children's Hospital so is kept fully employed. Alan and Barbara are well. Barbara is talking – and how she talks. Only single words yet, but no stopping.

He said there had been a polio epidemic so the children had been kept away from other children for the past eight months. They were planning to go with the children to a hotel in the National Park in January for two weeks, where there would be trout fishing, golf, walks and two active volcanoes, so he thought they would have a good time. He said that Alan got a tricycle for his fourth birthday which he seemed to live on.

In July 1949 Edna bought a plot of land in Victoria Avenue, which was also in Remuera, and sold the Lucerne Road house. They commissioned their friend and architect Vernon Brown to build them a new home. While they were waiting for the house to be built they moved in to a rented one in Meadowbank Avenue, just nearby. After our visit to New Zealand in 1998 and having seen the houses, I often wondered why they sold their beautiful home in Lucerne Road with its stunning views over Auckland. I was to discover the answer several years later.

Barbara and Alan

Above: Edna and Barbara, Lucerne Road

Left: Barbara on steps of house, Lucerne Road

Above: Edna, Barbara and Alan, Auckland Zoo

Below: Alan, Barbara and Poppy

Alan and Barbara on back garden wall of Lucerne Road

Alan, Barbara and Johnnie

Alan

Chapter Thirteen

Sheona

When Frank was about four he developed diphtheria. His sister Sheona was two at the time and their mother Isabel was pregnant with Mary. The family was living in Bradford in the suburb of Manningham, very near where Herbert's parents lived. Isabel was depressed and finding it hard to cope with the children, particularly as Herbert was difficult and demanding, so Sheona was sent to stay with Isabel's eldest sister Jane. Jane was married to Dr William Baigent; they had no children of their own and were only too pleased to help out Isabel and have Sheona to look after.

Jane and William Baigent lived in the Yorkshire market town of Northallerton at Dunston House, which they had named after Dunston Lodge, the lunatic asylum which Jane and Isabel's father, William Garbutt, had owned; Jane and most of her siblings were born in Dunston Lodge in Durham. Jane Baigent was born Jane Thornton Garbutt and Sheona had also been given the forenames Jane Thornton, although the family mostly called her Sheona. Herbert and Isabel had a fourth child, Bill, in 1905, who took up yet more of Isabel's time and energy. As the years passed Sheona spent more and more time with her aunt and uncle until they virtually adopted her; or indeed, as Sheona said, she adopted them. She described herself in her autobiography *Swan Feather*[1] as 'an only child with two brothers and one sister'. The Baigents would dearly have loved to adopt Sheona formally but they were too frightened to broach the subject with Herbert in case he decided to take Sheona back, and in the event Sheona grew up happily with her new parents and always referred to them as her mother and father. She described how she felt about her adoptive family: 'I think one father and one mother and one little girl is best.'

Jane Thornton Birkinshaw was born in 1901 at 6 The Terrace, Ovingham on Tyne near Newcastle. She was nicknamed Jennie, but did not like that name and later chose to be called Sheona, which is the gaelic name for Jane. As she was brought up by her aunt and uncle, rather than her natural parents, Sheona's childhood contrasted greatly to that of her siblings. She lived in a privileged world; silver-plated dishes on the table and always plenty to fill them, a cook and a house full of books. There were also two maids in Dunston House and other servants who came to light the boiler, wash the clothes and do the ironing. Dr Baigent was a respected physician and surgeon in Northallerton, which had its own hospital. He had a chauffeur to drive him round the countryside while visiting patients, and Sheona would often go out with him on his rounds. Dr Baigent was later to earn an OBE for his services to medicine.

Sheona

William Baigent's passion was fishing and he taught Sheona to fish so well that eventually he declared her to be better than himself. Sheona had learned to fish at the age of seven or eight when it had become possible to find waders small enough to fit her. She was taken fishing in Scotland by the Baigents and met and played with the author (of *Wind in the Willows*) Kenneth Grahame's son Mouse, who was tragically to commit suicide while a student at Oxford in 1920. Sheona was quite a tom-boy and thought nothing of riding bare-back over the heather or swimming naked in the river. She had governesses to teach her, and at the age of twelve went to boarding school at Skellfield near Ripon. Sheona told an amusing story of war time at school when she was fourteen, when her handsome cousin Ernest Wimberley of the Gordon Highlanders came to visit her, and he asked the headmistress whether he might take Sheona out to tea. The headmistress replied 'Captain Wimberley, I have the honour of my school to consider' and he responded 'and I have the honour of my Regiment'.

Sheona had an idyllic childhood, apart from the insecurities bequeathed by her natural parents, by whom she felt neither wanted nor needed. Nor did she ever have any strong daughterly attachment to Isabel. Sheona's view of her natural father was that all the Birkinshaws worked hard and made money with the exception of Herbert, and she only came to realise in later life what a hard time Herbert had given her siblings and also her mother Isabel. Herbert's niece Freda Scales had married a wealthy baronet and Herbert was always put out that his children did not 'marry well'.

Sheona felt that because Herbert had been sent away to Sligo to his mother's family during his school holidays he had been an unhappy child and that, perhaps, had made him the way he was. When Sheona was older, Herbert showed her a photo of himself in bow tie and boater; she thought he looked quite dashing, and for the first time understood why Isabel had married him.

Jane Baigent spent time reading to Sheona and made clothes for her, including her evening dresses. They would go blackberrying together on their cycles and tobogganing in the winter. One day the family went to a garden party in their newly-acquired car, wearing dust coats and veils over their hats to keep off the dust from the road, and the car broke down on the way. All the other guests passed by in their carriages looking frightfully superior. Sheona recalled that the speed limit for cars was twenty-eight miles an hour and the police would set traps to try and catch anyone who was speeding. These traps were manned by one policeman who would hide behind a haystack ready to jump out and accost any offending motorist.

Sheona saw her brother Frank regularly throughout their childhood, particularly when her parents, as she always referred to Jane and William Baigent, went away on holiday. She and Frank and Mary would be sent to stay with their grandmother Elizabeth Garbutt at Elizabeth's rented house in Ilkley, or at another one she stayed at in West Rainton in Northumberland. They also went to 30 Highbury in Newcastle where Granny Elizabeth lived most of the time with her two unmarried daughters Gus and Madge. There was a four-poster bed at Highbury and Frank and Sheona would produce plays using the bed as a stage. During their childhood she and Frank made a pact that when they were married they would always look out for each other's children, but Frank said that as the eldest, *his* children had to inherit the names Jane and Frank Thornton. (In the event it was Sheona's daughter Anne who acquired the Thornton name. Frank called his eldest daughter Jane but not Thornton and appointed Sheona as Jane's godmother.) Sheona was very fond of Frank and was touched when Frank told her that he had spent an hour and a half searching in the mud for a letter 'from a mere sister', as Sheona termed herself, which she had written to him during his time in the trenches. She told me that after the First War, and most likely after he had received his commission in the Territorial Army in 1926, Frank went to levees at Buckingham Palace. Levees were formal receptions held in the morning by the Sovereign. Frank must have had tails and white tie to wear at dances and on formal occasions, although Sheona always considered Frank bohemian because he did not wear a hat!

Sheona left school when she was seventeen and worked as a volunteer with the war wounded in the Rutson hospital in Northallerton. She was very active on the social scene and went to a hunt ball at Raby Castle in Durham, where there were dowagers in tiaras, boars' heads and champagne; it was the first event of its kind after the war. This was followed by the Bedale Hunt Ball, so Sheona was certainly moving in the 'right circles'. Occasionally Frank would accompany her to balls and point to points when he was home visiting the family. Sheona was invited to Switzerland with some friends of the Baigents, which was the first time she had been taken abroad. She was asked to bring a man with her to Switzerland to make the numbers even, so she took her first cousin Oliver Lodge. Sheona and Oliver had always regarded each other as 'a special person' and Oliver had even kept a letter she wrote to him from school.

However, Sheona had already met Grafton, an undergraduate at Brasenose College, Oxford, while fishing in Scotland. They shared a love of literature. He took her to dances and she described him as a glittering partner, and observed that a girl with a glamorous partner was more acceptable than a single one. He proposed to her at a ball beside the lily pond at Worcester College, Oxford, in June 1922, and Sheona said neither yes nor no to him. She described it as a weekend of glamour and misery: 'How can one know at that age?' She promised to think about it, but he said if it meant no, he could never see her again and Sheona could not bear that. In her heart she knew the truth was she was really in love with Oliver whom she wished to marry; unfortunately he had not got round to asking her!

The romance with Grafton continued with more declarations of love from him. A letter dated 23 April 1923 read:

> We had such a wonderful day today that it didn't seem so bad saying goodbye, but now I think I am sadder than I've ever been and miss you more than usual. But it is because I love you more. My darling I do want to say good night to you and to kiss you. I love you dearest mine, much more than I've ever done. I shall always love you.

The last letter she received from Grafton dated 23 June, 1923, read:

> I've absolutely nothing to tell you as a few hours ago I posted my last letter. Goodnight my own Sheona. God bless you darling.
>
> All my love – Your Grafton.

The amorous wooings were summed up in *Swan Feather*:

> Grafton encouraged me to read *The Canterbury Tales*, Malory's *Le Morte d'Arthur*, Donne, Herbert, Dryden, Pope. Oliver, on his way to see me, learned Keats's *Ode on a Grecian Urn*, many Shakespeare sonnets and Tennyson's *Ulysses*. One of them gave me a hat, the other a set of golf clubs that arrived by the same post. Father, justly irate because I was uncertain, capricious and moody, accused me of being like a film star. He could not think of anything worse to say about anyone.

Sheona eventually broke the news to Grafton that she could not marry him and he was naturally very hurt. He never married, and Sheona said the one thing she regretted in life was breaking his heart. Sheona mused on the reason for her decision, believing that 'Grafton required me to be glamorous. Oliver liked me exactly as I was.' She felt grateful to Grafton for all that she had learned from him and hoped he would find someone that would make him happier than she could. Sheona kept all Grafton's letters in one side of a wooden tea caddy where they remain to this day; the other side of the caddy contained those from Oliver.[2]

The tea caddy
with Grafton and Oliver's letters

Oliver's proposal eventually came in the form of a telegram: 'Marry me in Edinburgh on Thursday.' Sheona described in *Swan Feather* what happened next:

> I handed it [the telegram] to Mother. She made no observation, but stalked out of the dining room. When she returned, having crossed the road to the shop that sold corsets, violins and had a telephone, she said 'I have sent an answer'. 'What did you say?' I asked. 'Certainly not,' was her reply. 'I signed it Sheona.'

Oliver Lodge, who was eight years older than Sheona, was the son of Jane Baigent's sister Winifred.[3] As Isabel was also Winifred's sister and Sheona's natural mother, Sheona and Oliver were almost 'twice first cousins'. Winifred had married Dr Samuel Lodge; they had five sons, and the children of the two families had known each other all their lives.

Oliver's letters to Sheona were full of fun. One dated 3 April 1924 talked about 'getting married to the dearest girl in the whole world'. Oliver, Noll as he called himself, said he was astounded that Sheona's parents took the news of their engagement so calmly. He went on:

> Tell Uncle Willie[4] that when you are married you hope to be able to go and fish with him for weeks and weeks on end – in fact if you can do anything to liven up the drab life that you will have, I shall simply die of gratitude … Lionel [Oliver's brother] is very concerned at my capacity to look after you properly. He thinks I shall have to be very careful that you are not overworked.
>
> I send you 4¾ kisses and if you do not mind waiting for the balance until Friday, hope to be able to make up the difference then.
>
> Your loving lover - Noll

Another undated letter from Oliver read:

> My own dearest and nearest and nicest and bonniest, but rather far away, by far the biggest part of my heart, life sized embodiment of the most perfect little miniature that was ever painted, Sheona, whom I, Oliver, do love.
>
> Just a line to tell you that I am counting the seconds until I see you.

He told Sheona he had been to see the Cresswells, who were friends of the family, and compared the daughters to Sheona:

> I sat next to Primrose at dinner and felt so happy and pleased with myself because I had you. You have Ianthe's love of the country, Ruth's sympathy and understanding, Joan's cheeriness, when not

> depressed, and Primrose's prettiness multiplied by ten and two fifths, and rather a pretty figure besides.

He ended the letter by saying 'I love you between and during each breath … and am really and truly and thoroughly thankful because you are you'.

A letter dated 5 May from Oliver in London poured more adulation on Sheona:

> Dear Apple Blossom
>
> It is thoughtful of the authorities to ring church bells in London on Sunday mornings because they remind me of you.
>
> With all the love in the universe, Your wretchedly unworthy but incredibly fortunate lover - Noll

Another letter dated 17 May was written from the train 'between tunnels, Halifax to Bradford' and commented on Sheona's success at catching the most fish on her latest fishing trip. He continued:

> I am counting the seconds which lengthen into hours and the days which seem like weeks and the weeks which seem like years. I am beginning to fear that I shall be an old, old man before I see you again. Will you still be voting for me when you see me again and still imagine me as the nice kind grizzly you like and I should like to be? If you do we shall have a heavenly time. We will go to London and not bother particularly about anything. If we have a lot of money we will go to the Savoy or the Cecil and if we are 'stoney' well …. you can easily live on kisses.
>
> Your deaf, dumb and incapable but desperately happy lover – Noll.

A second letter, also dated 17 May, thanked Sheona for the trout she had sent him and mentioned the post he was applying for at the Bradford hospital and that he was worried he would not get it. Then he said 'what is money when, in the glittering language of the Oriental sage, I shall never wake up in the morning without discovering a treasure'. Another undated letter declared 'no endearments could express my love for you so what is the use of them'.

And yet more description as to how much he missed her:

> You have no idea how desolate the three weeks since I saw you last have been. I have been prowling about getting thinner and thinner and losing weight at every post in which there was no letter from you.

He then said that his mother had pointed out that perhaps Sheona was waiting for one from him. Eventually the long-awaited letter arrived and he said that he was 'overjoyed to find that you are still fond about me'.

On 19 May 1924 a telegram arrived addressed to Sheona which said that Oliver had been appointed Consulting Opthalmologist at the City of Bradford Hospital. He had also got the same appointment at St Luke's Hospital in Halifax. On hearing the news Sheona wrote to Oliver:

> Noll darling. I do think you are wonderful. Won't it be lovely for me to have a thoroughly self-satisfied and complacent husband to go for a honeymoon with. I will still be voting for you when I see you again, and you are still my very dear nice kind grizzly aren't you? … I don't care about clothes or furniture, I just want you … I still like you even more than fishing.

Oliver replied:

> My own bonnie wee lamb
>
> Just a line to say that I love you much more than you think I do, even if you can give a free reign to your imagination. I even like you better than I liked eating that enormous fish you sent me.

Oliver and Sheona were married at Lamesley Church on 24 June 1924 and had their reception at Farnacres in Durham, the home of Isabella Archer, one of the Garbutt cousins. Most of Sheona's family were at the wedding except her brother Frank, who was at that time studying medicine in London, and her sister Mary, also a student in London, although their brother Bill, then nineteen, was there. Another absentee from the wedding was Oliver's father Dr Lodge, who for some reason chose not to come. A stranger came up to Sheona after the wedding and gave her a kiss on the cheek; she was surprised to learn that it was her real father Herbert whom she had not recognised. Oliver and Sheona honeymooned in London where Oliver ate his dinners at the Inner Temple as he was also reading for the Bar because he thought it might be useful! They went to live in Halifax where Oliver's father had his consulting rooms. Halifax was an industrial town with mills belching out black smoke and was quite a change from what Sheona was used to, but she soon settled down in her role as surgeon's wife. A year after their marriage their first child Anne was born and ten years later another daughter, Fiona, arrived on the scene.

Sheona and Oliver frequently travelled to the Continent and on one occasion went on holiday to Paris. There were only three passengers on the plane and as the engines warmed up ready for take-off Sheona noticed that the door was wide open so she got up and locked it. The plane began to taxi across the field and suddenly stopped; there was great excitement when the crew realised that Sheona had locked the pilot out. It was quite a common occurrence for the pilot to leap on at the last minute, rather like a bus conductor.

Oliver and Sheona went to Germany several times; Oliver always combined his holidays with some work in the hospitals in the city they were visiting. They were in Germany in 1936 at the time of the Olympic Games, staying at the famous Adlon Hotel in Berlin. It was full of film stars and also a Maharajah with his entourage, and they danced with the Costa Rican Ambassador and his daughter. Hitler was appearing in the locality and they rushed out to see him but were arrested before they caught a glimpse of him. Oliver, thanks to his knowledge of the language, secured their release. Sheona and Oliver were quite naive about politics at the time and did not realise the significance of what was happening in Germany. In 1938 they planned a visit to Vienna and when they got to Victoria Station there were notices up saying 'Hitler invades Austria; people go there at their own risk'. They went nonetheless. They got to Innsbruck to find their hotel had been taken over by the army and theirs was the only table in the restaurant without a swastika on it. When they went to call on the surgeons they had come to visit, they found them gone; they had all been arrested. On the return journey they travelled on a train with a Jewish man and his wife who were terrified for their lives. The next morning they too had disappeared, having been rounded up by the blackshirts who seemed to be everywhere. Luckily Sheona and Oliver were left alone but when Sheona asked the wagon lit attendant what had happened to the Jewish couple he just shook his head and walked away. They saw tanks and troops everywhere. They had planned to visit Budapest but decided against it; they heard later that the man with whom they were going to stay had committed suicide. They returned home to the relative normality of England.

When the war started Oliver had hoped to obtain a commission in the Air Force as he had held commissions in both the Army and Navy in the First World War and thought he would have a change. However, he was told he was needed in the operating theatres at home looking after the wounded soldiers returning from the front.

After the war Oliver specialised in eye, ear, nose and throat surgery and was a pioneer in brain surgery. He was the first to plant radon seeds in tumours of the pituatry gland. He was a founder fellow of the International College of Surgeons and was invited as guest speaker to conferences throughout the world. One year he and Sheona went to Spain for a conference where they met Franco and his daughter at a party; they were told beforehand not to discuss politics. Oliver later went to South America for a conference, where he met Eva Peron, who, he said, was very beautiful.[5]

Wedding of Sheona and Oliver, 1924
at Farnacres, the home of Isabella Archer

Back row standing (from left to right): Rose and William Garbutt, the two Miss Dodgsons (relatives of Lewis Carroll), Dr Dick Garbutt and wife Margaret, two unknown ladies, Oliver and Sheona, Gus Garbutt, cousin Grace Howard, unknown lady, Herbert Birkinshaw, the Vicar of Lamesley and wife, Sam Johnson (husband of Alwyn, née Garbutt), Mary Thomson (née Garbutt)

Middle row seated: Madge Garbutt, Dr William Baigent, Isabella Archer, Kathleen Yeoman (Sheona's daughter Anne's godmother), Jane Baigent (née Garbutt), Mary Elizabeth Garbutt, Winifred Lodge (née Garbutt), Isabel Birkinshaw (née Garbutt), Aunt Dora Baigent

Front row sitting on grass: Bill Birkinshaw (son of Herbert and Isabel), Eleanor Martin (schoolfriend of Sheona), Dr Durham Lodge (best man and brother of Oliver), Malcolm Garbutt (son of Dr Dick Garbutt), Alwyn Johnson (daughter of William and Rose Garbutt), Rosalind (Ronnie) Garbutt (daughter of Dr Dick Garbutt), Lionel Lodge (brother of Oliver)

(See Garbutt tree 3 for Garbutt family, chapter 5)

Chapter Fourteen

Mary

It was a strange feeling to be sitting in the Archive Library of Churchill College, Cambridge, looking through my Aunt Mary's personal papers.[1] What was more extraordinary was to find some letters my parents had written to her and to her mother Isabel, over fifty years previously. My Aunt Mary, Frank's younger sister, married, as her second husband, Michael Stewart who became a Labour MP and then Foreign Secretary in the Wilson Government, and eventually a Life Peer. I met Mary and Michael on several occasions after we came back to England but I never warmed to them, particularly Mary, and I knew very little about her life, so what I discovered was a revelation.

I only came across this information by chance, as one day I was idly googling Michael's name and found that, after his death, all his personal and official papers had been lodged with the Churchill Archives Centre. I then began to wonder what had become of Mary's personal effects; she died before Michael and they had no children, so I assumed that all her papers and photographs would have been thrown out. I rang Michael's nephew to ask him whether he knew if any of Mary's family photographs had survived, and he said that the College had contacted his family and asked for Michael's papers, so that they could be kept for posterity and looked at by historians and researchers. I contacted the Archives Centre and asked them whether there were any of Mary's papers amongst Michael's collection and they said there were some personal documents belonging to Mary in the collection, but they had no idea what they were, and that I was very welcome to come up and have a look if I wished. Needless to say I accepted the offer with alacrity.

When I arrived at the College, expecting that I might find a couple of family photos at the most, I was extremely surprised to discover that Mary had left thirty-eight boxes of personal documents, letters, photos and diaries. For me it was an Aladdin's cave, a treasure trove, as I had thought that all her letters would have been destroyed; especially after what I found there. I checked again with Michael's nephew, and he assured me that Michael, before he died, had asked that both sets of papers be placed in the public domain.

I spent the next three months travelling weekly to Cambridge from London. Nothing in Mary's boxes was catalogued so I was randomly given letters to look at, a small pile at a time. When I came across letters from Michael to Mary I would go up the next week and ask to look in Michael's personal letters and would search for Mary's reply to particular questions or comments he had made. The days between visits became ones of eager anticipation as to what I would find on my next visit. Many of the letters my grandmother Isabel had written to Mary had been preserved and, even more amazingly, a letter from my mother written from New Zealand to Isabel, announcing my birth.

Mary was born Mary Elizabeth Henderson Birkinshaw in Bradford on 8 May 1903. She went to the High School for Girls in Birmingham, which came under the umbrella of the Foundation Schools of King Edward V1, in September 1913. Her termly fees started at four pounds rising to seven pounds by the time she left in 1923. During Mary's time at school the family moved to Hall Green in Birmingham and finally Alvechurch. She left school at the age of twenty, and then won a scholarship to Bedford College where she graduated with a BA in Philosophy in 1928. She went on to have a very fulfilling career.

Bill and Mary

Mary became a lecturer for the Workers' Educational Association (WEA), their ethos being to help ordinary people to aspire to more than ordinary achievements. At the same time, at the beginning of the war, she served as Senior Marshal for the St Pancras air raid shelter and worked in the hospital wards in Brentford. She joined the WAAF between 1941 and 1945 and was a psychiatric assistant in County Down during the latter part of the war, returning to the London Headquarters in 1944.

After the war she returned to the WEA as a tutor until 1964. She was a JP in London from 1949 and she was appointed Chairman of the East London Juvenile Court for ten years from 1956. She became a member of the Fabian Society Executive between 1950 and 1984, serving as Chairman in 1963-64. In 1966 she was appointed Chairman of the Governors of Charing Cross Hospital and held that appointment until 1974. She was also Honorary President of the Diplomatic Service Wives' Association. In December 1974 her career was crowned and her hard work rewarded when she was created a life peer, taking the title Baroness Stewart of Alvechurch and her place in the House of Lords. Alvechurch was the village where Mary grew up, just outside Birmingham.

However, life was not all easy for Mary. Her childhood was tough; there was not much money in the household, although her father Herbert was just about able to afford her school fees. These, according to the school records, were often paid late. Herbert was not an easy man and was a strict father and intensely disliked by Mary's brother Bill.

Mary kept a diary at certain periods of her life. She made an interesting comment on her life as a child:

> From Yorkshire we went to the Midlands where I recall most vividly we lived in a cottage in a Worcestershire village [Alvechurch] where we pumped water and carried it in buckets and used a privy down the garden and read by candlelight. Downstairs we had the luxury of two oil lamps in the sitting room and kitchen. Today this sounds like real hardship. Then to us as children it was just life and I can't recall feelings of envy for those better off.

Mary also commented about her father, recalling that everyone who knew him thought of him as a 'difficult man'. He had a voice like a 'sergeant-major in the Guards'. She explained how she coped with him:

> My reaction to him was one of avoidance. I returned from school as late as I dared – often doing my homework in the public library. On fine summer nights I slept in a camp bed in the garden where the trees rustling and the owls hooting were less disturbing than my father's voice. My mother was everything my father was not - tactful and with an intuitive grasp of the thoughts of those around her that enabled her to anticipate and avoid distressing situations. Our way of life made us the objects of pity.

Mary said she didn't dislike her father but she thought him one of the most selfish people she had ever known. He never paid the bills until forced to do so and he often bellowed and swore at her; most mornings she was greeted with 'Get up, you dirty little slut', and his bellows often 'followed us down the road to school'. Her mother Isabel had a constant struggle to feed and clothe her children and keep the peace. Mary was terrified of him although she says he treated her better than he treated her brothers as he wasn't so jealous of her. When her brother Frank, my father, was about seven and Mary was about two, and their mother was in bed shortly after Bill had been born, Herbert decided to leave home and 'go in search of a fortune in Bradford'. This would have been about 1905 when they were living in Gravelly Hill, Birmingham. As Herbert had all the money there was in his pocket and Isabel had none, she got out of bed, packed all the furniture into a van and set off after him to Bradford. Unfortunately there was no money to pay the van men to unload, as Herbert was not forthcoming, so they had to return to their home and find the money from another source in order to pay off the removers. Mary said this was just one of many similar incidents. Isabel's relatives would usually come to her rescue. Mary also had a sister Sheona, but she had been sent away when she was very young to be brought up by one of Isabel's sisters.

On 24 December 1931 Mary married her first husband Robert Goodyear; he was at the time a struggling novelist. They set up home together in Russell Court, in London. The marriage, however, proved to be ill-fated. There were stories that abounded in the family speculating about what had gone wrong, but it was not until I looked through Mary's papers that I discovered the truth. There were many letters in the Churchill Archives written to Mary from her husband Bob, as he was known.

Bob became one of Mary's students in January 1931, when she was lecturing for the WEA; he was at that time living in Luton and she in London. His first letter to her was addressed 'Dear Miss Birkinshaw' and apologised for missing a class. However, his letter revealed his attraction towards her. He wrote that his bad attendance was not caused by her or her presentation of the subject she was teaching, 'honestly I have never listened to anybody with greater pleasure'. He went on:

> I have never before been to a lecture and regretted that the lecturer was a lecturer who had come from high places and was decorated with degrees and things and who was generally shut away from more ordinary people by more or less impossible barriers to obstruct and discourage anybody who thought how nice it would be to know them personally.

He signed the letter 'Yours sincerely – R G Goodyear'.

By April his letters had progressed to 'Dear Mary' and 'Yours Bob'. In June he asked Mary to meet him on the steps of the Tate and said 'the only thing I've got to say to you my girl is – I love you – Bob'. Perhaps he proposed at that meeting as his next letter stated that he knew she had no intention of marrying him. Not deterred he wrote: 'We will be friends,' and added 'but I do desire you to marry me' and said he would 'drop the question and not refer to it again for a long time'. However, he persisted, saying 'you mustn't mind if I continue to call you darling and tell you now and then I adore you, because you are and I do'. He said 'no special significance need attach to the fact'. Bob must have proposed again in August as there was a letter from him to Mary saying 'I note with terrible calm that you will not marry me. Foolishly, perhaps, I add the word "yet".'

Nonetheless, by November Bob had persuaded Mary to marry him. He wrote to her from Luton saying 'I only know that I love you more than I have ever loved anything or anybody ever'. It appeared that Mary's father Herbert had asked them to consider postponing their marriage, probably because he suspected that Bob did not have very good prospects; Bob was at the time an advertisement clerk with the *Luton News*. Bob said about Herbert 'his point about babies is a most important one. And very obvious. We will not have one till we want one.'

By contrast, in his letter of 26 November, Bob wrote that Mary had made a good impression on his family and that 'Dad simply groped for laudatory adjectives' and couldn't imagine how 'I had managed to pick up with such a nice young woman'. And his letter of the next day to Mary:

> Your letter was lovelier than any gift I could conceive of. I was filled with happiness. Does it sometimes frighten you? Do you sometimes say: 'this is too good, too big. Happiness like this doesn't exist. Soon I must wake up?' But when I am reasonable again I know that my fears are foolish. We made it and it is ours to keep.
>
> Always – B.

After they were married, at the end of 1931, Bob and Mary lived in Luton and Bob wrote to her when she had gone away for a few days: 'I was glad to have your letter Mary B. I love you and I love you and I want you home again.' And another letter: 'It seems silly to sit down to write to you when I saw you but two and a half hours ago … I am counting the days before I hear from you.'

Tragically their marriage was not to last as eventually, after a few years, Bob decided he preferred the company of men, although, paradoxically, he continued to declare his love for Mary. It was quite clear that Bob loved Mary passionately and she loved him, as she continued to correspond and meet up with him after they had separated.

In 1934 Mary was working as a tutor for the WEA in Psychology and Sociology at a summer school where she first met Michael Stewart. He was at that time a school teacher and part-time tutor for the WEA in Economics and International Affairs. In his autobiography *Life and Labour*[2] Michael said that from the WEA came 'one unexpected and inestimable blessing'. He and Mary became friends and continued to meet up over the following years.

Michael Stewart was born in Bromley on 6 November 1906. He graduated from St John's College, Oxford, with a first-class BA in Philosophy and was President of the Oxford Union. He taught economics in various schools and at the University of London. During the war he served in the Middle East, joining the Intelligence Corps in 1942 and later transferring to the Army Educational Corps where he was promoted to Captain. In 1945 he became Labour MP for Fulham, which seat he held until 1979. He held various cabinet and shadow cabinet posts over the years, including Education, Foreign Secretary (1965-66 and 1968-70) and Secretary of State for Economic Affairs (1966-67). He became a life peer in July 1979 taking the title Baron Stewart of Fulham.

There were letters in the Churchill Archives from Michael to Mary dating from 1935, but while *their* romance was blossoming there were more letters to Mary from Bob.

One even more lyrical than usual letter from Bob likened Mary to a 'Mozart Sonata, in which a sweet tune rings and modulates and changes, now major now minor, sometimes allegro, sometimes andante cantabile. Always the same sweet tune in many phrases.'

In August 1938 Bob wrote to Mary in London from Luton in his usual vein: 'I was lonely and miserable and wanted to be with you. Just over a week and we're together again. I pine for you.' Another was addressed 'Darling Mary':

> How would it be if we went to the theatre next Saturday night? On second thoughts 'no'. The last time we went to a theatre you slept on my shoulder for the third Act. So no – definitely not. We'll perhaps go out for a little meal and have a quiet evening. I love you – B.

And an intriguing letter whose last paragraph indicated that one of his 'darling' friends was 'just visiting the abortionist'.

Even as late as 1939 he wrote to Mary: 'I love you so much but (and I say this quite detachedly without drama) I have no right to claim you and to insist upon living with you if I am not prepared to be your husband.' And a small card read: 'Dear Mary – My best love to you – and that is something you can believe in – Bob. Come back!' He also wrote: 'Time seems now-a-days no more to be measured by the sun and moon, but by the arrival of your letters.'

In one letter Bob mentioned to Mary, while she was away visiting friends in New York in June 1939, that he had been to visit her mother Isabel. Isabel had mistakenly thought he and some friends had wanted to stay and she had 'prepared beds and met every train during the day. She was lovely and ran about holding a hard-boiled egg.' Of Mary's father Herbert he said 'really I detest him – your Pa'.

Bob's letters were also an interesting reflection of the times. He wrote to Mary in July:

> Last night David [Bob's friend who was a ballet dancer] took me to a 'queer party' in Chelsea. It was given by the son of a Lord. Godfrey Winn [the actor and novelist and one-time lover of Somerset Maugham] was there. I talked to him and he was horrid. Also Anton Dolin [the ballet dancer] whom I liked.

And he added that there was someone else there who looked remarkably like the Duke of Kent 'who was in fact a cousin of the king'. The walls of the room were white and one was lined with mirrors and there were white jars of pink canna lilies. He continued:

> But the big joke, the supreme note of the evening were three stout whores who were paid to be there. They all sat together on a sofa drinking champagne and pretending to be ladies – until the champagne began to work.

In another revealing letter to Mary he said: 'Honestly, I wish I wasn't queer.'

On 2 September 1939, the day before war was officially declared, Bob wrote to Mary who was at that time teaching in Marlborough. He said he had just been sacked by MGM but there was some good news in that a friend of his had written to say 'she puts my two books among the beautiful things one has to be thankful for'. Bob had written two novels by that time, one of which was *I Lie Alone* (1935). He added to the end of the letter: 'Sunday morning. It's come now. I've just heard Chamberlain's speech. David rang up and put his receiver close to the radio.' Chamberlain was then the Conservative Prime Minister and his speech was the declaration of war on Germany. A coalition government was formed and Winston Churchill was made First Lord of the Admiralty, and in May became Prime Minister. Although Mary was an ardent socialist and never liked Chamberlain, she did admire Churchill.

In March Bob wrote again to Mary expressing his unhappiness. He said: 'Although it is madness for us – with me like I am – to envisage a future together, it is misery for me to be apart.' He said he lay awake at night thinking about her and 'cannot bear to see the years ahead without you'. He described his pain at thinking of other people who 'have a home and a woman and hot cross buns at Easter, and I in this horrible bondage must be alone and thwarted'. He said it would be madness to think anyone else could ever fill her place. He asked her to tell him if 'you think it is best for us to part' and said if he could find some psychoanalyst 'to release me from my chains I would go to him at once – tonight'. He went on to rationalise that he knew the pain would diminish with time and 'we shall both be happy again'. He said that if at least Mary could be happy that would be something, and that 'it is dreadful that I should have done this to you. I did not mean to. I did not.' He told her he had just been to the theatre and wrote eloquently of the night:

> The night is lovely beyond description. Something liquefies in me as I see that brilliant moon and the rare gold stars. It is too much.

And in the same letter a lovely description of the daffodils that a friend had brought him:

> These daffodils are beautiful, but their stalks are short and he has jammed them in pots so that just their heads hang over the side, like children looking out of train windows.

Michael was teaching in Frome in Somerset while Mary was living in London, so there were letters going back and forth between them. On 3 April 1940 Michael proposed marriage and Mary accepted. Mary wrote to Michael on 14 April:

> Last Monday on my way to Benfleet I saw a little country church in the middle of a field. The sun was shining. The birds were singing. The graveyard was covered with daffodils and primroses. It was so peaceful and I thought that is the church I'd like us to be married in.

She suggested they might have two farm labourers as witnesses but then added that you couldn't have a church service without kneeling down and saying and hearing lots of embarrassing things, and she wouldn't want to do that. She ended the letter: 'You have made me very happy.'

Michael, rather surprisingly, had also told Mary when he proposed on 3 April that he would not be able to consummate the marriage. Mary seemed to accept the fact but said 'as for you and me, sweetheart, I do wish very much that our marriage could be complete, so that we could have a child'. She went on to say that she had been pregnant by Bob but she had 'brought on a miscarriage - Bob didn't want a child and I didn't want a child that wasn't loved equally by both parents. Your child would have been different. I love you and you would have loved both of us.' Mary did ask him to tell her what the problem was as 'if I have full understanding I can face the situation'. In reply Michael said he was not keen to 'try something I have never felt attracted towards; I shall give you no pleasure and upset us both'. He said he had 'thought and thought how I could break this disability that stops our marriage from completeness' but had not come up with an answer. However, Mary clearly loved Michael enough for that fact not to get in the way, and she rationalised that they could adopt children instead.

In a later letter Michael told Mary something of his childhood. His father died when he was two and he had two elder sisters, so he was very much surrounded by women. He felt he was 'an odd sort of boy' and never could play games, but he had interests ahead of his age, the main one of which was politics. He had never had any girlfriends and had resigned himself to becoming a bachelor until Mary gave him 'the sweet and deepest happiness I have ever known'.

Six days later Mary wrote again to Michael saying how she loved to have his letters and went on to describe her feelings:

> With you I feel at peace and unafraid. I've never felt like that with anyone before. Sometimes I feel shy with you and thoughts and questions come in to my mind which I do not know how to express, and perhaps you too feel like that sometimes with me do you? But it does not seem to matter. Time will answer our questions. You wouldn't die without me would you? If you did I should become a spiritualist immediately!

Mary told Michael that she had lunch with Bob at Lyons Corner house and then walked with him in the park. She was discussing with him how best to obtain a mutual divorce so she could marry Michael, and said 'I feel there must be some way in which I can act which won't hurt anyone'.

In her next letter she said she had been to her solicitor about instigating divorce proceedings. He had told her that she must not be seen alone with a man in a place 'in which adultery could be committed', otherwise she might compromise the situation and she did not want to be seen as the guilty party. She said her friend Mollie was moaning that she would have to spend the summer chaperoning her. Her divorce would take about a year.

In May Mary wrote to Michael asking him if he would like to 'adopt one or two children if we couldn't have any of our own'. She said she would rather have 'our children because they would be partly you'. She went on to say 'there are so many buts', some of which because of the uncertainty of the war.

Mary wrote to Michael with a wonderful description of an event which took place in Westminster Abbey on 26 May 1940; it was the National Day of Prayer. It also happened to be the day the evacuation of Dunkirk began. Mary attended with her friend Mollie who was a journalist and she, Mary, went, as she put it, 'under false pretences'. She thought the guard mistook her for the Archbishop of Canterbury's wife and so she was allowed to stand with the VIPs and watch all the famous people coming out of the Abbey at the end of the service. She described it with amusement and very much with her socialist, and possibly republican, hat on:

> First came Churchill and his wife who slipped away before the king and queen. (Mollie, who knows, said that wasn't in keeping with Court etiquette). Then the queen, her smile more restrained than usual, with the king looking like a very raw aircraftsman, walking modestly behind, uncertain of himself but trying very hard to please. They drove off without ceremony though I'm sorry to say that Mrs Atlee *curtsied* when she shook hands with the queen. Then Queen Wilhelmina, obstructive as usual, *would* gossip at the door and hold up the Cabinet behind, while the Archbishop tried to edge her into her car. Next Chamberlain [who had recently resigned as Prime Minister to make way for Churchill] who was *cheered* by the deanery women - Mollie was so furious that she whispered 'let's start a counter demonstration'. Fortunately we remembered in time the dignity of the press and my temporary status as Archbishop's wife.

Following the Royalty came the cabinet ministers and ambassadors. Attlee, Lord Privy Seal at the time (Labour Prime Minister 1945-51) was 'quiet and modest in a corner'. Mary described the Archbishop as a 'nasty old man' and the Dean looking like 'any country vicar gossiping in the church doorway with his parishioners after the Sunday service'. Mary, in her letter, was rather scathing about some members of the coalition government from the Conservative Party who were dressed in silk hats and frock coats 'looking a bit crumpled as if they'd slept in their clothes the night before'. She said she could not imagine that the world's destiny depended on 'the actions of those ordinary looking men'. She asked Michael if he thought in a few years' time he would be facing the photographers at the Abbey door with her trying not to look too proud of him, she hovering behind? She says that 'perhaps it is fair to tell you before I marry you that I *won't* curtsey to the queen. Still I hope I *look* as charming as Mrs Attlee.'

In the same letter Mary said she had no news about the divorce. She asked Michael to tell his mother about their proposed marriage and said 'I'm afraid she won't think me good enough for you'. It was true that Michael's mother was not happy about Michael marrying a divorced woman. By contrast Mary said her own mother Isabel 'is anxious to meet you. She keeps the garden in special readiness for us, feeling we might turn up at any time.' Mary commented about the war and her hopes:

> It seems wrong of me to hope as *much* as I do that we shall both survive this war and help build the foundations of the new world. It's like asking for a special privilege for us when we know how many people must die. Fortunately I keep my childish quite irrational belief (the nearest thing I've got to a religion) that there is justice in our personal lives: no economic justice of course but justice in the distribution of happiness – so I feel if we do our jobs properly now, we shall be safe. But I do wish we could be together.

She asked that if Michael came to London why could they not join the London defence force together? She would not mind 'stalking a parachutist dressed as a nun and carrying a machine gun, a bicycle, a camera, an incendiary device and a week's ration, if you were with me'; in other words capturing an enemy who had parachuted into their midst in disguise, which had recently been done. She said 'we wouldn't shoot him, would we? We would sit down with him on Wimbledon Common, help him eat his ration and convert him to socialism.' And she added 'Oh dear Mickey, I get sillier and sillier!'

In another letter Mary asked him not to worry at all about her:

> Don't worry about me any more than you would worry about yourself because in a way we are one. I don't believe there is anything in the world I wouldn't do if you wanted me to, but perhaps that's because I couldn't imagine us differing about anything important.
>
> There's an air raid shelter just outside my window with an air raid warden looking just like a lavatory attendant sitting knitting at the top of the steps.

In her next letter Mary talked about her taking evacuees to Penzance:

> We meet in Mile End at 6am on Tuesday. The children will have to be up at 5am or before. Heaven knows what state they'll be in when they reach Penzance about 12 hours later. The average age is about 8. There are several of 3 or 4. They come from the poorest homes – numbers of them are from Limehouse – and will no doubt give their billetors a few shocks. They are very friendly – very dirty – and very excited about their journey.

Mary made the point that it was her theory that children were better off with their parents, taking their chances with the bombing, rather than being evacuated and having to leave their parents behind.

In the same letter Mary mentioned that Bob had been to see her solicitor and 'named the woman'. Presumably they were paying a woman to pretend to be his lover in order to help Mary get the divorce on grounds of his adultery as so often happened in those days when divorces were difficult to obtain. Homosexuality was illegal at the time so they could not divorce on those grounds. Bob had said he would not defend the suit.

Another letter started 'Darling – I've just been arrested'. Mary had been on her way to visit her sister Sheona and had been stopped by soldiers who asked to see her identity card. They decided her eyes were not grey and she looked younger than the woman in the photo and they assumed she was a spy, so she was locked up in a prison cell for a while until she could prove who she was.

In June 1940 Mary told Michael something more about her family and Frank in particular. First she discussed her father whom she considered to be quite cruel:

> My father wasn't a nice man. He was very selfish – he had no sense of social or personal responsibility. He was stupid and quite terrifyingly bad tempered.

Mary said that her brother Frank became like him in many ways, but that his selfishness and irresponsibility 'was tempered by cleverness and courage. He suffered considerably at my father's hands.' She felt it was because of this that Frank ran off to war. She said:

> He was in France within six months – was wounded – discharged because of his youth – joined up again in another regiment – acquired a number of medals ... After the war, as a result of a Government scheme, he went to the university and qualified as a doctor. Then followed several years during which we were constantly worrying lest he should be arrested for debt or worse than that – then to our great relief he went to New Zealand where he distinguished himself during the Great Earthquake by his enterprise and courage.

Mary said 'there were more years of irresponsible behaviour' on Frank's part. He was practising as a doctor during this time and when he returned to England on a visit she said there was 'more anxiety for us all'. He then returned to New Zealand, no doubt much to her relief, and 'has a good post under the New Zealand Government. He has a wife from whom he is separated and two children who adore him.' She told Michael that she was never close to Frank as he was a good deal older than her and away from home during most of her school days, but she and her other brother Bill had always been friends, even though they had little in common. Frank had apparently fought with his father 'but accepted him'. Bill, on the other hand, 'feared him'. She talked some more about Bill:

> He was an innocent, timid, friendly child ever anxious to believe the best of everybody and my father's behaviour often horrified him. And his love for my mother and hers for him did not make life easier for him. It aroused my father's jealousy and gave him a weapon against which they were both defenceless. He could hurt my mother most by attacking Bill. Outwardly Bill resisted my father but inwardly I think he was dominated by him.

Mary thought that Herbert's behaviour was the cause of many of Bill's difficulties in later years. In one letter she let slip her dislike of Frank by saying 'Brother Bill, my nice brother – Frank is the other one'.

Mary was perhaps, sadly, somewhat disingenuous towards Frank. He had, after all, been taken out of school at fifteen, made to get a job that he did not like, and a year later had run off to fight for his King and Country. She on the other hand had all her schooling paid for and then went straight on to university. The reason that Frank had a problem with money, according to Fay, was partly due to the fact that he would spend whatever he had on 'nice things' rather than practical ones. Having been brought up with 'make do and mend' and with the privations of fighting in a war, he no doubt yearned for a more indulgent way of life.

Mary herself was too afraid of Herbert to stand up to him as a child but 'I did what I wanted without permission and bore the inevitable rows afterward as best I could'. She felt it was cowardly of her and it meant she was in a 'more or less chronic state of anxiety'. However, she said she did not regret her childhood experiences and even her cowardly traits, and she said her own fears had given her a bond with people which she might not otherwise have had. Mary reckoned she had inherited 'a fair share of my father's vices and my mother's virtues'. And about Isabel she said:

> And from my mother I learnt how different the world might be from what it is. She is a delightful person … I wish you could see her entertaining the local lady bountifuls who sometimes call uninvited to patronise or to ask her to contribute to the church bazaar. Before they know where they are they find themselves eating a scrambled egg (usually at a very odd time). Mother takes it for granted that you are always hungry - possibly because she has been hungry so often herself.

When Mary reminisced in her letters about her own background of poverty she thought how amazing it was that Michael was not only someone who could support himself, but would be able to support her and their 'nine adopted refugee children'. This was a 'tongue in cheek' comment, but Mary was still hoping to have children somehow. Mary added that she would of course not be happy without a job of her own. Michael responded to that with

'I think perhaps we could manage with not quite as many as nine children – or have you set your heart on that number?' He went on to say that he didn't feel they needed any as being with her was happiness enough.

In a letter to Michael dated August 1940 Mary said she had been told by a friend that Bob was distressed at not having heard from her. Mary thought it was because 'it hurts Bob to think that I can be happy without him'; however Mary knew Bob still cared for her and wanted her happiness. And in reference to Michael she said 'I think of you and talk to the walls of my room about you' and that her belief in personal freedom 'conflicts with my desire to ask you to write very soon'.

Mary was an air raid warden in 1940 and was eventually made a senior marshal, which was unusual for a woman, and was in charge of three shelters. However, she said she was 'scared stiff in raids'. They would go out on patrol, fight fires, rescue people and do anything else that came along. Between patrols they 'played darts and struggled with crosswords'. Mary described one of the other shelter marshals as being 'rather a trial'. She would come on duty 'in a pink nightdress, high-heeled bedroom slippers and long hair streaming down her back'.

Mary talked about many of her adventures and the challenges in the shelters in letters to Michael, the letters sometimes written on headed notepaper from the Bonnington Hotel in Southampton Row where she was based. One evening, during a fire, she was in Lamb's Conduit Street clambering over the rooftops amongst the chimneys with another warden, Kelly, who was an Australian. They were trying to reach a building which was on fire further along the street and Mary described 'the moon shining pale above the burning buildings – the shooting stars of fire – the crash of the bombs dropping around us – the hum of the planes circling over us'. She called it 'terribly terrifying and yet somehow glorious'. Bombs were whistling overhead and they had to cling to the chimney pots. All the skylights were locked and they could not find a way down into the houses and as she thought of it as 'Wells's world to come' she suddenly remembered she was afraid of heights. She was trying to keep up with Kelly and the next thing she knew was that his leg had gone through a roof and he became trapped. However, he managed to extricate himself and Mary commented 'well, he's not a six foot prairie rider for nothing'. They eventually managed to open a skylight and 'fall down four flights of stairs to freedom'.

In her diary she wrote: 'We are a heterogeneous crowd at our post. We have a house-painter, a street-bookie, a lawyer, a woman journalist, a woman novelist, a night watchman, a teacher, a clerk or two, an ex-clergyman.' She said they had little in common 'save our preference for death rather than Nazi rule'.

An entry in the diary dated 31 January 1941 read:

> Walked through city this afternoon. Sightseers were so quiet and sad. It was like being at the funeral of someone you had loved very much. St Paul's standing blackened but unharmed amidst the ruins seemed grander and more important than ever.

By the end of May 1941 over 43,000 civilians in Britain had been killed and more than a million houses destroyed or damaged in the Blitz.

In a letter to Mary dated 2 April 1941 Michael was reminiscing about his proposal to her of the previous year when 'I asked you to marry me. The feeling of joy and certainty and warmth that I have from knowing we're betrothed seems now so much part of me that I find it difficult to believe it's only been a year.' In response Mary wrote saying how much she loved Michael and how she wanted to make him happy:

> I have loved and still do love a lot of people, but you are the only person with whom I have ever thought that I would like to live for always.

In early May Mary wrote that the sessions in the Old Bailey had been postponed for the first time ever because of the bombing and she was anxiously keeping her eye on the divorce court, which appeared to be functioning as normal, as her hearing was imminent. She eventually obtained her divorce on 26 May on the grounds of Bob's adultery, and wrote to Michael on 5 June 1941 saying how nice it was to be 'properly engaged'.

Just before they married Michael and Mary must have had a misunderstanding as Michael wrote:

> I don't know whether I really thought you meant you didn't want to marry me but you made my heart turn over inside me because you and marriage to you are the centre of my thoughts and feelings. Marriage is, first and foremost, the coming together of two people in affection and dear companionship for the sharing of every kind of emotion and interest; this I am sure of and believe like you that its success will turn on each party's knowing the mind and moods and feelings of the other and wanting to fit himself to them in kindness and understanding … Only a bit more than three weeks now, sweetheart, I love you with all my heart and think of you always.

Mary reassured him all was well and continued:

> I feel in my bones we'll be happy together, don't you? I don't think I ever conceived of the possibility of my being wholly happy and free from anxiety until quite recently. I've always found life interesting and I've always had someone to love and I've had lots of joyous moments but that isn't the same as being happy.

Ten days later Michael wrote from Frome in Somerset: 'In a fortnight sweetheart, we shall be married.' He said he was excited and pleased and loved Mary very much: 'We have waited a long time haven't we? We said it would be about a year – it's been rather longer.' Bob had written to Mary in June giving his blessing to her marriage with Michael, although still professing his love for her saying 'the years of my marriage to you were the happiest of my life'.

Mary booked a £2.14s wedding. She wanted to marry quietly but Michael wanted a reception. Mary said the difference between them was that Michael considered marriage primarily a social contract and for her it was a personal one. She asked him not to think of her as 'a disembodied spirit with an angelic nature hovering round you, will you?' She wanted 'to be loved physically even if we can't attain the heights of physical love'. Many friends had offered her their clothes' coupons for the event and she said she might well 'arrive at the Registry Office door in white satin and orange blossom'. In the event she wore a red dress.

Her friend Kelly, who ran the bomb shelter with her, had organised a pre-wedding party for her in his room in Guilford Street with their friend Mollie. That area of London was almost derelict from the bombing and they had no light nor gas nor fire, so Kelly lit a fire in a bucket and they made some tea and 'ate rolls and sardines with lettuce and rhubarb', as Mary related in her diary.

Mary and Michael married in August at the Holborn Registry Office; Mary was thirty-eight and Michael thirty-four. Mary's brother Bill and his wife Eileen were present. Michael wrote cryptically of the event in his autobiography *Life and Labour*: 'In 1941 we got married and lived happily ever after.' Michael had also recently been elected the prospective Member of Parliament for Fulham.

Bill would often ask Mary for advice as did Frank. Mary appeared to be the lynchpin for the family, especially while Frank was in New Zealand and Bill was in Nigeria during World War II. Mary was frequently helping the family out in one way or another and they had a great respect for her opinion. While Bill was overseas his wife Eileen was working in a munitions factory in Kent. Mary liked Eileen and called her and Bill 'a human couple'. Bill she referred to as 'a darling'.

In December 1941 Mary joined the WAAF. She had many interesting experiences, starting in the ranks and eventually becoming an officer in June 1942. On one day she might be lecturing to eight hundred people and on the next scrubbing the mess room floor. In January 1942 she wrote in her diary that she had decided that once the war was over, and if not before: 'I'm going to work like hell to get some domestic changes in our educational system'. She was horrified at the 'uncritical, unthinking people in this country. People need to be taught to think.'

In February 1943 Michael joined the Intelligence Corps and was sent to the Middle East. He and Mary would be apart for the next two years.

In August 1943 Mary wrote to Michael that she had heard from a friend that Bob's latest novel, *Mrs Loveday*,[3] 'has been a huge success – three impressions sold out immediately – the reviews have been remarkable. He dedicated it to me and gave me a copy via Mollie.'

Mary was offered a flat for Michael and herself to live in after the war by her army padre; he was also one of the canons at St Paul's Cathedral. It was in Amen Court just next to St Paul's and she told Michael about it with great excitement. She said she had told the padre that they 'weren't a bit ecclesiastical' and he didn't seem to mind. She said what she did not tell him was about their proposed 'adopted children'. Mary felt there would be plenty of parentless children in Europe after the war who would need looking after.

Mary's enigmatic comment in her diary in December 1944 about marriage was somewhat different from Michael's view of marriage:

> I can't live without loving people like Bob [her ex-husband] and John and Christopher [two friends]. My world would be empty without them. I need Michael to anchor me but I must be on a long leash so that I can wander sometimes out of sight of home.

She went on to say that there was a part of her that Michael would never understand 'though he would always be kind and sympathetic'. She said the world would be dreary 'if one were satisfied by one person. Certainly Michael would never be satisfied by me alone.' She said he needed his socialist activities 'just as I need my flights into the imagination – worlds created by other people'. Politics, she believed, was Michael's 'first love if not his only one', although he had told her he would always choose her over being an MP.

Michael returned to England in 1945 and rang Mary unexpectedly from Waterloo on his return from Cairo. Mary was at that time stationed at RAF Eastchurch in Kent. She ran into the garden and shouted the good news that Michael was finally home after their two-year separation. 'Everyone jumped up – Pip and one or two other men wheeled a handcart to the front of the mess and offered to push me up to London in it.' She was eventually driven to Sittingbourne and met Michael in London that evening. They had nowhere to stay and tried all the hotels. It was looking as though they might have to spend the night walking the streets and Mary said they felt like 'thwarted beggars – and then just when we were giving up hope the Russell Hotel receptionist, whom I heard refusing other people ahead of us, said to Michael "we can let you have a room, Captain". Michael thought she liked captains but I think she just realised how tired he was.'

In May 1945 Mary wrote to Michael that her latest idea was 'to join you in Parliament once you are secure there'. She said they would have to get a nursery school attached to the House of Commons so 'we can leave the children there each morning'! Michael was duly elected MP for Fulham in July of that year and Mary, while supporting him as an MP's loyal wife, continued with her own career.[4]

Mary in uniform

Chapter Fifteen

Bill

'I hated my father, absolutely hated him'. Karen, Bill's daughter, had often heard her father say this with great vehemence about his father Herbert, who, he said, had no redeeming features whatsoever. Bill never really explained to Karen why he felt so angry with Herbert but some family history research soon explained the reason; letters and diaries belonging to Bill's sister Mary, found in the Churchill Archives[1], were particularly illuminating in revealing Herbert's abominable behaviour towards his family.

William Thornton Birkinshaw, or Bill as we all called him, was born in the suburb of Manningham in Bradford on 11 March 1905, at 72 St Mary's Road, not far from where his father Herbert was born, and where Herbert's parents, John Richard and Annie, still lived. Six weeks later the family moved to Gravelly Hill, Birmingham. Bill was the youngest of four children, although his sister Sheona had already gone to live permanently with their aunt Jane Baigent by the time he was born. Bill did not see much of Sheona during his childhood except when he was ill and he was sent to the large and affluent Dunston House in Northallerton to Sheona's 'adopted' family. According to Sheona, who wrote about her childhood in later life, Bill adored playing with her toys, especially the circus, and she believed he secretly envied her.

In January 1914 Bill went to Aston Boys' School, part of the King Edward VI group of schools; the family by that time had moved to Erdington, Birmingham. The school record described Bill's father, Herbert, as being a 'Manufacturers' Agent'. In April 1918 when he was thirteen, Bill transferred to the Camp Hill School where he remained until he was eighteen. During this time the family moved again to Hall Green, and then to Selvas Cottage, Alvechurch, a small village outside Birmingham. According to the school records in 1914 the school fees were £1 12s 6d per term and by the time Bill left in 1923 they had risen to £3 per term. The Governors' Order Book of 1914 reflected the fact that the school fees were paid late that year for Bill and his sister Mary, so perhaps Herbert was going through a particularly hard time.

Herbert could be a harsh father, and one night he locked Bill out of the house because he had come home late. Bill had been told to be in at a certain time and on this occasion was ten minutes late. Herbert refused him entry and Bill had to sleep under the hedge in the snow all night. Mary described in her letters and diaries how cruel Herbert had been, particularly to Frank and Bill. She said that Herbert was intensely jealous of Bill, as Isabel doted on her youngest child and Herbert did not like it. Frank and Bill were very close, although there were seven years between them. In letters to me, Bill described

Frank, Mary and Bill

Bill and Mary

Frank as a 'wonderful brother' and said that 'there was no one in the world like him'. He said he had 'such an affection' for Frank and 'that is an understatement'. He said Frank had protected him from their father, and looked after him when he was hurt or ill. Bill said that even Mary did not know Frank as he had. Bill, like his brother, must have been a very forgiving son as he wrote to his parents frequently during his war years away from home, and dutifully looked after them in their old age.

Bill wrote me several letters after I asked him to tell me about my father and the family; this being after my mother had died in 1977. He said that one day, after Herbert died, he went to visit his mother Isabel at Barnt Green and found her in the process of burning old family letters, saying that no one would be interested in them. Bill managed to rescue some but most of the Birkinshaw ones had gone. He told me that his Grandmother Birkinshaw (Annie) was a very selfish woman and that the boys (Herbert and his brothers) were sent to boarding school in Sligo, Ireland, and were often left there for the holidays. Perhaps that was what had made Herbert become such a difficult man.

After finishing school Bill went to Birmingham University to study dentistry. He must have taken a couple of years out as he did not enrol at the university until he was twenty, according to the University archives. Perhaps he needed to take a job to earn money to pay his way through university. An article in *The Newark Advertiser,* dated 1978, written about Bill revealed the following:

> While at Birmingham University he had to earn money to support himself and joined repertory theatre, finding himself playing opposite players like Cedric Hardwick, Madeleine Carroll and Raymond Huntley. At one rehearsal for a production of 'The Applecart' George Bernard Shaw described him as 'my young apothecary'.

It was interesting that both Bill and Frank had met George Bernard Shaw, but at different times, Frank while he was producing radio plays in New Zealand.

The University records also showed that Bill was elected Assistant Secretary, then Honorary Secretary of the Guild of Undergraduates, between 1926 and 1928 after which he was elected President. The records also show that Bill failed some of his exams and had to retake them which was perhaps not surprising given all the other interests he had. In August 1928 Bill and his brother Frank were headline news in all the national papers when he and Frank were shipwrecked in the Thames Estuary, on which occasion they had nearly drowned.[2]

Half-way through his seven-year course Bill took a year off and obtained a commission in the Territorial Army (TA). Frank had also joined the TA while at university and had been attached to the Royal Army Medical Corps.

Unfortunately Bill also failed one of his final exams and left Birmingham University without graduating. He then went to London and finished his dentistry degree at Guy's Hospital, from which he graduated in 1932. The story was very similar to that of his brother Frank who moved from Birmingham to London University and failed his medical degree first time round. Their sister Mary was also living and working in London while Bill was a student there. Frank was living in New Zealand by this time.

After Bill qualified he did some locums in the Birmingham area, after which he worked at the London Omnibus Company clinic and then went into practice at St John's Wood in London, this according to an interview he gave in later years, when he was living in Southwell, near Nottingham, to *Leaves,* the Magazine of Southwell Cathedral.[3]

In 1937 Bill married his dental nurse Olive Woodard in London. Unfortunately, not long afterwards, Olive ran off with their best man and married him a year later. Bill was devastated. However, in 1939 he met and married Eileen Morden in London who was eleven years his junior. Her parents were actors and she was fun-loving with a wonderful sense of humour and also a sense of the ridiculous, according to my cousin Karen, their daughter. Bill's mother Isabel was devoted to Eileen and said how well Eileen looked after her whenever she was ill. Everyone thought Eileen charming and she was universally liked by friends and family.

At the outbreak of World War Two Bill joined the Army Dental Corps, and served for a time in Lisburn, Northern Ireland and then joined the West Africa Force in Nigeria where he was promoted to Major. *Leaves* reported that during his time in Lisburn Bill caught pneumonia, and when he was in Nigeria he survived a crash in an American plane.

In February 1943 Bill wrote to his mother from Nigeria describing the 'Ju-ju ceremony' at an African village which he had been to:

> First sacrifices were made to the Ju-ju, hens having their beaks slit through and the blood dashed on the Ju-ju. While the birds were still alive the feathers were plucked and stuck on the blooded parts. Then the male infants were presented to it being splattered with blood also, and a number of cattle were killed. The male children are thus given strength. If a female touches the Ju-ju though she would be completely barren. Then the dancing started, Africans wearing grotesque masks with bodies covered with white paint. There were some hundreds of them and they worked themselves into an absolute frenzy, leaping, yelling and shrieking through the forest. Young women who had been in 'fattening rooms' for two years or more to get fat and desirable for the men, came into our view, dressed in a string of beads – more or less. I managed to get a number of photographs, although the camera wasn't very popular, and they've come out extremely well.

Bill finished his letter by telling Isabel that he had ‘sent Pater a birthday cable’ and asked for his love to be given to his aunts Madge and Jennie.

In March 1943 Bill wrote to his parents to say he had been travelling and had done a thousand miles by train which took three days and nights, and he said that they had run out of drinking water on the journey but had managed to get by. He said he was now back at HQ with his unit in Nigeria after having had a few days’ rest swimming in the sea and meeting friends. He said he was living in a comfortable officers’ mess and had a large bush hut made of bamboo which was covered with thatch, through which the rain occasionally permeated.

In April 1943 Bill wrote to Mary saying he was sending a cheque to their aunt Madge for Isabel which should last her a year. He sent it to Madge rather than to Isabel in order to avoid Herbert getting hold of it. He said ‘Mother writes to me every week and I look forward to her letters tremendously’. His wife Eileen was working for the war effort in Rochester Kent, which Bill said he did not feel was a very safe area, because of the bombs, but he felt ‘awfully proud of her doing factory work’. He went on:

> My job at HQ is interesting. I’m in a pretty unhealthy spot as regards my living quarters but it’s not interfering with my work to any extent. I’ve got prickly heat which is a bit irritating, but I’m getting used to that quite cheerfully. Rats and ants have played a bit of havoc with some of my things, but again what a grand contrast it will be to return to civilization eventually. My idea of bliss at the moment is to be able to wear pyjamas and have a blanket and sheets instead of remaining stark naked and still pouring out gallons of sweat. But all the same I enjoy life, even here.
>
> Affectionately, Bill.

Bill suffered several bouts of fever and had a spell in hospital but otherwise kept pretty fit, he told his sister Mary in a letter. He described having a holiday with an American friend and the luxury they were living in:

> Now for a week I’m living in absolute luxury, with a real bed complete with mattress, bathroom and home comforts which only an American could introduce into such remote parts. Also it’s a joy to be out of uniform; mosquito proofed windows make mosquito nets and boots unnecessary. Normally we have to wear long boots, shirts with long sleeves, and ties and collars in the evening. In this climate it tends to be a bit trying, although of course one gets used to it.

Bill in uniform

Another letter arrived for Isabel and Herbert from Bill in August 1943:

> My dear Mother and Pater
>
> Today a parcel of 'Birmingham Mails' arrived from you … I found them most interesting and read all about the city's effort in the war week. Like Pater, I always like the cartoon and like Frank read all the advertisements.
>
> In my last letter I told you how I'd had a few bouts of minor illness, now I'm feeling grand and fit for anything – especially for a spot of service in the European zone of war when I return! In anticipation of that time I'm doing physical training, swimming – and incidentally, working like the devil. I'm getting plenty of variety in my work. Today for example I've paid a visit to the 68th. There I did some emergency work, including some Italians. Their teeth are just what one would expect – lousy. Then at HQ I saw a few naval patients and a 'Big Noise' of the tin mines, who travels down for treatment in his own private coach on the train.

He went on to comment to his parents about the 'marvellous Russian advances and the victories in Sicily and the Pacific'. He said that the two papers which were published in Nigeria were devoid of any war news, and he described the attitude of the average local:

> The average African does not know anything about the war anyway; my own orderlies, who are educated according to African standards, cannot even point to Nigeria on a map, and if asked if they have heard of America, Italy or Japan, just look blank and say 'No Sah'. The war is just a pleasant means of earning more money than they do in peace time, naturally they just want it to go on indefinitely.

Bill said in his letter that the government dental surgeon had gone on leave and had handed over his patients to him. That enabled Bill to do some private work and earn some extra money. He was saving up and planning to buy his own practice when he returned home after the war. In a letter to Mary in 1943 Bill said he wanted to buy a practice in a country town: 'Eileen will like it and I don't want to go to London again. Some real home life is indicated I think.'

On his return to England in 1943, by slow convoy, some of the ships were torpedoed. Again, according to the *Leaves'* profile, Bill then worked in air-sea rescue in Norfolk and sailed over a minefield to a pick-up off the coast of Denmark.

Bill joined Eileen in Rochester, and their much-loved daughter Karen was born in October 1944, after Eileen had had several miscarriages. Mary's somewhat acerbic comment in her diary was:

> I hope Eileen will be kind to the child. She didn't want a girl. I fear she will be resentful if Bill displays devotion as he undoubtedly will.

Mary went to visit the new arrival and in a later diary entry said she found Karen to be 'a remarkably well-behaved and good-looking baby who sleeps 20 hours out of 24'.

Bill and Eileen and Karen moved to Southwell and, according to another interview[4] Bill gave to a local paper, he set up a private practice in the town at 25 King Street 'virtually only with the clothes he stood up in'. All his possessions had been destroyed by a bomb on his London flat. Everyone rallied round and helped them with household necessities for which they were very grateful. After three years Bill moved and set up a dental practice in the large house at 10 Westgate in Southwell which he had managed to buy. He described the house in an earlier letter to his mother saying the garden was probably too large but that there was an orchard and they would be able to sell the produce. There was a greenhouse and 'a first-class asparagus bed' and a brick built summerhouse 'complete with claygate fireplace which Karen will like'. There were outbuildings including looseboxes in which he assured his mother he would not keep horses, but they would have a couple of cats. He said the most important aspect of the house was 'that Eileen is delighted'.

The interview went on to say that Bill 'made his mark' in Southwell, not only as a dental surgeon but in public life as well. He was a member of the Parish Council and chairman for one year, a member of the British Legion of which he had been president, an honorary life member of the local rugby club and a vice-president of the cricket club. He was also president of the Southwell Tennis Club, chairman of the local Infants School Managers and a school governor. He was a sidesman at the Minster, a commissioner of taxes, a committee member of the local Multiple Sclerosis Society and a member of the Newark Rotary Club. He was also interested in sketching and brass rubbing as well as walking.

Although Bill had made an interesting and fulfilling life for himself, the next few years were not to be easy.[5]

Chapter Sixteen

Isabel and Herbert

Isabel was born Isabella Henderson Garbutt in 1870, the fifth of eleven children. Her father William was the proprietor of a lunatic asylum, Dunston Lodge, in Whickham, near Gateshead, and her mother's family, the Hendersons, were farmers in Northumberland. Isabel, who was born at Dunston Lodge, had a happy and privileged upbringing with nurses and governesses to look after her.

Herbert Birkinshaw was born in Bradford in 1871 the son of a Yorkshire wool merchant and the ninth of ten children. Herbert was also in the wool business describing himself at different times as a stuff merchant, an agent, or a commercial traveller. He probably ran his own business at one time, but appeared never to be very successful at anything. Family gossip suggested that Herbert was the black sheep of his family and did not work as hard as his other brothers, which is maybe why he never appeared to have much money.

Three of Isabel's sisters had married doctors who worked in the asylum, and Isabel met Herbert while staying with one of them. Herbert and Isabel became engaged but Isabel soon realised she had made a mistake and wished to break off the engagement. However, one of her sisters had already committed such a sin and Isabel knew there was no way she could contribute to another slur on her family's good name.

Herbert and Isabel were married in the Church of St John the Evangelist, Birtley, which was not far from Whickham, on 3 August 1897. They started married life together at 6 The Terrace, Ovingham on Tyne near Newcastle where their first two children, Frank and Sheona, were born. They then moved, no doubt because of Herbert's job, to the suburb of Manningham in Bradford, where their third child Mary was born in May 1903.

A postcard from Herbert in Derby, dated 22 August 1904, to Isabel's unmarried sister Gus at West Rainton, a house the family rented not far from Whickham, announced the impending arrival there of Isabel, her mother and 'babys'. The following day Herbert sent a postcard to Isabel, this time from Bristol: 'Hope you arrived safely today and had a good journey. How is Frank? Write to Grand Hotel, Birmingham. Love to all – Herbert.' Another rather curious postcard from Herbert dated 10 September arrived at West Rainton addressed to Isabel. Herbert was writing from Matlock Bath, Derbyshire and said he had arrived safely and it was beautifully fine and that he was sending them some 'water to wash with on the Village Green!' (Matlock Bath water was supposed to have thermal and healing properties and people went there to 'take the cure'.) He said he hoped Frank was better and to 'kiss my little Mary for me'. He signed off 'love and kisses'.[1]

Bill, their fourth child, was also born in Bradford, but shortly after his birth the family were on the move again, this time to Gravelly Hill in Birmingham. The 1911 census described Herbert's job as 'agent for Bradford goods'. The house was described as having eight rooms, including the kitchen, so Herbert must have been doing quite well at that time. By 1913 they had moved to Erdington and a few years later to Hall Green, both suburbs of Birmingham. 1923 found them in Selvas Cottage in Alvechurch, a pretty village just outside Birmingham. The cottage in Alvechurch was at the end of a narrow lane and was a very basic house with no electricity or facilities. Herbert must really have fallen on hard times to have been living in such conditions. In 2009 we visited Alvechurch and discovered that the cottage had been extended and transformed into a beautiful, modern house.

Letters from Isabel to her daughter Mary, written during the Second World War and afterwards, as well as information from Mary's letters and diaries, which I discovered in the Churchill Archives Centre, provided snapshots of some of Herbert and Isabel's life together and that of their family.[2] Mary's letters revealed Herbert to be a bully both to Isabel and their children.

Isabel was the hub for all the family news and would keep everyone informed as to what the rest of the family were up to. Whenever Isabel received a letter she would forward it to her unmarried sisters Madge and Gus at 30 Highbury in Newcastle. They would forward it to Mary and then the letter would continue the rounds of the family.

Gus died in November 1933 aged sixty-two. After bequests to Isabel's children she left the remainder of her estate, worth in total about £4,500, to her sister Madge for her lifetime; this was then to be divided equally between Isabel's children on Madge's death. Gus obviously knew better than to leave money to Isabel as she believed that Herbert would soon appropriate it as was his custom whenever Isabel was given anything by her sisters.

Madge must have given some of this money to Isabel and Herbert to purchase land, as in 1934 they had a house built in Barnt Green, not far from Alvechurch where they were living at the time. In November of that year they accepted a tender for the building work of £741. The completed house was eventually featured in the February 1936 edition of the *Ideal Home* magazine. It was described as in the 'Dutch style' with pale green walls, white-painted steel casements, jet black wood frames and the rest pale primrose yellow. The roof was of glazed black pantiles and the facings were brick. Herbert called it Lebasi which was Isabel spelt backwards. We visited there at the same time as our trip to Alvechurch and, like Selvas Cottage, found it had been extended and modernised. However, unlike Selvas Cottage, when Herbert and Isabel first moved in to Lebasi it had all the mod cons of the period.

In letters to her husband Michael, Mary mentioned some of the problems Isabel had. Herbert never gave Isabel an allowance and Mary said he 'takes from her any money that he finds has been given to her'. Mary said that the

Lebasi, 1934 (from the Ideal Home *magazine)*

family would give Isabel money secretly which she hid round the house, but she hid it in such obvious places that 'father finds it during his nightly searches'. Even were she to keep the money from him, Mary said, Isabel would then give it to someone who needed it more than she did; Isabel would 'cadge money shamelessly from her relatives to buy food and clothes for us, but if anyone came to the house who was poorer than we were, we would go short of food'. Mary described Isabel as an 'adorable person' and said she did not know anyone who did not love her. Mary wrote 'she's so kind and generous and absurd and however hard hit she is, she always gets up and starts the battle over again'. Mary said it was the absurdity she liked best.

Once, Mary told Michael, Isabel used some money that Bill and Mary had given her to pay Frank's bills (Mary gave Isabel one pound a month). In June 1939 a policeman had come knocking at Isabel's door and told her about a debt that Frank owed to someone, and of course Isabel immediately paid it herself. Frank had by this time left the country and was living in New Zealand. Bill was very angry that Isabel had had to pay out when they knew Frank was earning £800 a year working in a hospital. Mary and Aunt Madge had also bailed Frank out in the past. As Mary said, Isabel may have been wrong 'but she was consistent – Frank's need was greater than ours'. Mary continued to say that Frank had a wife, from whom he was separated, and two daughters to support, but she considered him rather profligate with his money.

Mary said in another letter to Michael that although Isabel 'would literally shake with fear when father bullied her' she would not retaliate and 'after forty-five years he has failed to get her down'. Mary thought that 'nothing in the world could make her [Isabel] unkind or ungenerous or desert the people she loved'. Mary also thought that 'the last stand against Hitlerism would be made by people like Isabel'.

Isabel, in a letter to Mary, complained about her sister-in-law Emmeline who had moved in with them during the war. Emmeline was Herbert's younger brother Sidney's widow; she had no children. Sidney had run a laundry in Acton, which business had originally been owned by Emmeline's family. Emmeline was living in London with her brothers but suffered badly from nerves due to the bombing and came to live with Isabel and Herbert for a time. It appeared she almost drove the long-suffering Isabel to despair with her demands and complaints. In May 1943 Isabel, in a letter to Mary, said she had just taken Emmeline her breakfast upstairs and hoped 'she will be still for some time', and in another letter two days later reported that 'Emmeline gets into tempers about the most trivial things. She is very jealous and I think resents me, my family and husband.' Isabel complained she could not get on with anything as 'Emmeline will come and talk wherever I am and I have to give her my full attention', and that 'she talks incessantly about unpleasant subjects – operations and her departed husband'. However, Isabel said that Emmeline was happy and liked helping round the house and was managing to make her own bed and dust her room and also the sitting room for Isabel.

On another occasion Isabel wrote that Emmeline was in bed 'but there is nothing much the matter'. Isabel said that 'she does appreciate the way I look after her but she can be very disagreeable at times'. In June there was more of her hypochondria:

> Emmeline got very worried about a pain in her knee. I suggested rheumatism but that was not bad enough although I said how painful it could be. The doctor diagnosed rheumatism and suggested she should go for walks. I hear about Emmeline's health and that of all of her friends and relations at every meal and various other times. Now she thinks the doctor is wrong about the pain in her knee.

In June 1944 a telegram arrived at Lebasi from Frank and Edna in New Zealand announcing the arrival of their son Alan and saying how happy they were. Isabel wrote to Mary and said she expected Mary 'would be surprised at Edna having a son'. Perhaps this surprise was because Edna was already forty.

In September of that year, after the Liberation of Paris and with the Germans in retreat, Isabel, according to a letter she wrote to Mary, was celebrating the news that the end of the war was in sight. Even more exciting was the prospect of Emmeline returning to her home in London within the fortnight. However, Isabel did comment that Emmeline had said that 'no one has ever been so kind and sympathetic to her as I have been'. Six weeks later Emmeline was still at Barnt Green and Isabel wrote 'I am counting the days when Emmeline leaves on Thursday week'. She was to travel by train first class and had ordered a taxi at Euston to meet her. Sadly, Isabel said, she 'was going home to brothers whom she does not like'.

Isabel took a great pride in her garden, and in her letters would mention what flowers were out as each season came and went. In March 1945 there were crocuses, primroses and snowdrops. She also turned her attention to the complaints of her husband who was something of a hypochondriac and not one who paid compliments easily, as Isabel related to Mary:

> Pater paid you a compliment. He said that after myself you were very comforting and that is a great deal coming from Pater. He has stopped taking his temperature now so that is a good sign.

Isabel felt that Herbert was 'helpless without me' and 'really nervous alone at night' and that he couldn't do without her. She said that he would sit up until four in the morning 'so he won't be taken unawares by the air raids'. Herbert told his doctor one day in front of Isabel that 'if it were not for Isabel he would do away with himself'. The doctor told him he was selfish and just needed to cheer up. On one occasion Herbert asked a friend to phone the doctor to say he was dying. The friend said she would do nothing of the kind! When Isabel and Herbert were both ill, Herbert said how selfish it was of her to be ill at the same time. Herbert could, when he chose, be helpful, as when he was feeling better himself, Isabel reported to Mary, he had brought her a cup of tea and washed up for her.

Bill said in a letter to Mary that one time when he was home for the weekend his mother had a nasty cough. A friend told him that Isabel was nearly hysterical when Herbert had stalked into her room and called her a selfish old woman and he had turned the radio on full blast. (Herbert obviously liked to be the centre of attention and so hated Isabel to be ill.)

When Margaret returned to England from New Zealand in 1946 with Fay and Jane, she took the girls to visit Isabel who had not seen them since 1931 when Fay was born. In March 1947 Margaret, who was living in London, wrote to Isabel and told her she had moved to St John's Wood from Belsize Park and that they were now much more comfortable. Isabel told Mary that she thought Margaret's move was a mistake although she didn't say why. She also said that she had not told Herbert about it as she knew he would be angry. Isabel called Fay and Jane 'especially nice girls', and said how much Fay looked like Frank and said they seemed very attached to their father. Margaret told Isabel she was house-keeping for a professor and his violinist wife for three hours daily and was able to spend the mornings writing. She said the children were well and happy although there had been no electricity to run the turntables at Jane's pottery class, and 'Fay's school [she was at South Hampstead High] was closed down today for lack of coke'. The following July Jane passed her matriculation and was hoping her Uncle Selwyn (Margaret's brother) was going to get her a job in publishing, Margaret told Isabel.

On the occasions that Sheona wrote to her mother she addressed her as 'My dear Isabel' as she did not regard Isabel as being her mother. However, Sheona wrote to wish her parents well for their Golden Wedding on 3 August 1947 and apologised she could not be with them, but said that she and Oliver would drink their health in ginger beer. But Isabel had earlier told Mary not to celebrate their golden jubilee: 'Forget it', she said. Isabel obviously did not think that her marriage warranted celebrating. Sheona said she wished she lived nearer to Isabel in order to be able to help her when she was ill. Sheona had recently sent Isabel a food parcel containing turtle soup, a little sugar (it was still rationed at the time) and some calves-foot jelly. She suggested she might also send Isabel a cooked guinea fowl.

There was a surprisingly happy letter in September from Isabel to Mary describing an outing she had with Herbert and their grand-daughter Fay. Mary had sent her mother a pound and she spent it on a day out. They took the bus to Bromsgrove and then another one to Worcester, sitting in the front seat which 'just holds three people'. The views were beautiful and they had a picnic by the river. After lunch they visited the cathedral and went up the tower. They had tea at 'the White Tea Rooms' and returned home at 6.30. Fay was at that time nearly sixteen. Isabel commented that Fay had 'strong labour views' and she said that Fay had told them she had tried to reform the conservative views of her classmates, although to date she apparently had not managed it. Isabel said that in spite of Fay's political leanings 'Pater gets on splendidly with her' and that Fay 'just smiles when Pater says everything he does not like is the result of the Labour Government'.

In March 1949 Isabel wrote to Mary to say that she was not very well and that 'Pater brings my breakfast to bed every morning and does a lot for me'. Herbert must have mellowed somewhat. Isabel, in these later letters, often referred to Herbert as 'Dad' instead of 'Pater' which seemed a somewhat softer tone. She also told Mary that she had seen Margaret recently and described her as a wonderful person and very capable. Margaret had told Isabel that Jane was working in a bookshop and contributing to the rent of £6 6s a week and that she, Margaret, was making baskets for John Lewis's earning 2/6d an hour. Margaret was also working part-time for a dentist earning £2 10s a half day. Frank was sending her thirty shillings a week from New Zealand for Fay who was still at school and about to go off to university.

In the General Election of 1950 Isabel wrote to Mary to say how delighted she was that Michael had been re-elected in his Fulham constituency. She said she was indignant with Pater as 'he opened my voting paper to see for whom I had voted and then coming home called me a dirty little communist, but I am sure he was sorry as he has been very nice since'. She also told Mary that she had received a letter from Jane which she had not shown to Herbert as Jane was a socialist and Herbert would not like her views.

Isabel commented in a letter to Mary how she had talked to the pensions officer who came to visit them regarding Herbert's pension, and said to him how well the Labour Government looked after the poorer people. The officer agreed with Isabel that no one should vote anything but Labour when they saw all the distress there was around. When Herbert came in to the room and joined in the conversation he said how Labour was ruining him. However, despite his protestations, Herbert was much happier after he received his pension of twenty-six shillings a week, and consequently Isabel was also much better off. [3]

Isabel in the garden of Lebasi, 1938

Frank, 1940s.

Chapter Seventeen

Sad News

It was not until more than fifty years after the event that I discovered the circumstances surrounding my father's death. Mother had never spoken about it and I had never asked. This knowledge came unexpectedly in the form of a letter which I came across in 2003 in a box of photographs and letters belonging to Frank's first wife, Margaret, after she died. Her grandson Ben told me he had photos and letters belonging to his grandmother and he invited me to look through them. Isabel must have sent the letter to Margaret after Frank's death.

The letter was from my mother in New Zealand addressed to her mother-in-law Isabel in Barnt Green. It was dated 5 October 1949, three days after Frank died, and read:

> My dear Mother
>
> By this time you will have had the sad news of Frank's death. I asked the lawyer to send the cable to Mary so that she could let you and your husband and also Jane and Fay know. It is dreadful news to have to break to you. He had not been well for some time so that about six months ago we thought of selling things up and finding a quiet place for him to retire to and do very little. However, it is not so easy to sell a practice these days, people don't want to buy them, so we were unable to do that, and thought we would manage to cut down expenses by selling our large house and building a small one. Then Frank was going to take things a little easier. As a matter of fact we managed to arrange things so that he should get a regular rest each day and he felt better for it.

Edna went on to say that Frank knew he could 'go at any time' but they had hoped it would not be for many years to come. She said that he was so interested in the building of the new small house and would go each morning on his way into town to see how it was coming along. That Sunday Frank had taken the children to hear a band play in the park to amuse them, instead of having his usual rest. He brought them back and left them for her to give them their evening meal while he took the gardener back home in the car. She continued:

> At about 6 o'clock, when I had the children in the bath, a woman came in to tell me that she thought my husband was lying out in the road. Poor dear, he had managed to drive the car to the gate and stopped it and was just getting out when he slipped to the ground

> and couldn't get any further. He spoke to me when I went out and said he had a dreadful headache and wanted an aspirin, so I got some of the collecting crowd to carry him in and got him to bed, and he asked for aspirins and a warm rug and didn't know much more after that. He was unconscious at about 6.30 and by about ten past nine he was dead. I had Dr Roche in before he was unconscious and he and another doctor did all that was possible, but it must have been a very large haemorrhage and nothing could stop it, so he just died quickly. It was a wonderful way to die and he died uncomplainingly as he lived. He never made any fuss about the pain he so often suffered in the past months, and he couldn't have given less trouble to anyone.

My godmother Poppy had filled in a few more details in a letter she wrote to me in the 1980s, telling me that on the way back home Frank was not feeling well and was driving slowly very close to the kerb and knocked over a bicycle; luckily no one was on it. He managed to turn into the road outside the house and stumbled out of the car collapsing on the ground. Several people had followed him believing him to be drunk and they started to be abusive; they had also called the police. When Edna came out she realised immediately what had happened.

Edna told Isabel in her letter that Frank had just written two short articles for radio and he had been asked to do more so he was very pleased at that. Life was full for him and he was never bored. She said that Frank had told her he always knew he was going to die when he was fifty but that he said he 'had had a good life and done all he wanted to do and if it was to be that way, then he wouldn't complain.[1] Your son has been somebody to be proud of; I am certainly proud to have been his wife.' She described the funeral, which had been the previous day, saying she had asked the Air Force chaplain, whom Frank liked very much and who had christened me, to officiate. The ceremony was very short and dignified and Frank looked 'so peaceful and distinguished with his silver hair, then they covered him with a Union Jack'. She said the flowers were wonderful and the chapel was filled with his friends and patients who loved him. She had gone to a friend's house after the service and left another friend Maurice Brook to go to the crematorium with the other men. She said how much Frank loved his home and that he was 'a charming husband'. She talked more about him:

> I was just looking round a gathering of people, quite interesting people, the other day, and I said to him afterwards that none of the men there was a patch on him. He was very pleased, because he really was so much more interesting and lovable than most people one meets; there never was anyone like him … I keep finding myself thinking about something and saying to myself that I must

> tell Frank that, but of course then I have to pull myself up and realise that there will never be any more telling Frank anything. I think I shall always miss him most terribly. I met him in 1937, just twelve years ago, and we had hardly been away from each other since then. We had so much in common and seemed to know we were fond of each other right from the first. Well, it has been a wonderful twelve years. And now I must try and do what I can for the children alone. They are too young to realise quite what has happened, but they know that Daddy has gone forever and Alan is a little bit worried, and said yesterday 'Don't you die, Mummy' … they adored Frank so much that I can never fill the gap.

Edna said she had lost all interest in the new house but that they would have to have somewhere to live as they had to be out of the rented house the next March. She told Isabel she would send some recent photos of the children and said how like Frank Alan was and that 'Barbara is more like me and is a very sweet little thing just now and quite happy pottering about the house with whoever is here to do the housework'.

When Mary heard of Frank's death she wrote cryptically in her diary[2]:

> Cable from NZ that Frank died suddenly last night. Rang Bill who went to Barnt Green to break news to Mother. Rang Sheona. Told Fay [who happened to be with her]. It was a great shock to us all. Fabian local society meeting at House. Fay is staying with us until Thursday.

Fay remembered that Mary had been very kind to her.

Isabel wrote to Mary on 4 October to say what a shock the news of Frank's death had been and how good it was of Bill to come up. He had told Isabel how upset Eileen was to hear the news. Isabel said she has been working hard in the garden to stop herself worrying. She would write to Edna and would always keep in touch with her. After Isabel had read the letter from Edna she forwarded it to Mary with her own letter dated 14 October saying:

> I know you will feel very sad when you have read Edna's letter. I feel most dreadfully sorry for her and only wish I could see her, but I have always felt I knew her quite well and I had always kept in touch with her and Frank. I shall always be grateful to her for making Frank so happy. Will you send the letter back soon as I must send it to Bill to read and then to Madge?

When Sheona heard of Frank's death she wrote to Isabel:

Dearest Isabel

I wish I could be with you instead of writing – if it is humanly possible Oliver and I will come and see you within the next week or two – just for the day, not to stay the night. I am glad Bill can be with you now and that Mary & Michael are coming for the weekend.

I have been thinking lately that in spite of the tragedy and sorrow of death, the thing that matters is not when one dies, but how one lives, and as far as Frank is concerned you & Daddy can be proud and happy. He showed terrific courage and initiative in the First War both in the trenches and with Lawrence of Arabia. Whenever I hear Kiplings 'If' I think of him after the earthquake because of 'lose, and start again at your beginnings and never breathe a word about your loss'. Also he produced very fine and clever children, has done awfully good work as a doctor, and everyone has always liked him. I remember at a hunt ball at Northallerton when Frank was very young, a most alarming and critical man with a Boer War VC simply beaming upon him and obviously thinking that England couldn't quite be going to the dogs if she could still produce young men like that.

If my children turn out as well as Frank, Mary and Bill, I shall be more than content. Oliver is very distressed as he has always thought so highly of Frank.

We both send our love to you and Daddy and hope to see you soon.

Your loving – Sheona

Edna received a letter from Mary enclosing three pounds for her to buy flowers to put on Frank's grave. Edna replied on 25 October thanking her:

I have not been out to Frank's grave yet, I shall buy some nice flowers and take them out myself one day; so far I have not had the courage to go there. I went to the funeral service at the chapel, but not to the cemetery … I had a very dear friend of ours take the service. He is an Air Force chaplain and very fond of plays and play producing so he and Frank had much in common. He told me it was an honour to be asked to take the service.

Edna said in her letter that to Frank 'life was always such an interest … he was so vitally alive that this house is quite silent without him when the two children are in bed.' She said that Frank was writing some articles for the radio which he had called *Literary Fringes*[3] and had not had time to record them, but that a friend was going to read them over the radio as a tribute to Frank. Edna told Mary how fond and proud Frank was of Jane and Fay, although he was disappointed in Jane's premature marriage. He had even wanted to forego the holiday to Australia in 1947 they had had in order to get Jane to come to New Zealand instead of marrying, but she would not. Edna observed that she thought that marriage was Jane's real interest and it was a pity she had not waited as 'she would have had lots of choice as she promised to be very beautiful'.

Edna went on to say that her sister Mavis was coming over from Australia for a fortnight to help her, and Edna hoped to be able to spend Christmas with the family in Australia. Mary must have asked her whether she might return to England as Edna wrote: 'As to a trip to England, there is nothing I should like more, in fact I should like to live in England more than anywhere if one didn't depend on medical practice for a living.' She said that after much thought she would continue with the house building; the children 'love to go and watch the new house being built and are planning what kind of room they are to have when we go there … They are a sweet pair and full of life and plans.' She said she thought the children had come through with as little trauma as possible, but 'it was hard to have to tell them to go to bed quietly and quickly because Daddy was sick, and tell them he was dead when they woke'. She mentioned to Mary Alan's confusion as to what had happened to Frank:

> Alan suggested that there he was in his portrait, and when I took out an old photograph to put in my bedroom he wouldn't rest till I found another to put up in the sitting-room, and said I must take another one to the rooms [surgery]. Funny little things, one doesn't know what they are thinking. He talks to Daddy and asks him what he is doing up there on the wall all by himself. He is doing very well at school and likes it very much.

She ended on a wistful note saying: 'Well, goodnight, and I hope I see you all again some day. I suppose I'll get things sorted out soon.'

There were several obituaries in the national and local papers in New Zealand and a long obituary in the *Hauraki Plains Gazette* of 19 October 1949:

> News of the sudden death in Auckland recently of Dr Frank Birkinshaw was received in the Coromandel and surrounding district with widespread regret. As medical superintendent of the Coromandel and Mercury Bay hospitals for over five years, Dr Birkinshaw earned the affection and gratitude of many people both old and young. His cheery smile and happy knack of making his patients feel at ease will be long remembered by many people, a number of whom still went to him for advice after he left the district.

The obituary went on to say that Frank was the medical officer of the Loyal Hauraki (Masonic) Lodge and also a member and always took an interest in the affairs of the Order. It said that shortly after Frank arrived at Coromandel he started to plan the layout of the grounds at the hospital 'by utilising unemployed relief workers' and soon changed the appearance of the garden, and now the gardens were admired by many people and 'stand as one of the many tributes to his memory'. He also made many improvements to the hospital itself. The X-ray plant was set up, and a modern operating table was obtained as a result of 'his many petitions to the Board'. During the war he took a very active part in patriotic affairs; one of his ideas, 'that of the ugly man contest', resulted in over £360 being raised. He held first-aid classes 'which were attended by as many as forty at a time', and he organised ambulance services in the locality. He was also president of the Coromandel Returned Soldiers' Association for two years during the war period and 'he proved a good leader and helped to keep the returned men together and plan for the return of the younger men who were then on active service'. The article continued:

> As an organiser and leader Dr Birkinshaw's approach was irresistible and the force of his personality counted much in the success of the efforts that were so constantly being held for patriotic purposes. All these activities were carried out in addition to the exacting nature of his work which involved driving many miles over rough roads ... on his errands of mercy.

The Coromandel County Council stood in silence as a mark of respect and the article concluded by saying that 'public spirited men are all too few in these small country places'.

In November Edna received a letter of condolence from Alan Brassington who had known Frank in Christchurch and had also met Edna. He said that Frank had asked him to be the guardian of Jane and Fay many years before 'in case of calamity'. He said Frank was a 'wonderful person, far ahead of the times in many ways, and has been a deep influence on my outlook'. Alan had earlier written to another mutual friend of his and Frank, Maurice Brook, after he heard about Frank's death, the letter somehow ending up in Edna's possession:

> It was most thoughtful of you to write me so quickly about Frank, who has meant so very much to me in the past. You, who knew Frank, understand what an interesting and stimulating friend he was … I hated it when he left Christchurch … Frank wrote for the *Press* for years, a very bright column of Radio notes, which was read eagerly and wrangled over each week. It was provocative, witty, and ahead of the time.

He finished by saying what a vivid personality Frank had been and that they 'share the memory of a very dear friend'.

Edna's sister Mavis wrote to say she would come over to help and Edna replied to her:

> I got your letter yesterday saying you would probably be along on the 9th. If you come earlier it will be just as easy to handle, just get someone to send a cable during the day and we'll all be at the flying boat base to meet you. It is down at the quay and easy to get at. I do hope you have better weather than there is this week, but still there is only sea and sky to look at anyhow during the trip, so perhaps it is just as good to look at clouds!
>
> I have been pottering along with what there is of the practice, and as there is not a terrible lot at the moment I have been able to cope with things. I hope there will be more by the time you come.
>
> I don't think there is anything I want you to bring over. Alan has been worrying me to death for a geographical globe, but I found one of those and bought it for him. It hasn't been sent yet, but hope it will turn up today.
>
> I'm sorry if I have disappointed Margaret [Cadell, their cousin]. Would she like to come over after you go, or if I do manage Christmas perhaps she would like to come back with me? I think you will see that we would be tumbling over each other with another here and I am not good at coping just now with pushes and crowds. My children are terribly rackety and keep one fully occupied when one is at home; people say they are very healthy for doctors' children. I hope they remain so.
>
> Well, that's about all. We are all looking forward to seeing you, and I think you will be interested in our new house. It should have the roof on this week, then they can get going on the fittings, and no time to waste either, as we have to be out of the Meadowbank house by early March.
>
> With love to you all – Nannie [the nickname her family called her by]

Edna and the children went to Queensland, this time by flying boat, for Christmas of 1949 which they spent with Edna's father Jack who lived at Callandoon, near Goondiwindi, with his daughter Mavis and her son John. Jack had been widowed in 1920. Mavis too had been widowed, in 1943, when her husband, also called John, was killed by a Japanese sniper in New Guinea during the war. Callandoon was run by Edna and Mavis's younger brother Tony who also lived there with his wife Olive and their two children Gillie and Rorie. Tony had been a pilot in the Royal Australian Air Force and had

Above: John Thorn, Gillie Mackenzie, Alan and Barbara, and Rorie Mackenzie
Christmas 1949 at Callandoon
Below: with Grandfather Jack Mackenzie

met Olive while he was posted in Northern Scotland where she was serving in the WAAF.

Edna, Alan and I returned to New Zealand after the holiday and moved into the new house in Victoria Avenue in 1950. It was an unusual house built by the avant-garde architect Vernon Brown, who was a friend of Frank and Edna. It was painted in striking dark and light colours and had a garage underneath the house. Vernon Brown had previously built a house for some other mutual friends, Frank and Honey Haigh, Frank being a prominent Auckland lawyer. When Honey Haigh told Vernon Brown her mother had left her a grand piano which she wanted to put in the living room of her new house, Brown had retorted 'you're not having that awful thing in my lovely room'; Brown had to design a special alcove for it.[4] My mother also had a grand piano in her living room, but perhaps Brown had not noticed it. Frank Haigh was also a campaigner for progressive left wing causes. This group of friends, along with some others, including ARD Fairburn, Denis Glover and Frank Sargeson, a well-known short story writer, would meet for Sunday lunch parties at the Haigh house and were known as the Auckland Intelligentsia. In 1948 Sir Lawrence Olivier and Vivien Leigh, while on tour, visited the Haigh house. Vernon Brown's architecture became very sought after and was often commissioned by 'left-leaning academics, and professional people and artists who shunned uniformity', according to Peter Shaw's book *A History of New Zealand Architecture*.[5] Most of Brown's houses were in Remuera, the Auckland suburb, and made of weatherboard finished in white paint and creosote with a low pitched lean-to roof. Peter Shaw described them as being 'like a coconut with a bite taken out'.

The New Zealand Institute of Architects, in a recent exhibition of Vernon Brown Architecture in Auckland, gave a description of the 'Edna Birkinshaw' house, prefacing it with the fact that Dr Edna Mackenzie had married Frank Birkinshaw and 'bore him two more children, Barbara and Alan, who survived to adulthood despite living in this long north-facing three-bedroomed house with its precipitous unfenced concrete deck'. They described it as follows:

> With its monopitch roof and sliding glass doors, this was Vernon Brown's strongest modernist statement at this point ... A curving ply wall and inset Chinese ceramic panels are part of the unusual interior fittings, which also features recessed lighting, and glass walls dividing interior spaces.

Alan went to the primary school 'just over the fence' from the house and later to the King's Prep School close by. When I was old enough I went to 'kindy' as they called kindergarten.

Victoria Avenue house; With thanks to AGM Publishing Ltd. Home and Building *magazine 1951*

Victoria Avenue house - Chinese ceramic panels on wall

Short S30 Flying Boat, Auckland Harbour

In May 1950 Margaret, who was now living in London at 2 Wildwood Grove, Hampstead, received a letter from Edna's lawyers explaining the situation of Frank's estate. Edna, they said, wanted to make sure that Margaret knew why Jane and Fay were not to receive any money from the estate. At that time both the girls were at university, Jane at Exeter and Fay at St Andrew's. Frank had not left a will and under New Zealand law the widow was entitled to all the personal effects plus one thousand pounds absolutely. The total assets amounted to £2,674 less debts and bank overdraft of £944. The balance of the estate after the value of the personal effects was deducted was only £352 which would therefore go to Edna.

In March 1950 Isabel wrote to Mary to say she had heard from Edna who had sent her some photos of the children. Isabel said that Alan was a nice looking boy, but that Edna had said that Barbara 'takes a bad photo as she always screws her eyes up'. Isabel told Mary Herbert's opinion:

> Pater thinks Barbara very plain looking but I like her looks and I think you would. She has red hair and a very fair skin. Edna says she has hair the colour of hers. She is a fine looking child. Alan reads to her now.

On 16 June 1950 Edna wrote again to her mother-in-law:

> My dear Mamma,
>
> Today is Frank's birthday and I feel sad that he is not here to have a little celebration, as we always did. I sent you off a food parcel this morning, as a birthday gift from him. Alan had his birthday yesterday, turned six. He is very thrilled at being six and tomorrow, being Saturday, he is having his birthday party and having a few friends for the afternoon. I managed to get him a Swiss watch which goes on a chain in his pocket, and has a luminous dial.

Edna speculated in the letter as to whether she would be able to carry on with the practice for much longer as 'there are so many doctors now, especially in my line'. She was thinking of moving to somewhere more remote and doing a more general medical practice, and was looking out for any opportunities. That would of course be more difficult as far as the children's schooling was concerned. She told Isabel she had been planting bulbs and cuttings in the garden of the new house to make it feel more like home and that the surrounding view was very beautiful. She finished by saying 'I'll write again soon, today seems rather a sad day, but I thought you might like me to write'.

In July 1950 Isabel wrote to Mary to ask her to buy something for me for my birthday in August. She had enclosed a ten shilling note and suggested a small teddy bear. Isabel said of Herbert 'Dad is not at all interested in either Edna or the children'. Isabel also enclosed Edna's recent letter for Mary to read.

By 1951 Edna decided she could no longer stay in New Zealand and in October of that year she packed everything up and let the Victoria Avenue house to tenants. Earlier in the year Edna had taken Alan and myself for one last visit to Australia to say goodbye to her family. It was the last visit we made to Australia from New Zealand and the last time my mother would see her father, and Alan and I our grandfather; we would not set foot in Australia again for another eleven years. Edna had thought of moving to Sydney to live and work and be nearer her family, and had looked around for something suitable when she was there, but had not found anything.

According to Phyllis Fickling, who was our nanny at the time, and to whom I spoke many years later, I had not wanted to leave New Zealand, but nonetheless Edna, Alan and myself boarded a ship and headed for England. The ship was the *MV New Zealand Star*, a refrigerated cargo liner belonging to the Blue Star Line which only took a handful of passengers. According to the passenger list, which I found in the National Archives, only eight passengers left from Auckland, an architect and his wife, a mother and her two children and us three. We picked up another two passengers at Panama - a shipping agent and his wife. My brother remembered the ship stopping at Curaçao off the coast of Venezuela, probably to pick up supplies. We must have had a fairly comfortable voyage as all the cabins were first class and nearly all with en suite bathrooms, according to the ship's brochure of the time.[6] The brochure showed a grand piano in the lounge and described some of the ship's facilities as follows:

> Although ships are primarily intended for freight carrying, the passenger accommodation is dainty, commodious, well planned and decorated with that taste and forethought for which the Blue Star Line is so famous. A selection of books is provided for the use of passengers. Music and other entertainment is obtainable from a radio receiver.

The journey must have been particularly poignant for my mother, as twelve years earlier she and Frank had travelled on another Blue Star liner on their way to their new life in New Zealand.

The only thing I remember about the voyage was getting lost one day in the ship's long corridors while looking for our cabin. I could find neither my mother nor my brother, and I sat down on the floor, all alone, and cried.

APPENDIX

These four *Literary Fringes* were written by Frank in the 1940s to be read over the radio, and are lightly based on episodes in his life and on people he knew. They were commissioned by the New Zealand Broadcasting Corporation. Occasionally he used a pseudonym when writing, Barry Mansfield being his favourite. Unfortunately Frank died before he was able to broadcast them and after his death one of his friends was asked to read them as a tribute and memorial to him. They were then read again at a later date by a regular broadcaster and subsequently returned to Edna to keep. The money raised from the broadcasting fee was used to buy a tangible memorial to Frank, which was in the form of a chronometer clock engraved with his name, which was hung in the hospital at Coromandel. After the hospital closed in 1994 the clock was moved to the Coromandel School of Mines and Historical Museum where it remains on show.

In a letter many years later, Edna told Mary about the articles and Mary contacted the *New Statesman* who wanted to publish the first one. Unfortunately they dropped the idea as they were nervous about copyright.

This clock is dedicated to the memory of Frank Thornton Birkinshaw, MRCS. LRCP who was Superintendent of the Coromandel Hospital 1939-1944 and who died in Auckland 2 October 1949

Literary Fringes – No 1

The Hard Way to Hamlet by Barry Mansfield[1]

Reading Shakespeare is a thing that happens to practically everybody on earth who can read or write. Most of us make the approach the easy way; either we learn one of his plays at school, or an elderly aunt gives us his collected works for a birthday present, or we see *Hamlet* at the pictures with a dashing Prince and lovely Ophelia.

And talking of *Hamlet*, I approached *Hamlet* the hard way. Nothing easy about *Hamlet* at all. I read *Hamlet* right bang in the middle of the Arabian Desert, with a temperature of about 120 degrees Fahrenheit beating down on me from a cloudless glaring sky. And me, with a .45 Webley and Scott revolver in one hand, with a small crowd of unfriendly Bedouins watching me read *Hamlet* with the other hand, feeling very hot and very bothered!

It was in 1917. Me, I was very young, quite a lot under twenty, and a very unexceptionable 1st Air Mechanic in the Royal Flying Corps in a flight clipped of No 14 Squadron. Somebody said 'Here, you're to take Captain Lawrence up country' and I said, 'who's Captain Lawrence, and how am I going to take him?' And the somebody said, 'he's the wizard Lawrence, he is. He looks you in the fice and you does as 'e likes.'

So about twenty minutes later I had packed a Crossley Tender with rations for a week and loaded my revolver, and filled the tanks with water and slung a little washleather bag with ten sovereigns minted in Australia round my neck, and saw that my service rifle had plenty of ammunition and that I had twelve spare tyres and plenty of petrol and oil.

Captain Lawrence and I started from Aqaba, where there's still a little trouble going on by the way. It's a few mud huts and a broken down castle at the head of the Gulf of Aqaba, in the Red Sea. We went northwards and eastwards and we crossed the Hejaz Railway somewhere near the castle of Shobak, and then we were theoretically in enemy territory.

Captain Lawrence wasn't a very brilliant conversationalist. He said, after one day's travelling, on the morning of the second day, 'Do you like marmalade?' 'No' I said. He reflected on my reply for a few more miles and then said, 'I don't like marmalade either'.

Captain Lawrence – T E Lawrence – was about twenty-eight years old at the time. He was very untidily dressed. Like me, he was wearing a khaki shirt and shorts and the standard Bedouin headdress which all ranks wore in the desert. But at his side he carried, not a service revolver, but a very beautiful dagger in its sheath of gold wire. Lawrence was a small man, he came up only to my neck in height, he was slight, but he was muscularly lean. His complexion was of that light golden colour that is sometimes found in the native of Damascus.

However, this isn't a war story, but a literary 'conte'. On the afternoon of the second day, and still going east, the Crossley Tender hit a rock. The sump underneath the engine was made of aluminium, a hole was torn in the underside of this, and a gallon of oil poured over the sands of the desert. The conversation then went something like this:

Lawrence: Hit a rock eh?

Me: Yes, sir.

Lawrence: Bad, eh?

Me: Yes, sir.

Lawrence: Can't get any further, eh?

Me: Doesn't look like it.

Lawrence: Awkward, eh?

As a literary conversation this was negligible. But then I didn't know at the time that I was talking to a future literary genius and the future author of the *Seven Pillars of Wisdom*, and he didn't know that he was talking to a somewhat inconsequent Boswell. Had we both been able to foresee the future how different would our remarks to each other have been!

However, after a suitable interval, Lawrence decided to leave me with the water and the Crossley Tender. He himself would walk to Shobak, pick up some camels and obtain help for me in the shape of a new engine sump.

His parting conversation, very vividly remembered, was as follows:

Lawrence: I'm leaving the attaché case in the car.

Me: Yes, sir.

Lawrence: If there's any trouble sit on it.

Me: Yes, sir.

Lawrence: You'll be here for about twenty-four hours.

Me: Yes, sir.

Lawrence: If there's any real trouble, burn the car and the attaché case.

Me (somewhat doubtfully): Yes, sir.

Lawrence: I've got a volume of Shakespeare's tragedies here. I'll lend them to you. Have you read *Hamlet*?

Me: No sir,

Lawrence: Interesting story. Better read it. Hamlet was like me somehow. Always got himself into trouble without any logical reason.

Me: Yes, sir.

So Lawrence, with a waterbottle and haversack slung round him, walked off into the desert. I watched him until he became part of the mirage which always formed the desert horizon. And then I began to consider my own position. I was, as far as I knew, about forty miles inside Turkish, that is to say enemy, territory. I had a car that couldn't be made to go, water for two days and food for a week. If any Bedouins appeared, they would in all probability be unfriendly. They might shoot me. Or they might take me prisoner and hand me over to the Turks, which would be even more unpleasant. I also had three of Shakespeare's tragedies in a small volume, *Romeo and Juliet*, *Hamlet, Prince of Denmark*, and *Othello, the Moor of Venice.*

I had been instructed by Captain Lawrence to read *Hamlet*. I had two hours of daylight left, so I began to read *Hamlet*.

I finished Act 1:

> And still your fingers on your lips, I pray.
> The time is out of joint; O cursed spite,
> That ever I was born to set it right!
> Nay, come, let's go together.

It was nearly dark. I put *Hamlet, Prince of Denmark* on the front seat of the Crossley Tender. I put the attaché case under a cushion. I tied the lanyard of my revolver round my wrist. And I went off into a peaceful sleep.

Did I say a peaceful sleep? My mistake! I was awakened at dawn by a gentle tug at my wrist – the wrist to which was tied the lanyard of my revolver! I gave a yell. A Bedouin walked away with the majestic air of a man who wouldn't dream of stealing a man's revolver.

There was a small crowd squatting round the car. About fifteen or twenty men, about the same number of women and a few very small children. The men were well armed. They each had more than one rifle, and each had more than one knife. Most of them squinted. Their eyes were full of pus and crowded with flies. The women were shapeless masses of black, their faces were not visible. The children were just like any other dark brown children, friendly and very dirty.

'Good morning,' I said in my best Arabic. There was no reply. I tried my best winning smile. But there was no winning smile in return. I definitely hadn't the art of making friends and influencing people. The circle round the Crossley car was ominously silent. I decided that they were unfriendly Bedouins. I wondered how I was meant to interpret Lawrence's instructions. He had said: 'If there's any real trouble burn the car and the attaché case.' I wondered did he mean *me* to be part of the funeral pyre? It was a difficult situation.

You see, this hostile ring of Bedouins just sat still, and watched. They watched in silence while I opened a warm can of beef and ate it with two biscuits and washed it down with some warm water. I got out of the car and walked a step or two towards them, but I could sense their stiffening and their taking a firmer clutch on their rifles. So back I went to the car. Occasionally, one or other of them would rise and saunter towards the car and examine the headlamps with peculiar care. When they did this I stiffened and held my hand a little closer to my revolver. The sun rose higher in the sky. A few more Bedouins arrived, this time with a few goat-hair rugs, which they erected to make a crude lean-to tent. It looked as though they were going to make a day of it.

The women and children got bored, and vanished. The men stayed in their circle. They didn't discuss matters with each other. They just stayed put. Occasionally one or two would walk away and would be replaced by reinforcements.

Me, I didn't know what to do. Naturally I was very afraid. But Lawrence had told me to read *Hamlet*.

Out came *Hamlet*. I commenced Act Two. It was hot. Unbearably hot. Sweat fell from my face on to the pages of *Hamlet*, Act Two:

> What's Hecuba to him, or he to Hecuba,
> That he should weep for her? What would he do,
> Had he the motive and the cue for passion
> That I have, he would drown the stage with tears ……

The circle of Bedouins was still there. One of them sauntered up to the back of the Crossley Tender and picked up a blanket. He handled it for a few moments. I wondered whether I should make any gesture with my revolver. But thinking, I decided it might be my last gesture, so I thought better of it and watched him closely. He dropped the blanket and walked back to the circle.

At midday I drank more warm water and ate more warm bully beef and biscuit. I had reached Act Five by the early afternoon:

> How long will a man lie in the earth ere he rot?
> Faith, if he be not rotten before he die –
> He will last some eight year, or nine year …..

The Bedouins were becoming restless. They were also becoming more unpleasant in their behaviour. One of them shot at a head lamp of the Crossley, at point blank range. The glass and metal shattered simultaneously. A hit, a very palpable hit, I said to myself. But I didn't think it at all funny. I stopped reading *Hamlet* with some abruptness and clutched my revolver.

And then I heard the engine of a BE 2e 1915 model. The Bedouins heard it at the same time. The tension became suddenly slack. A message bag came fluttering down from the plane. I ran and picked it up. I put out a landing T. The plane landed ungracefully with a lot of bumping. That would be Lieutenant Makins. He always bumped when he landed. It was.

Well, I had been told to read *Hamlet*. And I'd read it the hard way. But I was very young. A year afterwards I was in hospital at Port Tewfik and I swapped my borrowed copy of Lawrence's *Tragedies of Shakespeare* for a pair of brown shoes which were too large for the jockey they belonged to. It was quite a pity, because the book was autographed!

Literary Fringes – No 2

How I nearly became a Poet

I really meant to tell you this evening how I was once kissed by an empress,[1] which is, of course, a most unusual occurrence; in fact I'm told that it is at the present time quite impossible, because world events have caused such a shortage of empresses, especially white empresses. Actually, I have an idea that white empresses are extinct.

But, instead, I'd like to tell you how I became a poet in London. And this account may give just a few pointers on how to approach poets, how to write verse, and how to get it published. And as all knowledge is based on experience, perhaps my own experiences may serve as a very inadequate guide.

First of all, of course, the prospective poet must arrive in London. If he comes from the English provinces, he may arrive penniless; if he comes from the Dominions, he should have a small income. If he comes from the United States, he *must* have a *large* income.

Me, I compromised. I arrived in London sometime in the nineteen twenties. I possessed a very well-cut double-breasted suit of Saxony tweed and made to measure by a good tailor. I also had some well-cut shirts and a presentable dinner jacket. The month before coming to London I had let my hair grow. This is very important, and I must strongly impress on all prospective poets that they *must* let their hair grow. I have met hundreds of poets, some of them quite well-established, and not one of them has short hair.

When I arrived in London I left my luggage at Euston Station in the cloakroom. The complete outfit consisted of a theatrical luggage basket in which was a camp-bed, five blankets, a small original portrait by Burne-Jones of a somewhat goitrous red-headed female, several silver photograph frames enclosing portraits of distant relatives and some assorted underwear and shoes.

The silver photograph frames, I say in all modesty, were a stroke of genius on my part. They were quite heavy, and were worth seven shillings of any pawnbroker's money. Under my arm, because it was too big for the basket, was an oriental rug. In my pockets were twenty one-pound notes, a few shillings in silver and a letter of introduction to an archdeacon. The money was to keep me for thirteen weeks.

I arrived from the country at Euston Station about mid-day and with my oriental rug tucked under my arm I took a No 14 bus to Bloomsbury, the poet's Mecca.

Now, what comes next is quite frankly a little incredible. You see, I expected to see poets by the dozen, and actually, as soon as I stepped off the bus at the Russell Hotel in Southampton Row, I did see a real, live one. There he was, Harold Monro, in person.[2] He was stroking his chin. He had dazzling teeth. I recognised him instantly because I had seen many photographs of him. He was the owner of the famous Poetry Bookshop. He was the idol of embryo writers in the early twenties. He was also probably the best, or one of the best, of the Georgian poets.

In cases like this, as you know, hesitation is fatal. So, with my oriental rug under my left arm, I went up to Harold Monro.

'You *are* Mr Monro, aren't you?' I said just a little doubtfully.

'I *am* Harold Monro,' he replied.

'I've just come to London,' I said.

'I knew it,' said Harold Monro. 'I can tell by your long hair. You write verse, and you want me to read it, and, if possible, to publish it.'

'I've never written any verse,' I replied sadly.

'In that case, I'm very happy to meet you,' said Harold Monro. 'It will give me the greatest possible pleasure to offer you some coffee. I live just round the corner.'

He strode away and I followed him, with my oriental rug tucked firmly under my arm. His house, the Poetry Book Shop, was only a few minutes away; a very beautiful Georgian house in a slum street off Theobald's Road, Devonshire Street to be exact. The street itself was sad and decrepit, but the Poetry Book Shop shone and glowed in a blaze of fresh paint.

We had coffee. I admired the shop, the poetry broadsheets, and the very decorative female who was apparently an assistant. Harold Monro looked at me, I thought a little sternly.

'You look too well-dressed for a poet,' said Harold Monro critically.

'But I'm not a poet,' I said. 'And anyway, I got an unexpected war gratuity, and I spent it on clothes.'

'Where are you going to live?' asked Harold Monro.

'I've no idea,' I said.

'Would you like to be a poet?' said Harold Monro, rather surprisingly.

'Isn't it rather difficult?' I said.

'Good Lord, no,' said Harold Monro. 'Being a poet is simply a matter of writing verse. And knowing what to do with it after you've written it.'

'Oh,' I said.

'I'll tell you what,' said Harold Monro, 'I've got a room upstairs I can let you have. There's a bathroom next to it and a gas stove on the landing.'

'I won't be able to afford it,' I said sadly.

You know, Harold Monro must have been a very persuasive poet, because I found myself following him upstairs. Two flights.

'Here it is,' said Harold Monro. Was it? It was. It was a large room. The ceiling was painted black. The walls were black. The floor was enamelled a bright orange. The Adam fireplace was painted black and the three very beautiful windows overlooking the slum of Devonshire Street were picked out in the same screaming shade of orange as was the floor.

'Good, isn't it?' said Harold Monro firmly.

'It's wonderful,' I said, rather weakly.

'Flecker[3] lived here for some time. It was *his* idea,' said HM. 'Anyway, it's yours. What furniture have you got?'

I undid the cord which held my oriental rug in position. It looked pale and wan as I laid it on the orange floor.

'Good,' said HM again, 'then you can bring anything else this afternoon. I'm going to Cornwall for three weeks' holiday tomorrow. If you're doing nothing at any time just open the shop and sell anything to anybody. But no credit, mind you, definitely no credit.'

I thought of the decorative assistant. Harold Monro must have read my thoughts. 'No,' he said, 'she won't be here either. You'd better give me three months' rent in advance.' 'How much?' I said. 'Five shillings a week, and you can look after the shop in your spare time.'

Well, I think you must admit that the offer sounded generous. I gave Harold Monro three pounds and five shillings for thirteen weeks' rent, and I thanked him and his extremely decorative assistant, and away I went to Euston Station to collect my wicker luggage basket. That evening I slept in the orange and black room on my camp bed, and admired a second-hand writing desk I had purchased in Theobald's Road for fourteen and sixpence. The silver photograph frames gleamed on the Adam mantelpiece. Mr Burne-Jones' goitrous masterpiece reposed chastely against a wall. I was on the way to becoming a poet.

The next morning I opened the shop at about ten o'clock.

At eleven o'clock a tall, thin man about thirty years old walked into the shop.

'Cambridge man?' he said.

'No,' I said, sadly.

'Oxford, perhaps?' he said with a touch of doubt in his voice.

'No.' I said, sadly.

'You're not a writer, then?'

'I hope to be,' I said.

'Not a hope old boy, not a hope. You can't expect to write unless you've been to one of the older universities.'

'No,' I said.

'Well, there it is old boy. Hard luck and that kind of thing. By the way, my name is Goldring, Douglas Goldring.[4] Of course you've read *Triumphal Ode*.'

'No,' I said. 'Pity,' he said and walked out of the shop.

In the afternoon a very friendly young man called Alec Waugh[5] came into the shop. He didn't seem to mind very much about my neither having been to Cambridge nor to Oxford. He told me that writing was one of the simplest things in the world. 'All you have to do,' he said, 'is to write eighty thousand words divided up into chapters. That makes an ordinary novel. If you want to write a serious novel you have to write a hundred and twenty thousand words.'

'It sounds simple,' I said.

'It is simple. And then all you have to do is to find a publisher.'

'Is that simple?' I said.

'Of course it's simple,' said Alec Waugh, happily. 'You see, my father is a publisher. He *has* to publish what I write. Take my young brother, Evelyn. He can't write for nuts, but he will! You mark my words. That's the only formula. Pen, paper, some spare time, and a father who's a publisher.'

'So you think I might become a writer?' I asked.

'No trouble at all,' said Alec. 'I'll fix it all up for you. I'll give you a ring later on in the week; there'll be a party or something we can go to.'

I was beginning to see the formula. All I needed was a father who was a publisher and who would send me to Cambridge or Oxford. It seemed quite simple.

The next day or so passed quietly and happily. I opened the shop when I liked and shut it when I liked. Dr. CEM Joad[6] came in and bought some books. He didn't wear a beard then. Several other writers and poets dropped in. Some gave me good advice and tried to borrow a few shillings, others didn't give me good advice. In the evenings I sat in front of my writing desk and began work on my first volume of sonnets.

But on the fourth day of my stay tragedy happened!

A very large, and to me very fearsome, woman entered the shop. 'Where,' she said, 'is Harold Monro?' 'I think in Cornwall,' I said. 'I am coming to live here,' she said. 'Does Harold Monro know?' I asked. 'Harold Monro certainly does know,' she said. 'He has allowed me to use one of his rooms. Here is the receipt.'

I got that sick feeling in the stomach and that dry feeling in the mouth, and that jellied feeling at the back of the knees. I just knew something was wrong. It was. She showed me the receipt, letting the room, *my* room, to one Clare Sheridan[7] for three months at one pound a week.

'Are you *the* Clare Sheridan?' I asked. 'I am,' she replied. 'You're a cousin of Winston Churchill?' 'I am,' she said firmly. 'And you've just returned from Russia.' 'I have,' she said. 'Where you sculpted the head of Lenin and Trotsky.' 'I did,' she said, grimly. 'And they tried to keep you in Russia by force, but they hadn't a chance?' 'They hadn't a single, little chance,' said Clare Sheridan. You know, I didn't have to think very much, I just knew.

There didn't seem to be very much point in fighting. The lady didn't look like the sort of person whom I could persuade by argument, or even by reading her my sonnets. So I took her upstairs. She didn't even blanch at the sight of the black and orange room. She stared at the oriental rug, though. The oriental rug of my delight.

'Is that your rug?' she asked. 'Yes,' I said. 'It's a Khizbah. Comes from Georgia. Not much good.' 'No,' I said. 'You can sleep here tonight. I'll move in tomorrow sometime.' 'Yes.'

You know I didn't have a single little chance. Like Lenin and Trotsky and the combined might of Soviet Russia, I didn't have a single chance against Clare Sheridan.

So me, I tossed that night on my little camp bed, and the next day I packed my poor belongings and went to Pimlico. I had had nearly one week of being a poet, and of meeting with poets and talking to poets and of writing sonnets.

But before I left the beautiful Georgian building in the slum street I left a little note on my fourteen and sixpenny writing desk. You see I knew that if Clare Sheridan put her elbows squarely on the writing desk it would simply collapse. So I left this little note: 'I would like you to have this, Clare Sheridan.' And then I went out and had a haircut.

Literary Fringes – No 3

How I nearly wrote a Thriller!

I had an idea that I might tell you the rather strange story of Katherine Mansfield and the sheet of pink blotting paper in the Gray's Inn Road. But Katherine Mansfield seems to have only a limited interest nowadays, so instead if you don't mind, I'll discuss the art of writing who-dun-its, and bang! bang! bang! three redskins bit the dusters. This latter class, the bang! bang! bangers! is really by far the easiest of any fiction to write. The only trouble about it is that it's shockingly badly paid. You see, a really fast writer working a forty-four hour week, can't earn as much as a good bricklayer working similar hours. You may not think this unfair, but it is because the writer has to buy fresh ribbons and, er – things, for his typewriter. The bricklayer doesn't have this extra expense as a rule.

Me, I had a very limited experience of writing this class of fiction. But although it was limited, it was in its way very spectacular.

This is how it happened.

One day I was travelling from Bristol to London in a Great Western express train. Third class, naturally. In the seat opposite me was a young man about the same age as myself. He was a good looking young man. His trousers were beautifully creased, his black shoes were highly polished, his thick brown hair was well brushed, he had a starched white collar, and, I think, yellow gloves. And he had that starry-eyed look on his face. The look of the eager young man who is filled with noble thoughts and good resolutions, and the resolve to set the Thames – or something – on fire.

We began to talk to each other.

His name was Allen Lane.[1] He was the nephew of John Lane, the well-known publisher, who had recently died. Young Allen Lane had been sent for from Bristol to take up a position in his uncle's firm.

Well, this was quite exciting. Me, I always thought of publishers as pie in the sky, bye and bye. Something that one didn't come across in real life. Something old and rather mouldy. And here was one, in the flesh, sitting opposite me.

Of course, I was writing a book at the time. I don't think I ever met anybody who wasn't writing a book at the time. All except Allen Lane, who'd just come from Bristol, and he thought about writers just about what I thought about publishers.

Well, we got on well together, and I saw quite a lot of him during the following month or so. He was given a minute cubby hole which he called his office in the famous establishment at the top end of the Albany, which is of course, or used to be, the haunt of London's eligible bachelors. He became friendly with lots of authors, went to the funeral of Anatole France, in Paris, and went to most of the necessary parties in the literary fringes. His clothes became even more meticulous and he began to be seen among the rightest kind of people in London.

Well, as I said, I was writing a book. And naturally I got stuck at chapter fourteen. My villain, a man known for some reason as 'The Tiger', was shipping cases of guns from Dymchurch to Spain. And my hero, who was a private eye called Barnard, was holding up the trucks in the Romney Marshes before they reached Dymchurch. My technical trouble was to find out the size of boat that could (a) anchor off Dymchurch and (b) get to Spain safely via the Bay of Biscay.

So you see, my boat had to be not too big, and certainly not too small.

So when I was telling Allen Lane about this, he came to the rescue. It seems that he knew a gun-runner, or at least a man who claimed to be a gun-runner. Allen Lane as a publisher had naturally to be very circumspect, but he wouldn't mind taking me to the Ham Bone Club where this man was to be found, and pointing him out to me. Then, of course, I could get all the information I wanted.

Off we went that night to the Ham Bone Club. It used to be in Ham Yard, just off Windmill Street, and only a hundred yards or so from Piccadilly Circus. It may be there still, but I expect the last war didn't help it much.[2]

And upstairs, sitting in a corner, behind a table, was the gun runner. He had two large diamonds deputising as shirt buttons, and a super size diamond, about four carats, stuck in a ring on one of his fingers. He was quite bald. Did I say bald? He *was*.

'This is Kevin Bull,' said Allen Lane.

'How do you do?' I said.

'Woof', said Kevin Bull, or words to that effect.

'I must go,' said Allen Lane, and he hurried away to the more right part of London's West End, if you see what I mean.

'What yer want?' said Kevin Bull.

'I've got some rifle cases on the beach at Dymchurch,' I said, 'and I want to know how to ….'

Now just as I said this I got a rather peculiar feeling at the pit of my stomach. And when I looked down to see where it was coming from, I saw that Kevin Bull's right hand was hidden under a newspaper, and from the end of the newspaper, which was lying rather untidily on the table, was the tip of an automatic. A .35 it was, I think. Very coy it looked.

Of course I didn't know what to do about it. I just cleared my throat in a gentle sort of manner. And waited. Kevin Bull waited as well. The tip of the barrel of the automatic kept on pointing at the pit of my stomach. There was a band in the next room. It went on playing. There was a bar at the other end of the room; lots of people were sitting up in front of it and chatting away gaily.

A girl waved to me from her table about twelve feet away. But I didn't feel a little bit like waving back.

'Spill,' said Kevin Bull.

I cleared my throat.

'You see, I'm writing a book. I've got stuck at chapter fourteen. I want your advice. At least I thought I wanted your advice.

'Writing a book, are yer?'

'Yes.'

There was the world of scorn in his voice. I noticed that the tip of the automatic no longer was under the newspaper. Kevin Bull leaned back and relaxed.

'Yer want advice about gun running?'

'Broadly speaking, yes,' I said.

'Keep out of it, see!'

'No good?' I asked.

'Good for some, no good for others, see!'

'Me, I see,' I said.

There was a pause. The orchestra went on playing quite happily. The bright hum of conversation continued. The pretty girl waved again. But somehow I wasn't really interested.

'Tell yer what,' said Kevin Bull. 'I'm going to Maldon tonight, see. Like to tag along?'

'Yes,' I said.

'All right,' he said. 'Ten o'clock. 34 Waterbank Crescent. Just this side of the Blackwall Tunnel.'

'All right,' I said.

Kevin Bull lost a certain amount of interest in me.

Well, about an hour and a half later, I was on my way to Waterbank Crescent on the bus. I got off at the Blackwall Tunnel; a few yards back was the road I wanted and a few yards down the road was a three-litre Bentley, a four-seater coupé. Kevin Bull was at the wheel of the Bentley. A somewhat bristly man was in the seat at the back. There was a small black leather suitcase on the floor in front of my seat.

'Get in,' said Kevin Bull.

I got in. I moved the suitcase on to my knee. It was very heavy for a small suitcase. We moved off, on the way to Stratford Broadway and Epping Forest, then to the Chelmsford Road.

'They're trying to douse me, see!' said Kevin Bull.

'Douse you?' I said.

'Douse me,' said Kevin Bull. 'Put me lights out, see.'

'Why?' I said.

'Habit of mine,' said Kevin Bull. 'Bad habit. I sell the guns to the Spaniards. Then I tell the other side. I get the money before the guns go aboard. Out goes the ship. The other side takes over, see. They sell me the guns back again. Spaniards don't like it. Can't take a joke, the Spaniards.'

By this time we had left London proper and were getting in to Epping Forest. If you don't know Epping Forest I might as well say that it's mainly grass and scattered trees, good roads running through, about twenty miles long and no lights and only a few buildings here and there.

I was thinking that Epping Forest was a perfect place for a murder!

Then Kevin Bull said: 'They're going to get Kevin Bull tonight.'

'Who are?' I said.

'They are,' said Kevin Bull. But it won't be Kevin Bull, see.'

'Er – who will it be,' I said. Rather faintly, I think I said it.

'Not me,' said Kevin Bull.

The Bentley gurgled along through Epping Forest; and at a particularly quiet and sinister looking part, he pulled up the car.

'Take the suitcase, Tiny,' he said to the man in the back seat.

Tiny leaned over and took the suitcase.

'Now get out, see,' said Kevin Bull.

I got out.

'Now sit down there, see,' said Kevin Bull.

I sat down.

I didn't feel at all happy. Quite frankly, I didn't like Kevin Bull and I didn't like Epping Forest. The ground I was sitting on was rather damp, and I felt sure I would catch my death of cold.

The man called Tiny got out of the car and opened the suitcase. In it there was a safety razor, some shaving cream, a suit of clothes the same colour as those worn by Kevin Bull, a small coil of rope, a pair of scissors and an automatic similar to the one worn by Kevin Bull. In the meantime Kevin Bull was sitting on the running board of the Bentley. He had an automatic as well. I had an idea that it seemed to be pointed mainly in my direction.

'D'yer see?' said Kevin Bull.

Do you know, I was too frightened even to reply. I was beginning to see, and what I saw I didn't like.

'It's a pity,' said Kevin Bull, 'it's a pity you'll never finish your novel.'

I was beginning to feel that the grass of Epping Forest was damper than ever. But also I began to stop worrying about catching my death of cold.

And then things suddenly began to happen.

They sometimes do. This time, they did.

Me, I was sitting on the grass. Brooding.

And then, quite suddenly: Bang! Bang!

Tiny was lying on the ground. Kevin Bull was lying on the ground. I knew I wasn't killed because my heart was beating so fast I couldn't think. But I knew I wasn't killed!

Then somebody came up to me, pushed me gently with his foot. 'Put him out of his misery?' he enquired of somebody else I couldn't see.

'I wouldn't do that,' I said. 'I'm no gun-runner. I'm a novelist.'

'Now that's very interesting,' said the man. But I noticed that he didn't sound very convinced. And he had an automatic in his hand. There were altogether too many automatics about, I thought.

'At least, I suppose I'm a novelist,' I added rather lamely.

'How come?' said the man.

'I got stuck at chapter fourteen,' I said'.

'Chapter fourteen of your first novel?' said the man.

'Yes,' I said.

'That's all right then,' he said. 'Every novelist does that in his first novel.'

Well, the tension seemed to die down a bit. Kevin Bull was dead. They tidied him up in the back of the Bentley. The man called Tiny was dead. They tidied him up on top of Kevin Bull. There were three other men who had been concerned with the hold up and shooting. One of them was called Hugh Clevely. The others I never knew. Hugh Clevely was a writer of mystery novels. But he was also connected with one side of the Spanish War. Kevin Bull had been doing a little double crossing, and Hugh Clevely had been asked to do a little liquidating.[3]

What about the suitcase?

Well, I rode with Hugh Clevely in the front of the Bentley while we continued our trip to Maldon. When we got there the bodies of Kevin Bull and Tiny were carried on to a yacht lying at mooring just off the Yacht Club premises.

It was about twelve o'clock. A lovely night. The full moon shone through the trees as we slid along the silver road.

But what about the suitcase? I expect that the scissors were for the use of Tiny to cut my hair with. The razor was for Tiny to shave my scalp with. Then the suit of clothes was to dress me in a way similar to Kevin Bull. And the automatic was for Tiny to shoot me through the face. And *there* would be a dead Kevin Bull, all ready for the inquest, while the real Kevin Bull would be free to wander away to pastures new.

Hugh Clevely drove me back to London.

He's now a very popular novelist.

Me, every time I read one of his thrillers I think of the Bang! Bangs! in Epping Forest. Somehow or other I never got beyond my chapter fourteen.

Literary Fringes - No 4

How I nearly became a Brilliant Conversationalist

When I was very young my father used to say: 'Barry, my boy, always remember, if you don't work, you can't expect to eat.'[1]

Of course, there wasn't any Social Security in those days, but I felt sure that my father was quite wrong. So, when I was in London I used to go and see Carlo Norway.[2] Often, that was. Carlo Norway lived in Store Street, off Tottenham Court Road, and he was a painter. He was a good painter, but people hadn't found it out at that time, all except a grocer. Carlo painted a portrait of the grocer's wife, and he got paid in sardines. Two hundred and eighteen tins of sardines. When I was hungry I used to go and see Carlo Norway. That was often. I used to buy a threepenny loaf of bread, and Carlo and I used to eat bread and sardines. Always bread and sardines.

One day Carlo said that there was no need for anybody to go hungry in a land of plenty. 'You can talk yourself out of it,' he said. 'I've tried,' I said. 'But it doesn't work.' 'If you can talk well,' said Carlo Norway, 'you can make friends. If you can make friends, they'll ask you out to dinner. Then you won't be hungry any more.' 'I know,' I said, 'I've seen the advertisements. How to become a brilliant conversationalist in twenty easy lessons.'

Carlo Norway opened another tin of sardines, and I cut another two slices of bread. We hadn't any butter, but he had some tea and no milk. 'Before you,' said Carlo Norway, 'sits one of England's foremost painters. Better than Augustus John. Better than Paul Nash. But I can't sell a picture.' 'I know,' I said sadly. 'Why not?' said Carlo Norway. 'I don't know,' I said. 'Simply because I can't talk,' said Carlo Norway. 'I can't sell myself, let alone my paintings.' 'I know,' I said sadly. 'I tell you what,' said Carlo Norway, 'I know a little club called the Cave of Harmony.[3] It's just filled with brilliant conversationalists. We'll go there next Saturday night. We'll see how it's done.'

So next Saturday night, at about half past ten, Carlo Norway and I went to the Cave of Harmony. It was in Charlotte Street, just on the fringes of Soho, and just on the other side of Tottenham Court Road. The Cave of Harmony became very famous later on, but at the time it was rather drab, mainly a long room with a small stage at one end, and a small dance band, and another room where you could buy sandwiches. Underneath the room, in the basement, there was a Negro night club, and there was a regular throb, throb, throb, from some drums underneath. The Cave of Harmony was run mainly by a young woman called Elsa Lanchester, who had flaming red hair and was very beautiful; and a man called Harold Scott. Well, the place was filled with people. Some were talking, some were dancing. The ones who talked were definitely brilliant conversationalists. That is to say, they kept on talking and didn't care who listened. So Carlo and I listened. The talk was all about black magic. It seemed that somebody had been studying black magic very hard and had got on the fourth dimension. And nobody could bring him back on to the common-or-garden third dimension. This was very sad for the poor man, who had quite a lot of money, and had gone down to Hastings to try to work out the tides.

I must say this is a bit complicated, but you see this young man was trying to prove that William the Conqueror hadn't landed at Hastings in 1066. He was trying to prove this by means of the tides, and he had also been studying black magic, and there he was, on the fourth dimension.

Well, Carlo Norway and I got a lot of information about black magic. It seemed that it was quite easy to dispose of anybody you don't like. You simply make a small wax image of the person concerned and then stick small pins with black heads in various parts of the anatomy of the wax image. If you want, say, to give the person rheumatism in the right knee, you simply stick a pin into the right knee of the image.

But if you want to kill a person, the technique is different. You have to make a clay image, and then put the image in a stream of slowly running water. It takes about a week for the clay image to be washed away to nothing, and during that time the person you are trying to kill simply withers away and dies.

Well, Carlo Norway and I kept on listening. And we heard about a man called Aleister Crowley, who was a very brilliant black magician.[4] It seems that he had wanted to dispose of a boy friend of one of Crowley's girl friends, if you see what I mean, and had told him to row out to sea in the Bay of Naples and throw away his oars. The man apparently did this and the oars floated ashore, but not the boat nor the boy friend. Aleister Crowley was such a brilliant black magician that, if he wanted to, he could make a pin rise from the table and stand on its point.

Well, Carlo Norway and I kept on listening. And in the end it was decided that a party of brilliant conversationalists were to go down to Hastings, with Aleister Crowley, and we'd try to bring back the poor young man, who had been studying tides and who was on the fourth dimension, back to the third dimension. (I *do* hope you can see what I mean.)

The next morning, that was Sunday, Carlo Norway and I were waiting at Waterloo Station together with five brilliant conversationalists and Aleister Crowley. It was a very important occasion indeed, because Carlo Norway had had to sell fifty-seven tins of sardines for our railway fares. And before we left home, Carlo Norway painted one of my cheeks with a daub of brown paint and then nicked his finger with a sardine tin opener and drew round the dab of paint on my cheek with his blood. 'What's this in aid of?' I asked. 'It's black magic,' said Carlo Norway.

We all got in a carriage, which we had to ourselves, on the train to Hastings. And then one of the brilliant conversationalists saw the dab of brown paint on my cheek with the daub of blood encircling it. 'Whatever's that on your face, Barry?' he said. 'That's St Anthony's Fire,' said Carlo Norway. 'It's known as erysipelas nowadays. It's very dangerous, and sometimes it's fatal.' 'Is it very infectious?' said the brilliant conversationalist. 'Dreadfully infectious,' said Carlo Norway. 'But Barry shouldn't be travelling with us,' said the brilliant conversationalist. 'He should be in bed, or in hospital, shouldn't he?' 'That's not necessary,' said Carlo Norway. 'You see, I've painted it with the blood of a black Munro.'

Well, the conversation became quite bright. Carlo explained that St Anthony's Fire could be cured almost immediately by painting on it the blood from a black cock. But as he hadn't the blood of a black cock, the blood of a black Munro was nearly as good. Carlo pointed out that the Munros as a clan didn't like donating their blood to other people. But he'd had no difficulty, because he was a guru. Everybody in the carriage, of course, knew what a guru was. Except me, that was. But I gathered that a guru was an esoteric teacher, and a very rare sort of person indeed.

Everybody was dreadfully impressed with Carlo Norway. All except Aleister Crowley, who looked a little glum, because he was a guru as well. Then the brilliant conversationalist said to Carlo Norway, rather doubtfully I thought: 'Aleister Crowley can make a pin stand up on its end by willing it to do so.' Carlo said in a rather superior voice: 'Any guru should be able to do that, but no self-respecting guru *would* do so.' Aleister Crowley said: 'I bet you you can't make a pin stand on its end.' Carlo Norway said: 'I don't bet. I am a guru and I have no money worth mentioning. I have merely fourteen and ninepence in ready money and seven tins of sardines in my pockets.' Alastair Crowley said: 'I will bet you fifty pounds to your fourteen and ninepence that you can't make a pin stand on its end by an effort of will.' And the other brilliant conversationalists all chipped in with bets of five pounds to a tin of sardines that Carlo couldn't make a pin stand on its end by an effort of his will. Me, I was worried. We'd already spent fifty-seven tins of sardines for the fares, and it looked as though we'd as good as lost another seven.

Well, we got to Hastings. And we all trooped into the waiting-room. We all sat round the large waiting-room table. Somebody produced a pin. 'You try first,' said Carlo Norway to Aleister Crowley. Aleister laid down the pin very carefully on the waiting-room table. Then he walked deoshins seven times round the table. Then he walked widdershins seven times round the table. Then Aleister Crowley took off his coat and rolled up his shirt sleeves. Then he muttered seven different incantations over the pin on the waiting-room table. Then he said: 'Rise – Pin.' The pin didn't rise. It stayed where it was. Aleister Crowley said: 'Rise – Pin.' The pin didn't rise. All the brilliant conversationalists looked very anxious. Me, I was just terrified. Carlo Norway looked quite calm. Aleister Crowley began to perspire rather profusely. He walked widdershins another seven times round the table, then he tried a few more special incantations. The pin stayed put. Then Aleister Crowley said that he felt rather tired. 'Another time, perhaps,' he said. Carlo Norway said, quite casually: 'It's really rather simple, you know.' Aleister Crowley was very cross. The brilliant conversationalists, all five of them, seemed rather worried, and not very conversational.

'You see,' said Carlo Norway, 'there's no need for a superior guru to do any of this widdershins and deoshins walking, and no need for any incantations.' Carlo Norway placed the pin on the table. 'There's not even any need to take off my coat,' he said. 'All I have to do is say: "Pin – Rise",' And as he said this, he put his hand over the pin on the waiting-room table and said: 'Pin – Rise.' Quite obediently, the pin rose. It stood up on its little head and waved its point gracefully in the air. The conversationalists just gaped. Carlo Norway said: 'Pin – Fall.' And quite obediently the pin fell back on the table. 'I will now ask my disciple to collect the bets,' said Carlo Norway. 'Fifty pounds from Aleister Crowley, and five pounds each from the others.' 'Barry,' he said, 'please collect seventy-five pounds.' I only collected seventy -three pounds, five shillings, because one of the brilliant conversationalists hadn't five pounds in his pocket.

'After this effort of will,' said Carlo Norway, 'my disciple and I will return to our home in London. If you have any difficulty in getting this poor friend of yours from the fourth dimension back on to the third, be sure to let me know.'

So Carlo Norway and I took the next train back to London. That night we had a really good meal at the Oxford Street Corner House. We ate good beef sandwiches; they were a change from sardines. And we drank Pilsener lager; it was a change from the tea with sugar and no milk. After we had eaten, I said to Carlo Norway: 'Are you really a guru?' 'What, me?' said Carlo. 'Yes, you,' I said. 'Good gracious, no,' said Carlo Norway. 'I'm a painter. And a very good painter. But I knew sooner or later during the day somebody or other would start talking about how Aleister Crowley can make a pin stand on its end.' 'And?' I said. 'And,' said Carlo Norway, 'I had a small magnet strapped under my shirt cuff. It's surprisingly simple to make a pin stand on its end when you enlist the aid of magnetism.'

Well, we had quite a lot of money for a short time. And Carlo and I had lots of good meals for some weeks. But somehow or other I never became a brilliant conversationalist. But, as Carlo Norway said: 'Actions speak louder than words.'

Oh, by the way, I never knew what became of the young man on the fourth dimension. I *do* hope that he isn't there still.

Source Notes

Chapter One - War

1. Frank's battalion, the 8th, of the Royal Warwickshire Regiment, consisted of about 1000 men, and along with the three other Royal Warwickshire Territorial battalions was part of 143rd Brigade and the 48th (South Midland) Division. The overwhelming majority of the 8th Battalion were working class.
2. Malcolm Brown *Tommy Goes to War*, Tempus Publishing 1999.
3. I gave all the originals of Frank's letters to the Imperial War Museum, London, on permanent loan. I have had to edit very little in Frank's letters; his spelling was impeccable!
4. 143rd Brigade War Diary, PRO WO95/2754. Battalion War Diary PRO WO95/2756. Both these are in the National Archives, Kew. Information from these diaries is used throughout this chapter.
5. Peter Caddick-Adams *By God They Can Fight! A History of 143rd Infantry Brigade 1908-1995.* Pub. 143rd (West Midlands) Brigade, Shrewsbury. 1995.
6. As above.
7. Aunt Jennie (Jane) and Aunt Gus were Isabel's sisters.
8. This latter point highlighted the fact that their equipment was poor, and certainly second-rate. Information from Robert David Williams BA (Hons). *A Social and Military History of the 1/8th Battalion, The Royal Warwickshire Regiment, in the Great War.* 1999.
9. Perhaps a friend rather than a family member.
10. Information from Robert Williams – see 8 above.
11. This letter is held with Mary's papers in the Churchill Archives Centre, Churchill College, Cambridge. *Stewart Papers.* (For the connection to the *Stewart Papers* see chapter 14)
12. Auntie Madge – another of Isabel's sisters.
13. Information from Commonwealth War Graves Commission. www.cwgc.org
14. Grannie – Herbert's mother, Annie.
15. Thrale – Frank's first cousin. He was the son of Isabel's eldest brother, William Garbutt.
16. From Peter Caddick-Adams' *By God They Can Fight.* See above.

Chapter Two—Arabia

1. For the story of John Thornton – see Chapter Four.
2. The RAF Museum drew my attention to *Cross & Cockade International*, a quarterly journal from The First World War Aviation Historical Society. Vol. 34, No 2, Summer 2003. The article was *Lawrence's Air Force* by Peter Wright and Roger Bragger. I contacted Roger by email and he was able to give me more information about 'X' flight for which I was very grateful.
3. PRO AIR/1/2250/209/47/1-3, war diary of 'X' Flight – National Archives, Kew.
4. The papers of the Reverend VD Siddons are preserved in the Imperial War Museum. His lecture on the Revolt in the Hejaz is categorised as VDS4.

5. *Pearson's Magazine* was a monthly magazine devoted to politics, literature and the arts.
6. The report of the mission and information about the Turkish pilot was extracted from the Joyce Papers in the Liddell Hart Centre for Military Archives, King's College, London. Place names in the report do not always correspond with the spelling on the maps dated around that time so I have tried to keep them consistent.
7. John Winterburn provided me with the information about the spur of the Hejaz railway from Aneiza to the Shobak area which was not marked on the map of 1918. This spur was constructed by the Ottomans to harvest wood from the forests at Shobak. John has been working on 'the Great Arab Revolt Project', investigating the history and archaeology of this event. I came across him while googling for information about places in Arabia. He has been very helpful in identifying some of Frank's Arabian photographs. John also helped me with the map of Jordan.
8. One of Makins' poor landings was amusingly referred to in the first of Frank's *Literary Fringes – The Hard Way to Hamlet.* I have included all four of Frank's *Literary Fringes* in the Appendix of this book.
9. See *The Hard Way to Hamlet*, as above.
10. Dr Vincent Orange, The Lord Deramore, Air Vice-Marshal D C Stapleton, Wing Commander E Donovan. *Winged Promises A History of No 14 Squadron, RAF 1915-1945.* The Royal Air Force Benevolent Fund enterprises, Glos. 1996.
11. The Medaille d'honneur, avec glaives (crossed swords) en bronze, was awarded to privates or corporals for service to the state of France.
12. *How I nearly became a Poet – Literary Fringes* reproduced in full in the Appendix.
13. James P Hynes. *Lawrence of Arabia's Secret Air Force.* Pen & Sword Aviation. Available August 2010. Based on the diary of Flight Sergeant George Hynes. I was put in touch with Jim Hynes by Squadron Leader Mike Napier (Retd) (whom I came across while googling) who is collecting information for 14 Squadron Association's Centenary Project.

Chapter Three – The Birkinshaw Ancestors

1. Information given to me by Ann Meltzer, my recently-discovered second cousin (see later in this chapter).
2. Surname information from website *House of Names* www.houseofnames.com. Accessed December 2008.
3. Information and obituary about John Richard provided by my recently-discovered second cousin Tim Illingworth (see later in this chapter).
4. John Richard applied for a passport in 1866 according to information from my Uncle Bill (Frank's brother).
5. Prunella Scales became a household name as Sybil Fawlty in the TV comedy 'Fawlty Towers' in which she played alongside John Cleese. She was awarded a CB in 1992.
6. Teresa Ransom *The Authorised Biography of Prunella Scales.* John Murray 2005. Some of the information in this chapter is taken from this source, and some also

was given to me by Tim Illingworth. Also thanks to Tim for providing copy of the photo of Freda Scales' wedding.

7. Letter given to me by my Uncle Bill.
8. Information from archivist of Kilkenny College, also from Kilkenny County Library and Sligo County Library.
9. I found John's war record in the online Australian Archives.
10. Migration records from www.ancestry.co.uk /www.findmypast.com.
11. I found Ross Shekleton with help from Burnley Library and the National Archives.
12. Information from various websites.
13. Kapunda was, incidentally, where John Birkinshaw Shekleton's wife Ida Blanche Clutterbuck came from, so perhaps there was a connection between the two families.
14. More about Emmeline's stay with Herbert and Isabel in chapter 16.
15. Information about his career from *Nature,* the International Weekly Journal of Science. (There are two portraits of Sir William Smith Jarratt by Bassano in the National Portrait Gallery in London, from which I was able to recognise Sir William in the photograph of Sidney and Emmeline's wedding.)
16. More about Herbert in chapter 16.

Chapter Four – The Mysterious John Thornton

1. Sheona was never officially adopted by her aunt and uncle although she used her new parents' surname and felt like their natural child.
2. Lieut-Colonel H.F.N. Jourdain, C.M.G. and Edward Fraser *The Connaught Rangers.* 3 volumes.
3. Information about John Thornton and the 94th Regiment, the Peninsular War and history of the time, taken from the above and: www.iprom.co.uk/archives/caithness/ptejohn.htm *The Caithness Archives: The Soldier who went to war in Spain.* Accessed December 2009. Details of the life of Field Marshal Arthur Wellesley 1st Duke of Wellington from various websites. War record of John Thornton – National Archives, Kew.
4. *Caithness Archives* – see above.

Chapter Five – The Hendersons and the Garbutts

1. In 2008 we visited Langleeford and met Walter Brown, the farmer. He was born in the farmhouse and has lived there all his life. He told us some of the local stories which I have incorporated here.
2. HJC Grierson Editor. *The Letters of Sir Walter Scott.* 12 vols London. Constable 1932-37.
3. *Reminiscences of Samuel Donkin of Northumbrian & Border Character, and of Local and General Topics, Social and Political, since the dawn of the present century.* Newcastle-upon-Tyne: Pub at the *Daily Journal* Office, Clayton Street, 1886.
4. Sheona Lodge *Swan Feather, Recollections in Poetry and Prose*. Flambard Press, Newcastle upon Tyne. 1993. Much of the information about the Hendersons and

Garbutts came from my Aunt Sheona who wrote extensively about them, and information also from her daughter Anne.

5. The portrait to which she refers was probably in fact the one of Elizabeth's grandfather William Henderson (1751-1830).
6. Information from Gateshead library, as is information about Dunston Lodge, to whom I am grateful for help.
7. D Lumley, transcriber *Echoes of Other Days, Some Leaves of Northern Lore*, Northumberland Press Ltd. 1930.
8. George Herring *A Day in a Private Lunatic Asylum; Being an Account of a Visit to Dunston Lodge, together with some details concerning the horrors of Lunatic Asylums in the earlier part of the present Century*. London: Walter Scott, 14 Paternoster Square and Newcastle-on-Tyne. 1884.
9. More about Herbert and Isabel in chapter 16.
10. Passenger lists obtained from the migration records from the National Archives, ancestry.co.uk and findmypast.com.
11. Information provided by my second cousin Geoffrey Allen, Katie and Herbert's grandson.

Chapter Six – Becoming a Doctor

1. Letter from the *Stewart Papers*, Churchill Archives Centre. See chapter 14.
2. Fay Weldon – I have taken various information from her autobiography *Auto Da Fay,* Flamingo 2002.
3. Online Oxford Dictionary of National Biography.
4. Information from The Royal Regiment of Fusiliers Museum (Royal Warwickshire).

Chapter Eight – Italy

1. Friends of Arthur Machen website: www.machensoc.demon.co.uk. Information about Arthur Machen was extracted from here. Accessed January 2010.
2. This diary was found amongst papers my brother had of some of Frank's articles, stories and radio plays.
3. See http://en.wikipedia.org/wiki/Kenneth_Dewar. Accessed February 2010. The Admiral did not like Bandmaster Barnacle's music and said 'I will not have a bugger like that on my ship' and nearly caused a mutiny! The *Royal Oak* was torpedoed by the Germans in 1939 while she was at anchor at Scapa Flow, Orkney, Scotland, with the loss of 833 lives.
4. Many crew lists are in the care of the Maritime History Archive in Newfoundland and prohibitively expensive to access - http://www.mun.ca/mha/. Passenger lists available from the National Archives through www.ancestry.co.uk and www.findmypast.com.

Chapter Nine – Earthquake

1 Information from Hawke's Bay Museum, Napier.

2 Letter from the Churchill Archives Centre, Churchill College, Cambridge, *Stewart papers*. See chapter 14.
3 Information about the Napier earthquake obtained from various websites.
4 I found this letter amongst Mother's papers after she died. Isabel must have returned it to Frank.

Chapter Ten – New Zealand 1930s

1. Information about all the ships mentioned in this chapter from migration records, National Archives Kew, and from the Printed Books Library, Guildhall, London.
2. Information from the Taranaki Base Hospital Library – *Hawera Hospital 100 years 1894-1994,* pb 1994 by Hawera Hospital Centennial Committee.
3. Fay Weldon. *Auto da Fay*. Flamingo 2002. Other information in this chapter is also taken from Fay's book.
4. Uncle Bill, Frank's younger brother, told me this story.
5. Margaret Jepson. *Via Panama*. London. H. Hamilton, 1934.
6. Gordon Ogilvie. *Denis Glover – His Life.* Random House, NZ 1999.
7. Denis Glover. *Hot Water Sailor,* Halstead Press, Sydney, 1962,
8. Lauris Edmonds, Ed. *The Letters of ARD Fairburn.* OUP 1981. Lauris Edmonds, incidentally, survived the 1931 Napier earthquake when she was a seven-year old girl.
9. Information from the N Z Archives, Nelson.
10. No records appear for Frank in the migration lists in the National Archives for this date, so he probably worked his passage as the ship's doctor. Crew members were not included in the passenger lists.

Chapter Eleven – Frank and Edna

1. I found Frank's discharge papers amongst my mother's documents after she died.
2. Information from the migration lists in the National Archives from www.findmypast.com.

Chapter Twelve - New Zealand 1940s

1. Churchill Archives Centre, Churchill College, Cambridge. *Stewart Papers*. The connection to the *Stewart Papers* is explained in Chapter 14. All letters and extracts from diaries are from this source, unless otherwise stated.
2. Information about Coromandel from various websites.
3. Fay Weldon. *Auto da Fay*. Flamingo 2002. Other information for this chapter also taken from this source.
4. New Zealand Archives, Nelson.
5. Letter found in Margaret's collection after she died. This collection is now with her grandson, Ben. Margaret kept photos and letters from Frank, bringing them back from New Zealand with her and keeping them as she moved from one place to another throughout her life.
6. From Margaret's collection.

7. Margaret's collection.
8. Margaret's collection.
9. National Archives, Kew. Migration Lists. www.ancestry.co.uk.
10. This Plan was found amongst the articles and plays in my brother's possession.
11. Margaret's collection.
12. Margaret's collection.

Chapter Thirteen – Sheona

1. Sheona Lodge - *Swan Feather, Recollections in Poetry and Prose*. Flambard Press, Newcastle upon Tyne. 1993. Information in this chapter is drawn from *Swan Feather* and Sheona's letters to me in the 1980s, as well as from recollections by her daughter Anne.
2. With thanks to my cousin Anne for allowing me the privilege of reading and reproducing some of her mother's letters (out of the tea caddy) from Grafton and Oliver.
3. See Family Tree 3, chapter 5.
4. Uncle Willie was William Baigent, Oliver's uncle and father-in-law to be. William was concerned he would lose Sheona as his fishing companion. See Family Tree 3, chapter 5.
5. The second part of Sheona's story continues in Book Three of this trilogy.

Chapter Fourteen - Mary

1. Churchill Archives Centre, Churchill College, Cambridge. *The Papers of Lord Stewart of Fulham and Baroness Stewart of Alvechurch.* Ref: GBR/0014/STWT. All information from Mary's letters and diaries in this chapter are from this source. Website http://janus.lib.cam.ac.uk.
2. Michael Stewart. *Life and Labour.* Sidgwick and Jackson 1980.
3. Bob's book was discussed in *The Creator as critic and other writings by E M Forster* by E M Forster and J M Heath. 2008. Website: books.google.co.uk. Accessed July 2010. *Mrs Loveday* was banned in Australia between 1945-58.
4. The second part of Mary's story continues in Book Three of this trilogy.

Chapter Fifteen – Bill

1. Churchill Archives Centre, Churchill College, Cambridge, *Stewart Papers.* All letters and extracts from Mary's diaries in this chapter are from this source, unless otherwise stated.
2. See chapter 7 - Shipwreck.
3. *Leaves* May 1985. The Magazine of the Cathedral and Parish Church of St Mary of Southwell.
4. Unfortunately there was no date or name of publication on this article.
5. The second part of Bill's story continues in Book Three of this trilogy.

Chapter Sixteen – Isabel and Herbert

1. Postcards found amongst my Aunt Sheona's papers.
2. Churchill Archives Centre, Churchill College, Cambridge. *Stewart Papers*. All the letters in this chapter are from this source. Information also taken from Mary's diaries.
3. More about Herbert and Isabel in Book Three of this trilogy.

Chapter Seventeen – Sad News

1. Frank was actually fifty-one when he died. However, his death certificate stated he was fifty and Mother had always believed he was born in 1899, which is what Frank had told her, whereas he was in fact born a year earlier.
2. Churchill Archives Centre, *Stewart Papers.* All the letters and diary extracts in this chapter are from this source, unless otherwise stated.
3. Frank's *Literary Fringes* are included in the appendix.
4. Information from the Historical Narrative of the website Historical Places Trust, www.historic.org.nz. Accessed 2008. Jones, Martin and Tania Mace, 'Haigh House (Former), 493 Pahi Road, Pahi', New Zealand Historic Places Trust registration report, August 2004.
5. Peter Shaw *A History of New Zealand Architecture.* Hodder Moa Becket, NZ 1997.
6. Blue Star Line website.

Appendix

The Hard Way to Hamlet

1. Frank's pseudonym.

How I nearly became a Poet

1. This was probably a reference to the story Frank told about receiving his Medaille d'honneur from the Empress Eugénie. She was the widow of Napoleon III who was the nephew of Napoleon Bonaparte.
2. Harold Monro was a poet and proprietor of The Poetry Bookshop in London.
3. Flecker was a poet and novelist who died in 1915.
4. Douglas Goldring was a writer and poet.
5. Alec Waugh was a novelist; the older brother of Evelyn Waugh.
6. Dr CEM Joad was a philosopher and broadcasting personality.
7. Clare Sheridan was a writer and sculptor and cousin of Winston Churchill.

How I nearly wrote a Thriller

1. Allen Lane travelled to London from Bristol in 1919 to take up his job with The Bodley Head, the firm his uncle John Allen had founded. Allen Lane eventually

took over the company and founded Penguin Books. Information from www.allenlane.org.uk. Accessed January 2010.

2. The Ham Bone Club became Cy Laurie's Skiffle Club in the 1950s. www.museumoflondon.org.uk. Accessed January 2010.
3. Hugh Clevely was a mystery writer and wrote some of the Sexton Blake novels. He co-wrote a novel with Edgar Jepson, Frank's father-in-law from his first marriage. Information from www.mysteryfile.com. Accessed January 2010.

How I nearly became a Brilliant Conversationalist

1. Frank sometimes used the name Barry Mansfield as a pseudonym for his writing.
2. Carlo Norway was a painter (probably rather a bad one) born in 1886.
3. The Cave of Harmony was founded by the actress Elsa Lanchester and her romantic partner Harold Scott. It was a midnight theatre which presented one-act plays by Pirandello and Checkhov. www.panicresearch.com/elsa_lanchester.html. Accessed January 2010.
4. Aleister Crowley, occultist and writer. Frank apparently saved his life on one occasion.